D0765615

LETTERS FROM NORTH AMERICA
AND THE PACIFIC
1898

LETTERS
FROM NORTH AMERICA
AND THE PACIFIC
1898

CHARLES PHILIPS TREVELYAN

With a Foreword by
Leonard Woolf

1969
CHATTO & WINDUS
LONDON

Published by
Chatto & Windus Ltd
42 William IV Street
London W.C.2

*

Clarke, Irwin & Co. Ltd.
Toronto

SBN 7011 1372 3

Printed in Great Britain by
R. & R. Clark, Limited, Edinburgh

CONTENTS

ACROSS THE PACIFIC, NEW ZEALAND
AND AUSTRALIA

PLATES

(*The Plates, with the exception of the picture of Sir George Trevelyan with Theodore Roosevelt, are from the original photographs taken by the Author on his journey.*)

Editor's note

The letters have been printed in full, with only most minor alterations or cutting of entirely irrelevant matter. For the convenience of the reader simple titles have been given to each letter, and footnotes have been added with brief information about important people, places and events.

FOREWORD

The letters to which I have been asked to write a foreword were written in 1898 by Charles Philips Trevelyan, eldest son of Sir George Otto Trevelyan, 2nd Baronet of Wallington, Cambo, Morpeth, Northumberland. The details and even the names are significant and important, for they belong to a class of society, a society, an era of history, a world which has ceased to exist and can never return. This is what gives to these letters their psychological, sociological, and historical interest. For in them Charles Trevelyan, aged 28, describes in detail to Sir George Otto and his family in Northumberland a nine months Odyssey with the famous Sidney and Beatrice Webb to the United States of America, New Zealand, and Australia. Like all Trevelyans of his and his father's generations he had a mind and a body of immense toughness; physically his energy and mentally his curiosity were indefatigable. He was born with a political spoon in his mouth and (probably from the first day he saw the world) he looked at it through the eyes of a Whig or Liberal statesman. It is through those eyes too that in these letters we see the picture of society and politics in America, New Zealand, and Australia—and in Cambo, Morpeth, Northumberland—just 16 years before they were finally destroyed by the shot which the Serbian student, Princip, fired at Serajevo. I shall say something about that picture, but before doing so, I should like to say something about Charles Trevelyan and his family.

When I went up to Trinity College, Cambridge, in 1899, I got to know George Macaulay Trevelyan, who had just been made a Fellow of the college, and later on his two older brothers, Charles and Bob. These three brothers were a formidable Trinity. They were the sons of Sir George Otto Trevelyan, who was a son of the 1st Bt. and of the sister of the great Macaulay. George Otto was born in 1838 and died in 1928. He was educated at Harrow and Trinity College, Cambridge, and had a long and distinguished political career, being an M.P. for 32 years and holding the high office of Chief Secretary for Ireland in Gladstone's Cabinet. He wrote the standard life of the great Macaulay. He inherited the baronetcy and a large, beautiful ancestral country mansion in Northumberland.

All three sons followed their father to Harrow and Trinity College, Cambridge. They were all three tremendously English; in each one saw a family likeness to the other two and all had an immense energy and vitality of mind and body. Charles was very goodlooking, but Bob and George were physically large, craggy, looming, with a curious clumsiness of body. When George laughed in the Great Court of Trinity—it sound like the raucous laughter of a great macaw—I think they could hear it far off in Johns on the one side and Clare on the other. 'You are not a Muscular Christian,' I once said to him, 'but you are next door to it, for you are a Muscular Agnostic', and he was rather pleased with the title. He and Charles were the leading spirits in the Lake Hunt. Every year at Whitsuntide they took a band of young men to the Lakes and there in a daily Hare and Hounds run they covered the hills and valleys of Cumberland. George was a member of the Sunday Tramps, that band of Muscular Agnostics or even Muscular Atheists which the strenuous agnostic of the previous generation, Leslie Stephen, led in vast walks over Surrey, often ending appropriately with a visit to George Meredith in his house on the Surrey hills. Meredith was the prophet, seer, and oracle of the Trevelyans' generation and one might hear George chanting 'Love in the Valley' in a strident singsong as he pounded over the hills of Westmorland or Surrey. There was an intellectual ferocity in George as a young man which could be intimidating to anyone who did not known him well or had any kind of intellectual wobble. Wobble was the one thing not tolerated by the Trevelyan brothers. George had an extremely good mind set in the hereditary mould of Victorian liberalism; on principle he was tolerant, but it would be an exasperated tolerance when confronted by a fool whom he knew that on principle he ought to suffer gladly. There was in his mind and in his outlook on the world and on history—you can see it clearly in his historical works—a curious and often contradictory mixture of matter-of-factness and romanticism.

Of these characteristics in George there were traces in both his brothers. Bob was a poet and a very endearing character. Pure poetry was not entirely consonant with the Trevelyan mould of intellectual liberalism in which the infant and adult Bob had been cast. But the strong romanticism in George, the thinner streak of romanticism in Charles, and Bob's poetry all had a similar psychological and possibly genetic origin. In each case they did not make an entirely comfortable fit with the positive intellectuality of the Trevelyan mind. In Bob's case his poetry suffered. His poems often begin well with real inspiration, but the afflatus does not last – the world of prose and intellect breaks through and breaks it up. Bob had a good mind – both he and George were Apostles – but there was a curious streak of ridiculousness in him – a mixture of Peter Schlemiel and Wagner's Reine Tor, an endearing combination. For instance in conversation his tongue would sometimes suddenly break loose and soar away into an argument or description, slightly absurd, irrelevant, fantastic, not entirely under his control, but extraordinarily funny. And he was prone to absurd contretemps, accidents or incidents. I remember two.

The first occurred in the 1914 war. Bob was on the side of the Conscientious Objectors and helped many of them. He had one day made an appointment with a General at the War Office in order to intercede on behalf of a C.O. who was being maltreated in the army. The night before the appointment he came and stayed with us at Richmond. He had made himself look very smart and respectable in a dark navy blue suit, new and spick and span, calculated to impress the General. After breakfast he took a book of his poetry out of his pocket and began reading a poem to us. To do this he put the book on the floor, he himself crouching over it in a kneeling position. The attitude and the occupation were characteristic of Bob. Unfortunately his bottom was too near the gas fire, and suddenly to my astonishment I saw a column of smoke rise from Bob's backside. A large hole was burnt in the seat of his new trousers. Virginia, a most incompetent sempstress, hurriedly sewed a patch into the garment.

The second incident occurred when we were living in Tavistock Square. Bob one day turned up unexpectedly at tea time. I told him that we should have to leave immediately after tea as I had to drive down to Chelsea to see Sibyl Colefax. 'In that case,' he said, 'you might take me with you as I'm staying in Chelsea with Logan (Pearsall Smith).' I of course agreed. That morning I had read in the *Times* that Clifford Allen, who had led the C.O.'s during the war, had accepted a peerage from Ramsay MacDonald, and I incautiously said to Bob: 'I always had my doubts about your friend Clifford–but how can he accept a peerage?' For the first and only time I saw Bob lose his temper. He became red in the face; words poured from his mouth which became slightly flecked with foam. I had insulted him by insulting his friend. 'I will not stay in your house to be insulted,' he said, seizing the teapot and pouring himself out another cup of tea. And then he hesitated, as the thought of having to find his way by bus to Chelsea instead of being driven in my car occurred to him. The words and the anger subsided. I drove him amicably, if slightly subdued, and dropped him in King's Road. He got out, but turned and put his head into the car, and said rather sheepishly: 'I'm sorry I lost my temper, Leonard.'

The streak of the Reine Tor comes out very clearly in this second trivial episode. It was this simplicity and absurdity superimposed upon the rugged Trevelyan intellectuality which appealed, I think, to G. E. Moore. Moore had an immense influence upon my generation at Cambridge, and also upon the generations which immediately preceded and followed mine. His standards were very high and intimacy with him was not easy. To become an intimate friend of his, to be accepted in his inner circle, one had to have some unusual quality of mind and character. The ultimate sign that one had been accepted was an invitation to come on Moore's reading party at Easter to Cornwall or Devon. Bob was always asked. Moore had a great affection for him. It was the simplicity which he liked and he shook with laughter over Bob's absurdities.

I never knew Charles as intimately as I knew Bob or as well as I know George. I never saw him at Cambridge. It was only after I returned to England in 1911 after seven years in the Ceylon Civil Service that I got to know him. It was in politics that I first met him during the 1914 war. Like the Buxtons and several other hereditary Liberals, he was already on the road from the Liberal Party into the Labour Party. This movement, which grew in strength until it emasculated the Liberal Party and has turned it into a political anachronism, was due to several causes: the cracks in the liberal principles of the Party even before the war; the war, which, like all wars, eroded liberalism and was therefore deadly to a Liberal Government responsible for conducting it; the political acrobatics of Lloyd George and the internecine suicidal vendetta between L. G. and Asquith. In 1914, when the war broke out, Charles was already on the road to political success in the Liberal Party, for since 1908 he had been Parliamentary Secretary, Board of Education. But he showed the obduracy of the Trevelyan principles and conscience – it was not the last time of his doing so – by resigning from the Government 'as a protest against the policy which involved Great Britain in the war'.

Charles's disapproval of the Liberal foreign policy and his resignation of office inevitably turned his attention to the problems of foreign relations and war and peace, and it was in this connection that I was drawn into personal contact with him. He was a very good-looking man. He was not as forceful as George nor as eccentric as Bob, but in many ways he was like them. They all three had a curious tang of precision and certainty in their voices, and George and Charles both had a habit, when they were speaking to you, of standing in front of you and looking both through you and over your head with a glint of misgiving in their eye as if they expected you to say something rather foolish. It was slightly disconcerting until one learnt that both of them were fundamentally benignant. Charles during the war joined Ramsay MacDonald, E. D. Morel, the Buxtons and others on the Left to found the Union of Democratic Control and he was on the Executive Committee. The U.D.C. tried to make people understand the disastrous results of the way in which the Great Powers conducted foreign affairs, the methods of power politics and secret diplomacy, which were direct causes of the 1914 war. I was a member of the U.D.C. though not on the Executive Committee. But I was actively engaged in the Fabian Society and League of Nations Society in trying to lay the foundations of a League of Nations, and from time to time I used to lunch with Ramsay and Charles and other members of the U.D.C. Executive at the 1917 Club to discuss problems, policies, and propaganda. But Charles's political heart was really given to education, and after the war, when he was elected a Labour M.P. for Newcastle and there were Labour Governments in 1924 and 1929–31, he almost of right returned to the Board of Education, this time as President with a seat in the Cabinet. In those years I did not see much of him politically for I was Secretary of the Labour Party Advisory Committees on International and Imperial Questions, and he had too much on his hands educationally in the House and the Cabinet to give much attention to other questions. But he was always extremely interested in international and imperial questions, and, on important occasions, he would find the time to discuss with me at his house in Great College Street the difficult problem of what line of policy the Labour Party should adopt. Then suddenly in 1931 he repeated the act of political honesty and courage which he had performed as a Liberal in 1914. He resigned from the Government and Cabinet. The cause and manner of his going showed both his social conscience and his social prescience. For he resigned as President of the Board of Education in protest against Ramsay MacDonald's failure to support him in this proposal to raise the school leaving age to 15.

I said at the beginning of this foreword that Charles's letters belong to a class and an era which no longer exists. To me that is one of the fascinating aspects of both the writer and the letters. In and around 1832 a political and social revolution began in Britain. It was to a great extent directed and extended for 80 years – until in fact 1914 – by a small social class, the upper middle professional class. The members of this class, or rather sub-class, were not aristocrats – though as the century waxed and waned intellectual aristocrats tended to coalesce with or even marry into it – they were well-to-do 'gentry'; their social aura was that of the country gentleman, with roots far back in an English county and a large country mansion. Some of them, of course, had been called by God to this estate from more lowly origins only recently, i.e. in the last 100 years, but they rapidly acquired the habits, outlook, psychology, and social smell of the British upper middle class. In their large houses they had large families; the sons went to Eton, Harrow, Winchester, Westminster, or occasionally some other public school; from the public school they went to Oxford or Cambridge, to a Naval College or Woolwich or Sandhurst. Then they went into the House of Commons, the Civil Service, the Law, the Indian Civil Service, the Colonial Service, or the Church. They became dons at Oxford or Cambridge or headmasters of Public Schools. The less intelligent went into the army or the navy. The government of Britain and of the Empire gradually came to be largely dominated by this class. You can see the process of change by comparing the Cabinets of the early years of the century with those of the early years of the 20th century. The majority of the early 19th century Cabinet Ministers came from the aristocracy, of the early 20th century from the upper middle class. If you examined the key posts in the English or Indian Civil Services or the High Court Bench of Judges or the Archbishoprics of Canterbury or York, you would almost inevitably find that they were comfortably occupied by members of the upper middle class, educated at one of the 'best' public schools and Oxford or Cambridge.

It is true that as the years went by and democracy kept creeping in, the lesser breeds of the middle middle class, or even the strata below that, began to make money and send their sons to Eton and Harrow, to Oxford or Cambridge, and so were able to break into the preserves of power. But so powerful is the influence or smell of the upper classes in England that the lesser breeds were immediately absorbed psychologically and socially in the small intellectual upper middle class and became to all intents and purposes indistinguishable from it. Most of them—from Benjamin Disraeli downwards—if they had the opportunity and the money, bought a country mansion.

The Trevelyans belonged to the original small intellectual upper middle class. Other families of the same kind were the Stracheys, the Stephens, the Darwins, the Youngs, the Arnolds, and the Arnold-Forsters. The Government and public services were full of them. They intermarried: George married the daughter of Mrs. Humphry Ward, a relation therefore of Arnolds, Huxleys, and Arnold-Forsters. Charles married a daughter of Sir Hugh Bell Bt., a sister of Gertrude Bell, from the centre of the professional upper middle class. It is fascinating to trace the effect of this, the psychology of this ruling class, in Charles Trevelyan's letters. He accepts, almost unconsciously, the fact that he is a member of an international élite with the privilege of entrée into Society—the society of the governing classes or 'top people'—in every country of the civilized (or uncivilized) world. The President of the United States of

America invites him to lunch at the White House as soon as he arrives in Washington. Governors of States, Judges of the Supreme Court, millionaires, Heads of Universities, ambassadors ask him to dinner and show him everything which he wants to see from a debate in Congress to a baseball match. Only once did one of the 'top people' hesitate to see Charles; but it was only because he did not realize who Charles was; as soon as he realized that Charles was a son of Sir George Otto Trevelyan, he opened his arms in welcome.

It was the same or even more so in New Zealand and Australia. Here, of course, he knew or knew of every one that mattered (including the public school they had been to) from the Governor-General and his A.D.C. down to the old Harrovian farming in the backwoods. There is a small incident recorded in one of the letters which reveals in an amusing, but significant, way the psychology of this upper middle class intellectual élite, its ambivalent attitude towards the aristocracy, a kind of social respect and intellectual contempt for it. Staying, as he so often did, at Government House—this time in Wellington, New Zealand—he went for a walk with a great grandson of the Duke of Wellington. 'He was a nice boy,' writes Charles, 'but I would have liked to have put him for a few weeks under old Nosy for training. He can't write a letter for his superior to sign half as well as any of the Board School boys Seddon may have jobbed into the Civil Service. He is the heir of the Dukedom, and began grumbling about death duties. I thought a great grandson of the Duke ought to be content to work for his living if necessary and not grumble at the taxes. "The Queen's Government, Sir, must be supported." So I gave him a little instruction in social radicalism and he did not seem to become less deferential. He is a good youth, and may be worthy to command a regiment in some Waterloo, but never an army. He has not alas! even got the nose.'

Charles, as I have said, was typically a member of this Victorian élite. He moves in the physical and spiritual atmosphere of Society and the ruling classes, in London, Washington, Samoa, New Zealand, and Australia, as a fish swims in water. He is a professional in the art of government, the technique of administration. It is from this point of view that he is passionately interested in history and politics, in the way people live,

xvi

how they are educated, how they rule or are ruled. But he is also pre-eminently an individual and a Trevelyan. Again and again in these letters he reminds me of George and, to a less extent perhaps, of Bob. There is his incredible energy and toughness. The extent of country which he covered in the three countries visited by him is immense. Wherever he went, every minute of his day was spent in interviewing every kind of person from statesmen to trade unionists and farmers. He inspected minutely every kind of institution and organization from a legislature or Supreme Court to a primary school. He went for days on long expeditions, camping in remote regions; he climbed mountains, herded cattle, shot and fished. Like his brothers, he went his own way. He walked if he wanted to walk. I can imagine him tramping along the hot dusty road from the Melbourne Races with the proletariat, when all the other grand people drove past him in state. He went on picnics and to dances, and he flirted with pretty young ladies.

He did all this with enormous zest and he writes about it vividly, with intelligence and humour. I end, as I began, by remarking that the class to which he belonged and the society which he described have passed away. They had their faults and their absurdities, as these letters show very clearly, but they also show that there were admirable things in the liberal tradition of public service, in the professional attitude of people like Charles Trevelyan to the art of government, to political principles and their social obligations.

Leonard Woolf

AMERICA

1. ACROSS THE ATLANTIC

*Somewhere south of Cape Breton which is
not in sight but is said to be an island.*

Tuesday, March 29, 1898

By the end of yesterday we had really begun to enjoy meals, to
play chess and to read not dully gaze at the pages of our books.
A diary could not begin till today.

On the 23rd we were seen off by a party of friends, all in some
sort of squash hat, except Bob.[1] Two were authors already,
Shaw[2] and Wallas,[3] two will be when we get back, Bob and
Hirst.[4] Mrs. Courteney[5] represented the Potters.

At Liverpool the Webbs[6] were met by the Holts, who being
managers of the line put them in a state cabin on deck. An
enthusiastic Fabian baronet also came from Yorkshire to see

[1] Robert Calverley Trevelyan (1872–1954), younger brother of
Charles. His first volume of poems was published in 1898.

[2] George Bernard Shaw (1856–1950), playwright.

[3] Graham Wallas (1858–1932), lecturer at London School of
Economics. His *Life of Francis Place* was published in 1898.

[4] Francis Hirst, author of a biography of Adam Smith.

[5] Sister of Mrs. Webb.

[6] Sidney James Webb, Baron Passfield (1859–1947). Social reformer and historian. Joined Fabian Society in 1885 and with
Sidney Olivier (later Lord Olivier) and Graham Wallas, greatly
influenced the Society's policy. In 1891 Webb took part in the Progressive campaign for the London County Council, and in 1892 was
returned as member for Deptford, retaining this seat until 1910. In
1892 Webb married Beatrice Potter (1858–1943), the 8th of 9
beautiful sisters. She was already enquiring into conditions of
London life and work. In 1894 the Webbs published a *History of
Trade Unionism*, followed in 1897 by *Industrial Democracy*. In 1895
they were instrumental in starting the London School of Economics,
to which they both were devoted. From 1915–1925 Sidney was a
member of the Labour Party Executive, and in 1922 was returned
to Parliament for Seaham. He was President of the Board of Trade
in the first Labour Government, 1924, and Secretary of State for
Colonies in 1929. He resigned in 1931. The Webbs travelled several
times in Russia, and in 1935 their *Soviet Communism, a New Civilization?* was published. In 1944 Sidney received the O.M.

3

them off. O'Rorke and Jones, both Reverend and in black, came to see me off.

We had some beautiful views of the Welsh coast on the way out, and wondered if the old man of England[1] would still be living among them when we came back.

Next morning, 24th, after a decent passage, we found ourselves in Queenstown harbour, a lovely morning; the white houses, blue water, green hills and yellow gorse making as pretty a sight as was needed of the beautiful island. I took some photos. Then the inevitable Irish steerage passengers came on. A jolly fellow with a turn-up nose, and a limp, and a yellow and black woollen collar, and a brogue, immediately constituted himself Mark Tapley and M.C. of the Irish jig dancing. And before they were out of the harbour the fiddle was going and instead of wullaloo and lamentations they were all smiling and trying to forget. Some cheerful Irish women were allowed on board to sell bog-oak ornaments, green hankerchiefs and Kenmare lace.

Then we started. The coast was clearer than when the French entered Bantry Bay, and there were one or two castles to be seen along the cliffs which I am told Pitt put up since, being rather flustered by the near shave we had of Hoche becoming Lord Lieutenant.

All went pretty well until the evening. Merriment was a little forced at dinner. But most of us got through the night. I need not try to record the pleasures and interests of the next three days, the 25th, 26th, and 27th. They do not present themselves consecutively to the recollection. All but about half a dozen out of the 160 saloon passengers admit they never had a worse time. I was not actually sick much; but all that could be done was to walk up and down the rolling and lurching decks, to sit looking glumly out over the whitening waves rolled up in rugs, to say a cheerful sentence now and then, to read a page now and then, to go to dinner and eat a little bit of beef or chicken and run up again for the air, to be tossed about in your bunk at night, the whole ship cracking, groaning, banging, jumping, rolling, palpitating, smelling, etc. I never spent three days of more unadulterated misery. It was not that I have not been more miserable. But I have never been so absolutely without

[1] Gladstone (1809–1898).

4

some compensating comfort or pleasure. By the 28th yesterday we were a good deal happier and are beginning to know each other better, to talk, play chess, and eat freely. Today I am as fit as a fiddle, getting up at 6 o'clock and writing this before 8.30 breakfast without a trifle even of squeamishness. Olivier, by the way, Joe Chamberlain's emissary from the Colonial Office to America re Sugar Question in West Indies, old Fabian, present eminent Civil Servant, is with us – did I tell you? He, damn him, has been quite well all the time, and has been writing despatches, calculating what the tariffs in cents work out to be in £s, composing works of his own, and generally making himself disagreeably active to the irritation of the incapacitated. Webb however was a good set off, who was as bad as possible. No one would have thought that the green haggard little man who appeared on deck for an hour a day had controlled the policy of the Metropolis.

For our fellow-passengers – there are no fierce men, there is hardly any poker. Three gentlemen of Texas, who look more like Irish A.D.Cs. than farmers, are the most flashy of the party. One has a pretty American wife. There are two Scotchmen whom I like. There are a lot of business men with whom I talk about the tariff and Interstate Commerce Commission. But on the whole the company is dull. The best man is a tall competent looking engineer from near Brighouse who has built a railway a thousand miles up the Amazon and is now practically boss of the State of Amazonas in Brazil. He runs the place. He is going to have a sort of revolution soon and make an independent state of which he is evidently going to be president. Read the 'Man of Mark' and put a competent Yorkshireman in the place of the silly clerk. I will show you if I can a photo of the future President of Amazonas. The ladies are uninteresting. The best of them with whom I have made friends is a Miss Jackson, but she has been so ill that I have not seen much of her. I have also talked to a languid lady from Newport, who reads things and whose husband does not with emphasis.

Since breakfast I have found an old acquaintance of Mark and Robert Philips, much excited at meeting me, one Richard Sykes. Know ye of him? If so, let me hear. He has a town called after him in the very part of Dakota to which I have intended going, and owns much land. He will introduce me to the

5

Western farmer. It is a good stroke of luck. I made his acquaintance over Captain Mahan's books.

The ship is a grand place, or would be if on land. It is the most comfortable of hotels, jolly stewards—mine Tay, Pay, O'Connor—very good eating, a decent Scotch Captain, nice officers, excellent library almost entirely novels except Macaulay's Life. The only objection to our life, barring the seasickness, is that we are so entirely separated from the people who run the ship while at work. There is no one to ask the meaning of a rope or the character of the ship on the horizon.

March 30

Up in the morning by six in hopes of getting a first view of America. Great disappointment. The water like a mill-pond, but pouring rain obscures the view, so I turn in here to finish letter to you. The last day was real pleasure. It was very calm and everyone was in good humour, wondering they ever were ill.

Like Swift to Stella I must end my letters at a date and begin the next one on the evening of the same day. So here this must end. Love to England.

Yours
C. P. T.

2. NEW YORK AND WASHINGTON

Hotel Westminster,
Irving Place, N.Y.

Wednesday, March 30

We passed Sandy Hook about nine o'clock, the weather gloomy and dull so that the view of the New York Harbour was not what it might have been. On the left as we went in we passed Lafayette Island where the southern prisoners were shut up.[1] They could not have had more room than in Libby prison. But the natural sanitary advantages were no doubt superior. On the same side is Fort Wadsworth with three generations of fortifica-

[1] During Civil War 1861–1866.

6

tion—first little ? pounders (sic) of the last century—secondly, a stone fort by the water's edge of the middle century like Ft. Sumpter—thirdly, the wooden green ridge, screening unseen batteries.

(March 30. They are said today to be blowing up the wooden summer walk and round it in preparation for war.[1])

Then on into the inner harbour, with quick paddle steamers shooting across to New Brighton and New Jersey, yachts at anchor, ships being towed up by steamers into port, with the colossal Liberty statue in the midst, holding aloft its torch. Then we began working slowly up the Hudson—On our right was New York. First was a green garden, very unwarlike, the Battery, at the tip of the City's nose—Behind rise about thirty huge buildings some 16 storeys high. At first you think them store-rooms. But they are really Wall Street and the business quarters of the new world, the few acres where the whole machine of politics and society is worked from. The offices are piled one on the top of the other to save the precious space, no smoke coming from chimneys but little puffs of white steam from the heating engines flickering all over the huge castles. About eleven we got on shore, saying goodbye to our fellow passengers, wife of episcopalian methodist bishop of Africa especially effusive, having discovered at last moment my relationship to Macaulay. 'I guess, young man, it's a great responsibility. May the Lord bless you.' Our luggage was searched without undue fuss and expedited by waggon. We went off in a car. The car was full and we had to stand at the back. We had to hold on tight. It lurched more than the ship. Later we found that this lurching is confined to the horse trams running down the side streets. The electric cars that go down the main avenues and Broadway at about 15 miles an hour are very steady, and comfortable, if you can get a seat. But you generally can't. You stand in the middle hanging onto straps on the ledge outside. This is because no one ever takes a cab, no one ever walks if he can help it. The cars follow as close as they can to one another, but cannot accommodate the mass. For long distances the overhead railways are very pleasant, as quick as the underground but airy, and not disfiguring the town much,

[1] In support of insurgents in Cuba, against the repressive rule of Spain.

nor in any way endangering traffic even in the streets over which they run. Altogether I like the system of progression here.

We have gone to this quiet but comfortable hotel in the centre of the town exactly between the residential and business quarters, 'used by diplomats' says Baedeker, so we thought we would go for Olivier's sake as he is going in that capacity to Washington. Very nice nigger boys, who talk in cheery frankly familiar way, do the answering of bells and running of errands. The waiting is done by a mixed European set of waiters. We have got a sitting room and are on the American plan, i.e. ex-pension. In the evening to see the American rendering of Tess of the D'Urbervilles. We all agreed the situation to be impossible, or at least unconvincing. The whole play worked out rather melodramatically. But it was far better than it would have been in England. The actors and actresses were far more natural than with us, and though none but Mrs. Fiske, the Tess, were really good they all were up to a decent standard. Above all none were vulgar or coarse. So to bed in a hot room. They do not understand the value of air in New York indoors, though they keep purer air out of doors than in any other great city. I walked without gloves from lunch to tea and did not need to wash my hands. Poor Halifax, poorer London. Mrs. Webb called it 'an elegant city' in her diary when she was here as a girl. We all agree with her. Certainly the first impression is that of a foreign continental city with its broad, bright boulevards.

Thursday, March 31

Got up early after a bad night in a stuffy room. No doubt partly due to tittupping by sea, because at times the hotel seems to rock gently like the saloon of the 'Teutonic'. But as a first duty I went and got my room changed to an airy one upstairs. Then I went out to have my boots blacked. No midnight porter here cleans your boots while you sleep. But you go out into the streets where every few hundred yards are raised chairs on which you may sit and have your boots comfortably blacked by a licensed bootblack, who generally speaks some foreign tongue. It is a very good position from which to watch the people going in to their work at the stores (shops) in the morning. The average man looks much healthier and less worn

8

than in London and I do not yet see the signs of the nervous pressure so much talked about. The city is bristling and active, but not more so than London. The feeling of foreignness is disappearing today. The language and the universal activity are so unlike a French or German city. I am beginning to feel as if I were among our own people. This has grown more quickly with seeing a variety of interesting people today. We went to lunch at a restaurant with Mr. Graham Brooks, a friend of the Webbs a political and economic writer and enquirer. The Rev. Rainsford a very active social reform clergyman, but *very* unclerical, sat next me. We had a capital talk about shooting in the Rockies and politics. Seth Low was the other guest. He is President of Columbia University N.Y. and was the Reform Candidate for the Mayoralty against Tammany[1] last year. We had a most interesting talk with him. We thought him very capable, probably more of a practical man than a student, though with not quite the dash or presence for a very good candidate. He was on the whole very hopeful in his views. In the afternoon I went with Bob Ferguson, (Ronald's brother) who is exceedingly hospitable, to see several people. Hewitt Papa knows, late Mayor of N.Y. He is rich, with a house furnished in English fashion, with stately butler etc., talks of Aunt Alice,[2] and has a country house up the Hudson. Talkative daughters.

Then to see Cameron, three times Senator for Pennsylvania, and now Republican boss of that state. He showed more of the reputed American traits than anyone I have met yet. We found him smoking in his bedroom. As we settled down to talk, he drew his cuspidor (Angl. spittoon) to him, and 'guessed Bryan[3] would have won if the price of corn had not gone up.'

In the evening I went alone to a native American play 'Far Down East' depicting a modern puritan family in Massachusetts. The acting was not very good, but thoroughly natural

[1] The popular name for the Democratic Party in New York City and State.

[2] Younger sister of Sir George Otto Trevelyan ('G. O. T.'), married Stratford Dugdale.

[3] William Jennings Bryan (1860–1925). Populist and free-silver Democrat candidate for Presidency. He was narrowly defeated by Republican candidate, William McKinley, in 1897.

and very enjoyable. One incident during the performance was remarkable to me. After the first act a gruff not uncourteous voice asked to pass me in my row in the dress circle. A policeman in full dress pushed past and sat through the next act looking on and talking to a group of his friends. He did take his hat off. But what would the Criterion think of having a Bobby dropping in to have a look. Outside their chief duty seemed to be to converse with the passers by, preferably the women. Such is one side of Tammany.

Friday, April 1

Getting very much at home in New York today. The best part of the morning I spent with a representative of the religious world, Rev. Josiah Strong who was a man of the best religious sort, entirely devoted to utilizing the Churches for world progress and social reform. He is a keen advocate of Arbitration and English Alliance, and is using his very considerable position to educate the new generation here to a higher standard of citizenship. It is rapidly becoming evident to me that the United States does not in any way lack the very earnest, philanthropic, public spirited class that abound in England. Indifference to social or political wrong is not a characteristic of the people. They are quite as much alive to it as we are.

In the afternoon down to the other end of the town to Wall Street, where I had an hour's conversation with Bacon, Manager of the Pierpoint Morgan Bank, contrast enough to Strong. Had a long talk on Cuba, Silver, etc. He is going to do his best to get me into Congress on Monday. Went down to see the Battery in the beautiful evening light, a lovely view of sea and land. Then out to tea with the Chandlers with whom Hester Lyttleton stayed. You can tell her how much I liked them if you see her. Unfortunately I could not do more than this short visit of $\frac{3}{4}$ hour.

Dined with the Hewitts and went with them to Buffalo Bill after. It was still good fun. This time there was added a squad of 12 Cubans mostly officers wounded in the war, carrying the Cuban banner. They rode round in turns, their names and wounds called out to the audience, and cheered as they galloped past. Of course the war is the chief topic. It is not worth while here discussing its probability because by the time this letter reaches you the question will be settled. But today it seems inevitable. Bacon in the City thought so, where they do not like or want war, though they acquiesce. I must say this that the attitude of the country is most admirable. The majority genuinely do not want to fight though of course many think it will be good fun. But there are hardly any people, and certainly no party who have not definitely made up their minds that it is a matter of duty to turn the abominable Spaniard out of Cuba and have done with the miserable condition once and for all. On this occasion the Senate does not represent opinion. It is true that the Maine[1] explosion has been one of the causes of unanimity, but mere desire for vengeance is not the leading motive and the Maine is only a minor point in the argument against Spain. I very much hope that, if there be war, it will be appreciated in England that it is a war purely for humanity and not for aggrandizement. The general approval of England so far has pleased the Americans very much.

Everything is betokening war. The papers are crammed from beginning to end, with rumours, with statements (generally lies), with calculations of the Spanish navy, with plans of campaign, with lives of admirals, with pictures of ships. One paper had the Ballad of the Revenge all over its front page. Another had an autograph letter from Grant[2] asking that his grandson be given a nomination to the army and then an announcement that the young man now 16, was dying to fight the Spaniards. The sensationalism of the papers is unbelievable till you see them. It is also incredible how little interesting or reliable information they give. On the whole they are the worst of the great American institutions, tawdry, vulgar, vicious, lying, foolish. But on the whole they follow, do not lead opinion. Few believe their facts, though many are tickled by their conceits and inventions. I enclose with this another packet of the Maine Disaster, which I explain how to work in my note. (Apply the red glow of a match to the point on paper where torch is being held by Spaniard). Did you ever see a cleverer political cartoon.

[1] American battleship, blown up in Havana harbour, Cuba, in 1898, for which the Spaniards were blamed.
[2] Ulysses S. Grant (1822–1885), Union General in Civil War, President of U.S.A. 1868.

The way of advertising news at the Newspaper offices is original. It is all written out in large hand in ink or charcoal and posted up the height of a man's head. It is much pleasanter to read than printed capitals. You see crowds round it all day.

Saturday, April 2

Indeed you were wise to advise me to have an inside pocket to my waistcoat. Webb mislaid his pocket-book twice and has finally lost it with the form of application for his circular notes in it! Probably it was stolen in a car. Fortunately he has not lost the notes, so he has only to wait until he can get a new application form. Meanwhile I, who have my money all safe have to finance them. So I spent part of this morning down at Wall St. again drawing money. After that I saw Albert Shaw, Editor of the American Edition of the Review of Reviews, an interesting, vigorous, youngish Western man, with whom I talked long, and from whom I have got a good lot of introductions westwards.

Lunch at Columbia University with President Seth Low and the Professors. Afterwards we went over the buildings which are new. It is the old university endowed by George II with £3,400, now enlarged by private munificence to a great university of a modern model type. The central building is a Library given by Low himself, round it other schools. The mere mechanical perfection and excellence of building and arrangement astounded us. There were engines for electricity and warming fit to run the hugest cotton mill in Halifax. There were boarded running tracks indoors sloped at the corners. There were baths lit by submarine electricity, ideally perfect lecture rooms, a grand reading room, Beautiful system of library arrangement. Poor Trinity men gaze aghast, and ask where Trinity will be in this next generation. Somehow perhaps the library will fill quicker from the brains of the old college than the ingenuity of the new. But there is no doubt that when a thing is done here, it is the best that the time can make. It brought home to me that the two systems could never be comparable. But it shows clearly to me the desire for learning and consequent certainty of its eventual growth here.

Visited Godkin, Editor of Nation & Evening Post, respectable English sort of papers. A very English household.

Dined with Whitridge. Mr. Mat Arnold had just arrived. A pleasant dinner. Then on with Whitridge to finish up my first stay in N.Y. with a visit to the Century Club, the literary and intellectual centre of the City, a mixture of the Savile and Athenaeum. Once a month there is a great congregation of people. Fortunately we hit off the right Saturday. I talked to Chamberlain, rather a fire-eating champion of arbitration, but from whom I got some information. I saw Schuz, once a republican Cabinet Minister with Hayes, now a supporter of Seth Low and the Independent Reformers in New York. He is President of the Civil Service Reform Association. I spoke to the Editor of the Century, Gilder. Saw also Colonel Waring who organized the Street cleaning under the reform administration. But the man I was most pleased to meet was W. D. Howells,[1] a charming, quiet, enthusiastic little man, very keen about the moral side of politics, though not taking part in them. He was very pleased to hear about your writing. Altogether a most pleasant evening and good end up to the first visit of the tour.

Sunday, April 3

Left New York for Washington. Graham Brooks saw us off at New Jersey side. The first glimpse of rural America not inspiring. The whole line is disfigured with endless advertisements of Schenk's Mandrake Pills and Sapolio etc. to an extent unheard of at home. Every wooden barn within 300 yards of railway was ornamented with huge lettering. The country at once brings back recollections of the photos of the Civil War in the Century. There is a great deal of low wood, beech, oak and birch, which has never been cleared, generally a good deal of water lying in it, sometimes mere marsh land. The intervening clearings are very lightly tilled, the soil in most places apparently merely scratched for sowing. Many tracts are covered with long coarse grass or reed. The fences are very light wood. The roads appear to be merely dirt roads, sand tracks, that would soon be dug up by waggons or artillery. The houses are universally wooden, generally painted bright white, sometimes red brown. It all

[1] William Dean Howells (1837–1920), novelist and critic, leader of American letters, editor of *Atlantic Monthly*, editor and friend of Henry James and Mark Twain.

13

gives the idea of a country which is only half developed, even there in New Jersey and Pennsylvania; the natural resources not half utilized yet, the land not half cleared. What a country, if this is the part of it that is most filled up.

Reached Washington. Found a crowded Hotel. Manager says there was never such a crowd before except at time of an Inauguration.

Monday, April 4

Morning news more peaceable. The President is not as was expected to send his final message to the Congress today.

Out with Webb to present introductions. First round by White House. It is a worthy building for a democratic king, not over large, It is quite white, with a garden of pretty coloured flowers in front. All round are flowering trees and bushes. Simple architecture, no gaudiness. Beautiful magnolias and a green lawn with slim park railings separate it from the road. The gates are open to pedestrians, and carriages, and anyone who has business, or thinks he has, can walk up unchallenged. Below it rises the colossal obelisk to Washington. On one side the Treasury, on the other the Army and Navy Departments guard it. We went to the Navy, passing in between two giant anchors, to visit Roosevelt the Secretary. At the top of the stairs was the model of the Maine. We went into a waiting room whence we were shown into a clerk's room, into which Roosevelt came in a few minutes. He greeted us courteously and forcefully, settling in a moment that we were to lunch with him. The way he did it showed him to be a man who knew how to deal with his fellows, and we went off understanding how he had been able to cure the corruption of the Tammany police in his 3 years of office. More of him presently. Then we went to the British Embassy and saw Pauncefote, a respectable elderly diplomatist, who moved us from one room to another, until we had got out of the draught. He was very pleasant and will help us to get into the Senate. But never was democratic effectiveness and aristocratic dilatoriness more marked than passing from Roosevelt to Pauncefote.

Then we went to see the head of the Washington Labour Bureau, and got more introductions from him. We shall see more of him presently, name Errol Wright.

THE AUTHOR IN CHICAGO

THE WEBBS CROSSING
THE PACIFIC

SIR GEORGE
TREVELYAN, THE
AUTHOR'S FATHER,
AND THEODORE
ROOSEVELT

Then to lunch with Roosevelt, who is rampantly for war. He is an absolutely fearless man, who went into New York politics with ideas which he now admits were impractical of a reform movement uncompromisingly righteous in everything. He learnt to compromise as he explained to us by bitter experience, but still keeps his vigorous enthusiasms. He is burnt up with rage at the Spanish atrocities and longs for war. He is raging against the callous powers of the stock exchange. McKinley[1] has heard some plain speaking from him. He is clearly a very noble and practical character, and will go further than any man I have yet seen. He is a brilliant and epigrammatic talker which makes him the life of any company. If he fails in making a big name for himself, it will be because of some act of jovial daring. He is dying to fight himself at this moment, and if an army did go to Cuba, he would go with it and throw up his secretaryship.

After this most interesting lunch we went off to the Capitol. It is a magnificent thing. I have never seen St. Peter's; but it is far the most adequate building for its intention I have ever seen. It is huge, it is strong, it is reasonably simple, it stands well, it is of beautiful white stone mixed with marble. It has a very fine dome of white stone also. In every way it represents a great nation and its best aspirations. It strikes awe. By it is a beautiful new building, the Congress Library. We immediately made friends with the doorkeeper of the Senate, a gentleman of great importance, looking like a clever clerk as so many responsible Americans do. He sent us all over the building under charge of one of his attendants. With the usual love of mechanical processes which characterizes America we were taken first to see how the ventilating fan worked. It was very good, but not quite as interesting as Guy Fawkes' vault. Then we went into the gallery of the Senate, above half as big again as the School Board and arranged like it except for large galleries all round. It looked very decorous and businesslike, but we did not stay as only uninteresting private bills were under discussion. From these we walked through many palatial lobbies to the House of Representatives. There is full access to the lobbies and the galleries and the place was alive with sightseers and lobbyists. The House of Representatives was a very different sight to the

[1] William McKinley, President 1897–1901. Assassinated in office.

Senate. It was a huge hall, big enough to hold every member's desk and revolving easy chair. Huge galleries are round all sides. There is no restriction on at any rate moderate talking in the galleries, so that a steady hum pervades them. The talking in the chamber is quite immoderate. There was a railway bill under discussion. Two members, one proposing an amendment, the other in charge of the bill and opposing stood up together and conversed with one another, the shorthand reporter in the gangway between them. When they had done and both sat down, the clerk told the President, who was in a rocking chair on the dais talking with three members, that the debate was at an end and he put the question, which was carried with some alteration – and so on. Meanwhile all the other members, some 60 or so in the room carried on conversation about other things. Small messenger boys lolled in some of the empty arm chairs towards the back. In a sofa just below us, behind the seats, lay a representative asleep *and snoring*! Now I do not say that business cannot be transacted under such conditions, but it is interestingly different to the House of Commons where the attendance may be small but at least regards the speakers as in possession of the house. However I daresay we shall see a different sight when the Presidents message on Cuba has reached Congress tomorrow or the next day. That story you will have to wait for. Tomorrow in any case we spend at the Senate, where we have a sheaf of interesting introductions.

Bless you all.
Charles Trevelyan

3. WASHINGTON. MOUNT VERNON

Written in the gallery of the Senate House, Washington, while waiting for the opening of the session in which President McKinley is going to send his Message about the war with Spain.

April 6, 1898

Tuesday, April 5

(Day before) A sudden spell of cold weather. Snow falling most of the morning.

Went to the Capitol to see Senators. Spent an hour first in the new Library of Congress, a gorgeous palace. The stairway is very fine, all grey and white marble. The decoration is very bold and coloured. But the effect is not unpleasantly gaudy. Some modern French pictures in the inner rooms are bad and vicious. But the hall is the best new public interior I have seen.

Over the main entrance to the library are the heads of half a dozen great English and American writers. The English are represented by Macaulay and Scott. I am inclined to think G. O. T.[1] is the best known English living writer. Everybody asks about him because of the Life.[1]

Then to the Senate, where I stayed for some hours, interviewing Senators in the Marble Room, the comfortable inner lobby of the Senate. First I saw Cabot Lodge, who is one of the most active Republicans, very pro-american, who has written much against the tendency of Americans to defer to English opinion & I believe is a good deal responsible for the loss of the Arbitration Treaty. He is a friend of Aunt Alice – I am going to dine with him today (Wednesday). Then I saw an old Senator Hawley to whom Bryce[2] gave me an introduction, who was

---

[1] Sir George Otto Trevelyan (1838–1928), father of Charles. He was the son of Sir Charles Edward Trevelyan, who married Hannah, sister of Lord Macaulay. G. O. T. wrote the *Life and Letters of Lord Macaulay* (1876), one of the best known of all biographies in the English language.

[2] James, Viscount Bryce (1838–1922), jurist, historian, and politician. He wrote *The American Commonwealth*, first published in 1888, revised editions 1893 and 1895. It gives a thorough picture of the political system of the country and is recognized as a standard work in America.

rather ancient and sleepy, but very kind. He gave me an oyster lunch and passed me on to others. While with him we met Mr. Smith of the Philadelphia Press, who had sat next G. O. T. at some dinner and said that he knew more about the American war than anyone in America.

Next I had a long talk with a young Independent Bryanite from South Dakota. As I rather expected, the spirit in which he took things was very much the same as our own social reformers, Liberals & Progressives, at home, only they are not yet definite enough in their issues. It is not even certain that Silver will be the real fight. But I think it looks like it. For the next man I saw was Jones, the leader of the Democratic Party in the Senate, who did not lay stress on anything except Silver – He was an oldish man, serious and sensible, but not a quick thinker or commanding personality. He was very much of the boss type, knowing the expedient.

In the evening I called on Mrs. Cabot Lodge, a very nice bright lady.

We dined with Wright, head of the Labour Bureau with one or two other quiet people. It was interesting as showing the style of a quiet American household. They gave us a less pretentious dinner than the same class in England, the profusion being in the way of ice-cream, which in deference to them I eat for the first time, and found to be good. Wright is a keen fellow, very progressive – not nearly as good as I. L. Smith, but quite worthy of the position.

We sat up till late in the bar of the Hotel drinking lemon squashes. It was rather poor, but I shall begin cock-tails and American Drinks at Chicago – with Albert Shaw.

Wednesday, April 6

A beautiful though cold day, propitious for the declaration of war if there is to be one – America is delighted at the English refusing to join the Concert of Europe in proposals of mediation. They feel that they come too late to be genuine, and are only an excuse for bolstering up Spain. The good feeling to England and the consciousness that the great future depends upon our good relations in time to come, is quite universal among the thinking people and as far as I have seen among the whole population. It is certainly quite as strong as our friendliness to America. But I shall have a lot to say about that, and cannot begin a dissertation now.

We are now seated in the gallery of the Senate – Time 10.15, house meets at 12. Pauncefote has got us into the diplomatic gallery just opposite the Speaker. All the sitting room in the other galleries is already crowded. Files of people are waiting in the passages outside for the chance of standing room some time hence. The greater excitement will be in the House of Representatives. But it will be pretty keen here. If the Spanish ambassador comes & sits in front of us, I shall join the cheering if there is any strong declaration. There are as many women as men almost in the room at this moment. The ladies' galleries are nearly as large as the men's, though not so exclusive. Men can go in with ladies.

1 *o'clock*. The Message has not yet come. It is said to be delayed till 3 o'clock, until a cablegram is received from Havana, we suppose to say that the Consul has left. The House is discussing the Appropriation Bill – rather dull details – expenditure on paint of White House and cost of Yellowstone Park. I have just taken a photo of the gallery – 'Waiting for the President's Message'.

Later. Alas! We were miserably done out of our drama. At about 1.30 some one moved that the House sit in executive session, which means clearing the galleries. The listening multitude groaned low. But out we all had to go. We went off to get lunch; but before the oysters were out before us the news came that the doors were again open. So we rushed back. But we were soon told that the Message was not coming. It has been postponed until Monday next.

So off we went, the day ending flatly for us.

I went to see the battle of Gettysburg[1] panorama, a very mildewed one but excellent. Pickett's charge is the central feature, you standing at the Bloody Angle, where I hope really to stand on Wednesday. By the way we heard them voting

---

[1] In 1863 the Confederate Army under Robert E. Lee invaded Pennsylvania, but was intercepted by the Union force at Gettysburg, and after a three-day battle fell back to the Potomac. Pickett's desperate charge on the final day, facing terrific fire, was one of the most gallant episodes of the Civil War, but failed.

supplies for Gettysburg, $50,000, and for Chickamauga[1] which they have made into National Parks. They are now going to do the same with Shiloh,[2] voting I think for the first time $55,000 for it.

After this I visited the Tuckermans, a charming mother and middle aged daughter who are the centre of polite society here. Then on to call at the Embassy, where afternoon tea was being run by a bouncing handsome Bostonian girl, a contrast to the rather staid shy English girls round her.

In the evening a most interesting dinner with Cabot Lodge. Willy Chandler, a queer fellow, who has had Cuban adventures, backs Tammany and does all sorts of daring and incongruous things. But the life and soul of the party – as of all parties where he is present – was Roosevelt. Of course all the talk was about the war. I had a most interesting half hour, hearing about all the commanders of the American battle ships, the probable naval policy, the methods of warfare. Then we got on to discussing the military qualities of the races – G. O. T. would find him the best companion in the world. But to have a talk at such a time, when he has got the navy in hand which will probably be fighting in a week, is delightfully exciting. He bore out what we had heard about Mahan.[3] He says he has no executive power at all, no decision and nerve and that he will not have command, but that they are using him as adviser. He and Mahan are very strong on smashing the Spanish fleet, before spending energy in an attack on Havana – arguing from old historical lessons. The fleet are straining to be at the nearest Spaniards. But probably the wiser policy of attacking the Spanish fleet will prevail. I can tell you it is an exciting thing living in the midst of a nation preparing for war.

I have got my photos now. Some are very good. I send some. But the best, those I took of you, Papa & Booa[4] before I left, I

[1] Battle of the Civil War.
[2] Battle of the Civil War.
[3] Captain A. T. Mahan insisted on the importance of sea power and on the duty of spreading the benefits of American civilisation overseas.
[4] Mrs. Prestwich, devoted Nurse to the three Trevelyan brothers. She remained with the family and acted as amanuensis to G. O. T., deciphering his close-written, and often cross-written, scrawl, which she copied out in long hand for most of his books, before the days of typewriters.

keep because I want them by me. They are better than stilted shop photos.

Thursday, April 7

Went up the Washington Monument, the highest solid building in the world. It is a huge stone obelisk, very simple and impressive. It is so big that there is room inside for a very big lift and a wide stair-case and landings all the way up. I walked up, taking $\frac{1}{4}$ hour heavy climbing, in preference to waiting 40 minutes for a place in the lift. A magnificent view of the city from the top, except that the Capitol did not stand out, any more than the elevation of Mont Martre is recognizable from the top of the Eiffel.

To lunch with Roosevelt at a Restaurant. Party consisted of the Tuckerman ladies, both charming but not very politically wise, and consequently uproariously chaffed by Roosevelt for their 'sucking dove' attitude about Spain; a Dr. Reece, a very intelligent New York reformer, a German with an astounding mixture of German and American accent; Senator Proctor, a great civil service reformer; W. Chandler whom I explained yesterday; Bob Ferguson; an unknown and ourselves. First we had put before us a dish of what we thought was meant for soup a nasty reddish mess at bottom of plate, which I vainly tried to refuse. However the nigger waiter insisted, and presently oysters began to be dropped into the said mess, until we had had more than was good for us and we were able forcibly to prevent any more being put on our plates. Then we had 'ruddy duck' and boiled housing round it. It was better than Wallington wild-duck – then coffee. A most unEnglish lunch certainly! Roosevelt again in tearing spirits.

Then Webb and I to the House to see the Speaker, who is extremely unlike Peel or Sully. He runs the House. He appears to manage the whole order of business, to interview and influence the members, to push his own party. He is a rum cove. He does not talk unless he has something to say, sits in his chair rocking and looks at you. Then says bang out in idiomatic and often expletive English what he thinks. A blunt forcible individual! He sent us up into the gallery with his secretary. Certainly the worst said about the House is hardly too bad. A debate was going on about an increase of the army. The opportunity of course was taken to discuss the Cuban question. The country in general is very angry at the present delay, having worked itself up to the expectation of a declaration by the President yesterday. Before we came in a Democrat had made a violent attack upon him. Now a respectable looking Ohio Member, Grosvenor, was defending him, on the perfectly justifiable ground that he wishes to save the Americans in Cuba. He asserted that he was not influenced by the moneyed interests, which is the usual accusation, in his delay. The speech was sensible enough, but in any case would have been a poor oratorial effort. But every two minutes he was interrupted. In the first place they have an extraordinary procedure by which they settle, to begin with, how long a man is to be allowed to speak – then if he has not done they extend it. Neither side as a rule object to extension but generally they have different ideas as to the length desirable. That causes three minutes shouting every quarter of an hour. Then every three minutes some opponent would get up and insist on being heard, ask the speaker a question or challenge a statement and remain standing until he had been answered. Occasionally there would be a fire of repartee, and always the freest language! No sensation was caused by a member saying that his hon. friend had told an untruth. Once without any expostulation the speaker called out 'God help the men who have *you* for an advocate'. Meanwhile dozens of members stood in the space in front of the speaker's chair or lounged up the aisles between the chairs, or sauntered out of the smoking rooms which opened on the House to take a few whiffs behind the chairs. The Speaker occasionally rapped with his hammer and when the noise made everyone inaudible shouted 'The House will be in Order', until reasonable quiet was restored. This went on for some three quarters of an hour, when Grosvenor sat down, though he might have done it half an hour before or half an hour later for all the difference it would have made to the effectiveness of his argument. Immediately at least a dozen of his friends sitting round him shook him warmly by the hand. After him the leader of the Democratic party, Bailey of Texas, a most sleek, conceited, ineffective, preachy young man got up and made a bad speech explanatory of his position. Of course the assembly is not to be compared to our House of Commons. It has not the authority and there-

22

fore not the personel. But I expected something better. The Senate alone pretends to authority, dignity or competence.

This night we went to a play of Shaw's which happened to be acting here, the 'Devil's Disciple'. It was very amusing and there was a good and appreciative house. It was much better acted than 'Arms & the Man', but I do not think it was so amusing. It has a good deal of the melodrama in it, and as the conclusion is Burgoyne's surrender, it is flattering to this great people.

Friday, April 8

Today we have spent chiefly with Democratic and Populist politicians. In the morning we were introduced by Kyle to Senator Allen, Bryan's chief of staff in the last campaign. He was a fine old boy, who had been a private in the war, and had a son who was dying to enlist to fight Spain. He was not a deeply versed thinker, but was very shrewd, and his opinions were thoroughly sensible. In the difficult economic questions they have to face he was led by party programme. But his feeling was right and right also in his complete friendliness to England. I find in none of them any of that hostility of which we heard so much, and I am getting to be very hopeful of the future of our relations. He received us in his shirt-sleeves, and expectorated freely into a huge cuspidor. Generally in the East expectoration is less now than in the average English city, though there are more spittoons about, and a few notices against it linger on in the cars. Out west I expect to find more of it still in practice.

After him I saw the head of the Education Bureau an interesting and cultivated man, Dr. Harris.

In the afternoon I saw my first game of baseball, a kind of glorified rounders. I don't think it could come up to cricket however well played and however skilful. I took some photos of it, which will enable me to explain it.

This evening we had Congressman Simpson of Kansas to see us, another rough sensible Western Populist.

Saturday, April 9

Went to see Mount Vernon, the home of Washington. It is on the Potomac, about 15 miles from Washington. I went by car along an electric line. As we approached Mount Vernon there was a rather steep ascent and our full cars stuck the first time, and we ran back to level ground again, then rushed at it like a horse that has refused a jump. This time we just crawled up. It is evident that one of the chief difficulties of electric locomotion in the present is their inability to get special force for emergencies. The steerer of the train has less means of creating power than the steam engineer. Mount Vernon is a very pretty white wooden house with a red tiled roof. It is on the top of the Virginia bank of the Potomac. The slopes are clothed in woods and the view up and down and across the river was very beautiful, even now when the trees were not in leaf. The Washingtons must have been very substantial people. The house is simple wood, but no one built in anything else in those days, nor indeed now except in towns. But there are plenty of rooms and good sized ones, some 6 on each of three floors. A good deal of the old carpeting and furniture has been preserved or recovered, and it shows a pretty high standard of taste and comfort. Other of the rooms have been furnished by various state governments, most of them with furniture appropriate to the period. But Wisconsin has exhibited its patriotism by giving a wholesale order to some modern upholsterer in Milwaukee, and has filled the chamber allotted to it with modern chairs, chests of drawers, and bed-hangings after the style of a middle-class bedroom in an English provincial town. Altogether I do not think the reverential or sentimental strain is strongly developed yet in the Yankee. Of the hundreds at the place today, no one but myself took off his hat before Washington's tomb. The relics were not particularly interesting. But the whole surroundings in spite of tourists and oyster patties at the entrance were very real. Behind the house away from the river ran two sets of buildings, on one side the stables, and kitchen, and barns; on the other the slave lodgings. In front was a clear lawn for Mr. and Mrs. Washington to step out onto and tell the truth on. I would not mind it much in exchange for Wallington, if you could add grouse moors and mountains six miles off.

Back again to Washington. Had an hour and half talk with Senator Fairbanks about Immigration and other things.

In the evening to dine with Sir Julian Pauncefote, who was very kind and friendly. He is a most fatherly old boy, quite solid, respectable, diplomatic, stupid, imperturbable as a British Ambassador should be. His daughters are the natural result, nice and stupid, such a contrast to the American average girl. Tell Hester Lyttleton that she has created quite a sensation in the East by her liveliness and phil-Americanism. Miss Bayard, the Chandlers and others besides are full of her.

So ends the stay at Washington. No, not quite. I had unpleasant tenantry in my couch the night; but—

Sunday, April 10

I hope by the time I meet Buckler at Baltimore whither I am being hustled on the Pennsylvanian railroad this Sunday morning, my features will have resumed their accustomed regularity.

Of course most of the talk now is of war. I have said little about it, because it alters from day to day. That it should come is inevitable. All but a few financiers and timid ladies have absolutely made up their minds that Spain shall go and at once. It is hardly conceivable that Spain will go. Those are the unvarying factors. With them no other issue is possible. In some ways it is a pity to leave the East just now. But I should see nothing if I stayed really; and if there is to be land fighting and arming of the people, the West will probably rise to it more vigorously and spontaneously than any other part of the country.

Today I am beginning my solitary journey. But I have got such shoals of introductions that I cannot get lost.

Love to England.
Charles Trevelyan

4. BALTIMORE AND GETTYSBURG

Sunday, April 10

Baltimore is in a charming country and the Buckler's house is in the nicest part of it. Today Buckler took me for a walk to an institution called a country club where we had lunch on oysters and duck. There are no comfortable little inns as in England, and those who want a Sunday lunch out of town have to provide themselves a place to eat it in. We walked home across country, through woods and fields, stopping for tea at the house of an old millionaire of sixty-five who had recently married a wife of 20 summers. Spent a quiet, pleasant evening. Round the house at night-time the marsh-frogs keep up a perpetual twittering song, and are especially musical after rain.

Monday, April 11

Buckler had some business at Annapolis. So I went with him. It is the capital of Maryland, a sleepy old town with a history. Its only modern claim to fame is that it has the naval academy of the U.S.A. We spent some time walking about in the cheerful sunny grounds and barracks where the middies are training. Then we went to the old state-house. It is a fresh looking brick building with a wooden dome, but all quite old. In the room where the Senate of the State now meets Washington came in 1783 to resign his commission. There too, so say local records, the treaty of peace was signed with Great Britain. The historian remembers something about a Paris treaty. But perhaps the discrepancy can be somehow reconciled. Certainly there met the First Constitutional Convention at which 5 states were represented in 1786, the year before the great Convention. Old coaches with nigger drivers still rumble about the streets, looking verily as if they remembered the day when they drove Jefferson and Washington from the cars to the State House to begin constitution making. There is an old church too in an old square, with an ugly modern inside. The American Episcopalian prayer-book which I studied is an almost exact adaptation of the Church of England book, minus the Athanasian creed. It was adopted by the prelates in 1789, when the civil breach had become permanent with the mother-country. The Peggy Stewart was burnt in Annapolis harbour at the time when Boston harbour was black with unexpected tea. Oddly enough the national prejudice against tea-taxing is abiding. While they make sugar, clothes, iron and all else dear for the consumer by almost prohibitive duties, they let in tea free, outdoing us in free trade in that one article. Wm. Buckler drove me through the bright town of Baltimore on our return. Nothing noticeable except the very mean habitation of the Johns Hopkins University, perhaps the best research institution in the States, but housed in scrubby new buildings in the centre of the town.

The President's Message has come. It is too long to comment on. I think it will mean war. I do not think he can possibly ensure pacification in Cuba without ejecting Spain, and force I think is necessary for that. The tone of the Message is very good. But he omits to say the one essential thing – the Spanish troops must go. Nothing else really matters, and that would enable him to demand a clear answer at once. As it is Spain will only shilly-shally and gain strength for a contest which it has determined to undertake. However he is now committed to saving Cuba, and it is now only a question of time.

A very nice lawyer, Buckler's partner, dined here. In this country there are not separate solicitors and barristers. Consequently as one man cannot do all the work of both classes, men form partnerships. Some do the solicitoring others the court pleading and pool the profits. Buckler says it works well, though it generally prevents the prodigious individual profits our few leading lawyers get in England.

Tuesday, April 12

An absolutely quiet day. Read Browning in the morning. Lunched with Buckler and Keyser, a copper manufacturer, at the Maryland Club. Read up Gettysburg in the Peabody Library. A bright fellow, Howard to dinner.

There is in Baltimore a man, Jerome Bonaparte. He has the well-known features. He is grandson of Jerome, brother to Napoleon, who made what became a mésalliance as soon as Napoleon became emperor, and was forced to divorce his American wife and marry in his proper station a second time. But he left a family, whose offspring is the present Bonaparte, who occasionally bursts out as an eloquent and rather effective city reformer. But apparently he will never be President.

Wednesday, April 13

Started early for Gettysburg. On arriving here I at once ordered a carriage. It was a sort of buggy for two, the driver being a guide as well. He drove a very big, unshapely horse that shed white hairs on us all the afternoon. My guide had not seen the fight, being a boy of five in the Cumberland valley on the Western side of the Blue Mountains at the time of the war. But he knew all about it, and told his tale sensibly and not over-sensationally, very soon recognizing that I was no child on a battle ground and not being too elementary. It is a splendid battle to see. The ridges are very distinct, and the positions obvious. But they are emphasized by a very careful marking out of the whole ground. Round almost all the front of the Federal position on the first and third days a barbed wire has been run. But the wonderful things are the monuments. Almost every battery has placed a gun where it did most work. The Bloody Angle and Rickett's Battery at the entrance to the cemetery are crowded with guns. Everywhere where a regiment stood is a monument, solid and generally ugly, sometimes a figure, running or shooting, sometimes a trophy of arms, some-times a mere marble block with an inscription. They are not offensive however, and do not spoil the ground. They mark the keenness of the people to signalize the fame of those who fought, and they help you to understand the fight. It enables you to see without difficulty from the Round Top, the horrible gap in the line made by Sickles' advance. That question I want to read a lot about. I want to know where Sickles was supposed to have been expected to stand. If he was expected to hold the line of the Lower Round Top along the Cemetery Ridge, it was sheer folly advancing. But if he was posted half way to the Peach Orchard, there was every inducement for him I must say to advance as far as the Peach Orchard. It would have commanded him if he had not. It commands the approach from the West. It is the obvious key to all positions in front of the Round Top and Cemetery Ridge.

On the other hand he must have exposed his right flank badly; and the utter blatancy of leaving the Round Top un-defended, until Warren seized it on his own authority, is almost incredible. It makes me very much want to get at the Century accounts again. There are hardly any Confederate monuments. There is one where Armistead fell in the Bloody Angle. There is one page of a giant double scroll on which the names of the regiments are inscribed that made and repelled Pickett's charge. It stands at the grove which was the high water mark

28

of the rebellion. There is one other on Culp's Hill to a Maryland regiment that made a valiant dash on the third day to recover the position from which Johnson was pushed in the morning. All the others, and they are hundreds, are to Federal regiments. It makes the field the record of the cause as well as of the military events. The rows of graves in the war cemetery, where Lincoln made his greatest speech, are most impressive. Otherwise at present I cannot describe the battle. It took 4 hours to see, and will take a lot of talking over. But we must have maps and my photos to talk it over successfully. I hope they come out well. If they do, they will illustrate it a great deal. The Lutheran Seminary still stands on its ridge. The old gate to the Cemetery is the same as ever. The house in which Meade had his head quarters, the barn from which Pickett's charge started, the Devil's Den, the woods on the Round Tops and Culp's Hill, the wall at Bloody Angle, and the High-Water Mark grove are all as they were, or scrupulously repaired exactly as they were. Only the Peach Orchard has lost it Peach Trees like Hougoumont[1] has lost its wood. But it is a clearly marked field still. The town is not much bigger than it was, only increased by a few villas belonging to the professors of the College which is here.

I may say some more, explanatory of my photos, if they succeed a fortnight hence, and now, gentlemen, I am open to questions – Pause – As no one seems to want to ask the speaker anything, his account must be taken as giving universal satisfaction. So, goodbye. Love to all.

Yours aff.
Charles Trevelyan

5. PITTSBURG

Gettysburg

Thursday, April 14

When I had got down this morning the fame of me had penetrated to high official circles. There are three National

---

[1] Chateau on the field of the Battle of Waterloo 1815, defended by Wellington's troops. With the farm of La Haye Sainte, this formed the front line of Wellington's position.

Commissioners who look after the Field, one a Confederate, two Federal, old soldiers all. The Confederate came to look me up and carried me off to their office. We had a good talk about the battle. He had been on Longstreet's right the second day, and had taken part in the charge on the Lower Round Top, which Warren was just in time to repel. One of the two Federal Commissioners who was present had been wounded on the second day, while driving off the attack on Sickles' exposed right wing in the gap between his line and Hancock's. Then my Confederate friend showed me a set of plans of the three battles, at different hours, more elaborate than Siborne's of Waterloo. Before starting I walked again through the cemetery, 'the final resting place of those who here gave their lives that the nation might live.'

Now I am on my way to Pittsburg. We have passed through the Alleghenies. They are fine hills clad everywhere with wood. Not a hill-top that we could see had been cleared. Only the valleys were settled and cultivated. On the whole I thought they would be grander. It was the same sort of disappointment as the Rhine. It was all very good but not magnificent. The immense tract they cover is the wonderful part. Here we are now running into the Pittsburg coaling district at 5.30. Since 11 o'clock I have been travelling in fast trains, more than half the time in the hills, and the whole time in the one state of Pennsylvania. I have not got out of one state, travelling during the time it takes to get from King's Cross to Scots Gap[1] and at about the same average pace.

This evening I went to the Melodrama 'Cuba's Vow', Cuba being the heroine of a tale of Cuban independence. The hero is of course an American naval officer, with his attendant Jack tars who are exactly the English tar in dress and popular character for joviality and devil-may-care. The villainess is the Spanish governor's wife. Her accomplice is a sneaking, murderous Spaniard. Her husband is professional ravisher to the Havana prison. Gomez and Maceo strut about the stage in insurgent white waving the Cuban banner. The Maine is blown up in tableau. The gallery howls with delight at the victories of the Cubans or Americans, and roars with hatred whenever the Spaniards come on the stage.

[1] The railway station for Wallington.

A PICNIC WITH STUDENTS FROM GRINNELL COLLEGE

INDIANS AT LEECH LAKE, MINNESOTA

MAIN STREET IN LINCOLN, NEBRASKA

GOVERNORS AND PROFESSORS, COLORADO UNIVERSITY

Friday, April 15

Pittsburg is not like an Eastern City. It is Newcastle, Liverpool, Leeds over again. A cloud of smoke hangs over it by day. The glow of scores of furnaces light the river banks by night. It stands at the junction of two great rivers, the Monongahela which flows down today in a turbid yellowy stream, and the Allegheny which is blackish. They join at the nose of the city where Fort Duquesne stood. A hundred and fifty years ago the whole country was desolate except for the little French block-house at the river junction. Today the old block-house stands in a little green patch off a filthy slum-street. It has just been rescued from being a tenement by some historical ladies. It now stands humbly in the midst of this roaring city of 600,000 inhabitants, the only relic of the old days of primitive barter. It became Fort Pitt and named the town when the English once got to it. The *first* time they failed if you remember. For eight miles up the river Monongahela is the industrial suburb of Braddock, built on the hill-slope. At the bottom day and night the Carnegie and Bessemer furnaces roar, forgetting the fate of the stupid general who on the same ground paraded his red-coats before the Indian sharp-shooters, and had to run away and die, poor man, in spite of his regulation drill and swearing. There I spent today seeing the works where the Bessemer rails are turned out. On the other side of the river is Homestead where the great strike was and the Duquesne works, all three of them under Carnegie and Co. There is no need to describe them, even if possible. The great peculiarity of course is the natural gas. Enormous supplies of it are stored up in different parts of Pennsylvania, West Virginia, and Indiana, in the porous earth below the coal. It is apparently of the same nature as the oil of other districts. It is used for manufacturing, and heating all the houses of Pittsburg. It is being shamefully wasted, and cannot last many years longer. When first found it was allowed to escape in incredible volume. I was told how at one place for many months an enormous volume was emitted volcano-like from one of the borings. A farmer who lived two miles off said that the roar and vibration of the flame often shook his windows and that he could generally read by the light of it at night. They control it now and use it, by pipes, carrying it for hundreds of miles. But they waste it carelessly, not reckoning on its limitation. Here in this town there are just the same industrial questions as at home. The industries have grown up uncontrolled because of the discovery of coal, gas, and iron. The city has collected hap-hazard to carry on the work. All nations are jumbled up here, the poor living in tenement dens or wooden shanties thrown up or dumped down (better expression) with very little reference to roads or situation, whenever a new house is wanted. It is a most chaotic city, and as yet there is no public spirit or public consciousness to make the conditions healthy or decent. Carnegie has given libraries, a Park and organs to several dozen churches. Some of the other millionaires have done the same. Otherwise the town is chaos. Few, uncomfortable and crowded cars run down the main streets, except where the Pennsylvania railroad has got the right of way by a municipal job. There you cannot cross the street often till a huge elephant of a luggage train, a quarter of a mile long has got itself past at the rate of about six miles an hour, with intolerable roaring and whistling of steam and ringing of bells. You are pulled up the steep hills by cars with only two slender ropes and no catch-brakes in the event of the ropes snapping. This, up inclines as steep as Lauterbrunn–Mürren. Devil a bit the city alderman cares who has pocketed his fee or his shares from the Company. Companies levy black-mail at all the four bridges over Allegheny, the Salford to their Manchester. You pay 5c=3d a horse carriage, 1c for yourself on foot. The streets, except where cars run, are so bad you could not possibly find a track to bicycle on. The smoke pours out of the chimneys absolutely unchecked, in torrents that would appal even a Halifax man. It is industrial greatness with all the worst industrial abuses on the grandest scale. The class of manufacturer I have met is not pleasing. There is profound contempt and dislike of Unions and all their ways, much worse than in England. A certain De Armit was recommended to me to tell me about mining, being a great controller of pits and 'having fought the unions like the devil'. He certainly was a choice specimen of the hell-brood. He was well-nigh drunk with whiskey at 5 in the afternoon at the best town club, and as coarse a fighting-cock as I have often seen. Not much chance of conciliation with such a man. His fierce competence was

32

evident. But he was nothing but a selfish, violent money-maker. All the men I meet here are rough; but they are a good breed and shrewd and friendly. With their immense natural resources they will do great things. I absolutely trust them to evolve order out of their social disorder in time. A jolly Irish American has been doing the honours for me, one O'Neill, an editor of the Pittsburg Despatch. He knows everybody and wants me to do everything. He has the entrée to all the theatres. Tonight he introduced me to a very clever interesting man, Magee, the leading lawyer of the Municipality–(Rings, Trusts, corrupt corporations etc. always attach the best lawyers) – Then he took us to a vulgar but highly amusing play by an actress May Irwin, who sings pretty nigger songs written by herself, and might have been a considerable actress if she had not descended to low comedy. Here in Pittsburg the stage is as vile as in London. In New York I mentioned its freedom from coarseness. Here it is as coarse as it can be short of outrage, though very humorous.

By the way O'Neill's uncle, to whom I had an introduction, is now his step-father, having married his mother on his father's death. But there are no hands held up in holy horror here.

Saturday, April 16

Today – again accompanied by a sardonic-looking but good natured manager of Carnegie & Co. named Wagner – to see a mine. We went by car (rail) fifty miles up the Monongahela to California. We passed one town of several hundred inhabitants new this last twelve-month, another of some thousands, only five years old. The valley is full of coal-pits and glass factoires. The glass is now all in one ring, and we passed some works that had been 'shut down' by the trust. The names of the firms are almost all English, not Swede, German or Jew, in this neighbourhood, I am pleased to say; Fawcett, Snodgrass (!) etc. Our pit was interesting, because of the extraordinary ease with which the coal was extracted compared with England. There was no shaft, merely a slightly sloping tunnel run into the side of the hill along the river. One small engine slowly and without ceasing winds a rope to which the trucks are hitched. They run out to a pier from which they are tipped into barges, which drop down the river, 40 miles, to Carnegies. The side lines are worked by mules. There is no gas, and we wore our lights in our caps as they do in Lanarkshire. A small furnace, so small that you could stand four paces off without being scorched was all that was necessary to keep the mine far more airy and cool than Ashington[1] colliery with its elaborate appliances. It is a good thing they are not within shipping distance of England. The cost of production must be about $\frac{1}{3}$ of what it is with us. The miners are a very fluctuating population. Hungarians, Swedes, Irish etc. The Americans are a minority. They have got 8 hours in this mine, and are fighting for it elsewhere, apparently successfully. Only one shift is worked a day. The whole district round Pittsburg is underlaid with coal. But it has only been worked near the rivers. A tremendous prospect for it. I see no reason why there should not be six millions in 25 years where there are 600,000 now.

The size of the country and its resources are beginning to take hold of my imagination. I begin to see why the American is always asking for appreciation. His country is a marvel – though all his institutions are not. And he does want the foreigner to feel what is the greatest fact to him. He has a right to swagger. I find him quite amenable to criticism about his institutions.

On our way back we looked into the Normal college for training teachers at California, a state institution, *not* run by any church *for* any church, as our teachers' colleges are. Men and girls are taught together, dine together, have clubs together, are housed in different wings. It works admirably and the heads say it makes the men so much gentler. Fancy a Harrow boy picking flowers of an afternoon, as these youths were! Not that they neglected games. There is one great difference between the teaching profession here and in England. Here in the greater number of cases it is only a stepping stone. A man does not go to a Public (Board) school expecting to teach there all his life. He looks eventually to law, business etc. The lads I saw were very intelligent. On the way back we passed one of the steamers with a paddle at the back, which are used to shove the coal and other barges up and down the rivers.

[1] Mining village in Northumberland.

It was the 'Little Bill' famous for having conveyed the Pinker-ton[1] men to the landing-stage.

O'Neill took me to the most popular theatre tonight, a play, decently respectable, with decently respectable variety enter-tainment after it. The stalls were packed with nice young men, I suppose clerks, but with the look of small college men, and their young women. A monstrously bad 'Remember the Maine' was sung monstrously badly, and the audience with all the will in the world could not rise to it. But when the comic man came on and said that he would not keep them long, but that anyone who left the room he would know to be a —— Spaniard–there were yells. The air is quite electrical now. As we came out, the Saturday night crowds were looking up at the huge news posters, announcing that the Senate by 57–21 are for recognizing Cuban independence. The ordinary man does not care about the independence. What he does care about is kicking the Spaniard out of Cuba. That he is going to do. The quarrel about recognition and the clashing opinion of the houses is sure to get squared or the public will lose its temper.

Friend Roosevelt has resigned to my immense disgust in order to take a command in the army. No man has the right to resign a position of such supreme importance as the command of the Admiralty at such a juncture. I am going to tell him so.

Sunday, April 17

A drive round the town this morning. It was spoilt by a thunder shower, but I got a photo or two.

This afternoon I went out to the heights above the town. There I sat down on some benches from which the respectable workingman was engaged in admiring his city. A nice little man looking very like an English engineer came and sat down by me. We got into talk. He was a founder. He told me all about his Union which was pretty strong and was properly recog-nized by the masters who were themselves federated. I got a

---

[1] Allan Pinkerton (1819–1884), chief of a Chicago Detective Agency, employed by the Union Government in 1861 to discover details of a plot to destroy the railroad and to assassinate Lincoln, the President-elect, on his way to Washington. Pinkerton headed an organization for obtaining military information from the Con-federate Army.

35

good deal of interesting information from him. Finally it turned out that he was born in Pittsburg, though of Swiss parentage, his parents having come to America as young people. There was not a sign of the foreigner in him. He seemed to be of the sturdy, self-reliant, sensible type of workman you find in Yorkshire or Northumberland, and his Yankee accent betrayed nothing of his origin. It was very interesting to see how rapid the transition to complete Anglo-Saxon character could be.

Monday, April 18

At the Auditorium in Chicago in a room on the 5th floor looking out over the Lake, with a strong lake breeze blowing in at the window. I had a very comfortable journey in a Pullman last night sleeping all the way through Ohio and Indiana. We took about ¾ of an hour entering Chicago, from the first busy suburbs to the centre. It seems to cover more space than London even. They are more lavish of land. The living houses are built separate in the outskirts not joining as a rule as in London – No more at present.

Yours affectionately to all,
Charles Trevelyan

6. CHICAGO. THE WAR BEGINS

The Auditorium,
Chicago

Monday, April 18

This letter has to be written up from recollection at the end of an interesting week in Chicago of seeing, hearing and talking. So I will begin with a general account.

The first thing about Chicago is that it is seemingly unlimited. We took fifty minutes entering it, steaming rather slowly past endless streets, over endless crossings, among endless lines of rails flowing in broad streams into the centre of the city. We certainly passed through more town than you do in getting to any great London station. They take plenty of room for everything. The great railway corporations were able to acquire unlimited land, while our railways had to toilsomely buy and litigate for every precious foot they used. The same ease of acquiring land has led to the building of houses in much looser order than in London. Except in the centre of the city the houses are generally separate, even the poorer ones where the workers live. In the suburb through which I am now passing each house – I should think belonging to small city clerks – has its own width of space between its next neighbour.

The people are very like any big English town, mixed prosperity and poverty. State Street is full of fine ladies at fine shops in the afternoon like Piccadilly and Oxford Street. Madison and La Salle streets are like the city with big banks and exchanges. Street cars and fast local trains carry crowds to and from work from the suburbs. Only imagine Liverpool placed on the shore of a sweet watered, tideless sea, and you have Chicago. Anything more externally prosaic or English cannot be imagined. The streets are badly paved, horrid for bicycling, either with badly laid stone or mud. The parks are extensive and well kept, with bold statues of war heroes and others, and full of low, pleasant trees. The chief noticeable difference is the foreign speech of so many men and women – most noticeable of all the Irish brogue of every policeman. But more of that great political race presently.

Today I spent in preparing to see people. I went to Hull House, a sort of Toynbee Hall,[1] run by Miss Addams, a most splendid woman, who has an enormous influence and acquaintance, and in the smaller society of Chicago is a greater fact than the Toynbee people. I found that arrangements had been made for my reception there. But as I had gone to the Auditorium I determined to stay and see what a great American Hotel was like.

Miss Addams then took me round to a meeting of religious reformers, where I saw some interesting people.

In the evening Mr. H. D. Lloyd, who wrote 'Wealth and Commonwealth', a great exposure of the godless methods of the Trusts especially the Standard Oil Co., invited me to a public

[1] Pioneer University settlement and social service centre in East London, founded in 1884 by Canon Barnett and named after Arnold Toynbee, social reformer and economist.

dinner of the Dutch Americans in Chicago at one of the best restaurants to celebrate the birthday of William of Orange. The room was decorated with scenery displaying a street and canal in Amsterdam. The Menu was in Dutch–'Rundvleesch'. 'Gebraden Nieuw Nederlandsche Jonge Esnde'. After dinner long pipes were brought in, decorated with orange ribbon, which we placidly smoked like Dutch burghers while the speeches went on. All the talk was about Spain and the war. It was very interesting. These people had two patriotisms, the old pride in the race of dyke-diggers and sea-dogs of Holland, and the enthusiasm for the great new land of the star spangled banner. They recalled in glowing periods how their fathers had been the first to rise against Spain in the days of her might, how they had beaten Alva and his trained batallions. Now in the days of her national decrepitude they were glad to be able to strike again a blow at the country that their fathers fought and hated. The speeches were some of them really good, though most of them were rather spread-eagle. But throughout there was one note running and one only, that the war with Spain was undertaken to destroy the power for evil of the brutal Spaniard. 'That war is holy that conquers despotism, that peace may reign'. Then there was a very florid speech about Dutch art, ending 'Therefore shine on, o magic light of Rembrandt–from sky and cross and tomb, shine on'. Finally there came the Mayor of one of the suburb towns of Chicago, Evanston, who made a long speech of about half an hour on Municipal Reform, the sort of speech we should have on a political platform–and good for that purpose. I was greatly interested, though it naturally bored the others at 11 P.M. But it was very interesting to see that municipal reform should be at any rate so theoretically accepted as desirable by the better class, that the sort of speech Tweedmouth might make about the L.C.C. at the Annual Meeting of the London Reform Union was not regarded as offensive, only as rather tedious, by an audience of rich citizens. The standard of speaking was greatly higher than in England. The best speech was by Lloyd, who made what we regard as a pattern, bright, thoughtful after dinner speech. The other less good men, instead of prosing dully for half an hour each on some grovelling topic in ill-set sentences, spoke out clearly on interesting and lively topics, always finished in style,

and erring only on the side of grandiloquence. It was vastly
more amusing than an English Corporation feast.

Tuesday, April 19

Lunched at Hull House. Miss Addams has round her all the
reformers and all the best elements in the city. Today I saw
Miss Kelley who had been Factory Inspector of Illinois; but the
present governor, a corrupt dog who has succeeded Altgeld,
turned her out and appointed a man who leaves the laws to be
a dead letter. During her term of office the state Legislature
passed a law restricting the hours of women's labour. The
Supreme Court of the State–bossed and manipulated as usual
by the great capitalist trusts–declared such a law unconstitu-
tional as infringing the right of free contract!

There has just been a great municipal contest here between
the reformers and the corrupt aldermen of the City Council.
Hull House has hitherto taken no direct part. This time it
threw itself into the contest. They had found it impossible to
hold aloof any longer. As an instance of the sort of thing they
have to see done. The Board of Education–a decent body
appointed by the Mayor, & corresponding to our School
Board–found a new school absolutely necessary close to Hull
House, where there is an utterly crowded, inadequate, badly
built school at present. They were offered an excellent site just
where they wanted to build. But the sanction of sites and
building lies finally not with any Education Department but
with the City Alderman. These worthy rulers sent word to the
owner of the site that they were quite ready to buy the site for
the Education Board if $1000 out of the $13,000 were returned
to them. As the vendor happened to be honest he would not
pay the black-mail and the Aldermen refused the school.
Johnny Powers, the most notorious rascal of the lot represents
Hull House. So when Hull House determined to oppose him
he swore in public that he would clear Hull House out of his
ward within a year. By dint of bribery, cajolery, etc. he got in
and is the boss of a better but still corrupt council. So Hull
House is girding up its loins to fight. Today the coping off some
brick pillars at the entrance has been knocked off and carried
away. Poor Miss Addams hung her head humorously and said
'I suppose this is the beginning of the disintegration'. Of course

39

there is no use calling in the police. They are Irish, and the friends of Power are Irish, corruption is maintained by the Irish. The priests have attacked Hull House, accusing it of infidelity—which certainly is not unknown there—and of seducing the Catholic youth, which *is* unknown. Power stimulates their antipathy by giving a whole new system of heating to their church. Here the Irish schools have no Education department to improve them. And 6000 children out of 10,000 are taught in the district by priest-managed schools which inspectors don't visit. The Irish are often called the 'ruling race' here. In the City Hall I saw lists of all the persons eligible for positions of any sort under the City government. In all the lists more than half were Irish names. In the police list *at least 4 out of 5 were Irish.*

Wednesday, April 20

Did not do much till the evening when I went to dine at Hull House. After dinner there was a reception for me. I stood in the middle of the room and a whole succession of people, chiefly municipal reformers, education authorities and university dons were introduced, shook hands, passed a word, and went by. I suppose there were about 100 people. Then we adjourned to a big room for a discussion. I was asked to speak on anything I pleased, so I gave them a twenty minutes speech on the hopes of an Anglo-Saxon alliance between America and Great Britain. As usual the most complete friendliness was expressed by all the succeeding speakers, and everyone said that the anti-English feeling, such as it is, is most superficial. There is no doubt of the universal desire for a closer connection. Of course I have not been able to see English papers. But I gather—it certainly is the general opinion here—that we are generally taking the side of the States in the war. If I had not so much to do, I should have written home before to explain to our papers if it requires explaining, that the States have brought on war most reluctantly, that they want above all things not to have Cuba on their hands, that the sole reason for intervention has been the general horror at the Spanish atrocities. There never was a war, less selfishly undertaken, or more reluctantly, more purely for humanitarian reasons. Our nation ought to be with this nation heart and soul. They are going to clear out a barbarous people, solely because of their barbarity, and not because that barbarity is an excuse for self-aggrandizement. No one who has not been over here can in the least appreciate the deep-seated unwillingness of the ordinary American to meddle with anything outside his own country. It is part of his political and national creed that foreign complications are the bane of the older peoples and must be kept out of his own politics. If by any means Spain could have been induced to withdraw her troops without the use of force, any sort of autonomous government would have been accepted that secured life & property, there would have been no war. No one in England must suppose that the war was brought on by noisy bluster in Congress. Of course all men did not urge intervention. But the vast majority did; and there was no effective minority in or out of political circles that cared to exert themselves to prevent it. Only a very few of the Eastern business interests were indifferent to what the bulk of their nation perceived to be their duty, the kicking out of the Spaniard. Should we have delayed to eject Turkey from Crete or Armenia, if Spain had been our only possible opponent and they had lain no further from our shores than the Dutch coast? The horrors of Cuba are proved by the recent consular reports to equal those of Crete & Armenia. And our people ought to show the fullest-hearted sympathy with the other half of the race which is doing what they failed to do two years ago. The belief that England appreciates what they are doing really delights the heart of these simple energetic people. It would be a terrible disappointment and sore to them if English sympathy were withdrawn. If it is continued, it will do more to cement the good-will between the two countries than a dozen negotiations between Olney & Salisbury.[1]

Thursday, April 21

Today war has become certain. The President forwarded his Ultimatum to Spain, but the Spanish government has replied by giving Woodford, the U.S.A. ambassador, orders to leave. But in Chicago there is little to indicate war except the papers. The Latin peoples would be standing at the corners gesticulating.

[1] Secretaries of State for Foreign Affairs of U.S.A. and Great Britain respectively.

Here business goes on just as usual. There are a good many unwonted stars and stripes run up on business houses and in front of villas in the suburbs. Resolutions are being passed by public bodies (especially the corrupt ones, Tammany leading) to permit their employees to join the army, retaining their full pay & having their places again when they return. Two or three locomotive engines are carrying the Cuban flag. The business men of Chicago hold a dinner tomorrow, at which I am to be present, to approve the action of the government and give their curse to Spain. In a calm Anglo-Saxon way they accept what has come, are not doing it carelessly, but see no reason why Chicago should become hysterical over it. So I with the rest am going on with my business.

Today I went to the industrial sights of Chicago. The Stock Yards, where Armour and Co. slaughter 6,000 hogs, 5,000 sheep and 2,500 cattle a day, was the chief interest. I was well prepared for the horrible sight. It surpasses anything in loathsomeness I ever hope to see. The Cock-pit of a three decker must have been nothing to it. The sight of the slaughtering is pretty bad, and the torrents of blood. The squawking of the pigs is discordant mixed with shoutings and clashings of machinery. The disembowelling and cutting up would be enough for one alone on most days. But worst of all is the smell. It is indescribable, and no other smell is possible for hours afterwards. I cannot say that I think the processes needlessly cruel for the beasts. The hogs are killed much quicker than they would be in a farmer's yard. They have a hook put round one leg and are swung up by machinery. In a few seconds their throat is cut by an unerring butcher and in a few more seconds they have done struggling. It is horrible to see the blood pour out. But if you kill meat at all, it is not badly done. There is no suspense for the other beasts, as I have heard it said. Though hundreds are in pens within earshot in the same shed, they are either placidly trotting about or callously sleeping till their turn comes. The cattle are knocked on the head, then picked up and swung round to a butcher who cuts their throats and catches the blood in a bucket. But the system must brutalize the men. I felt a viler animal altogether after coming out. The smell and reek alone seem to saturate you with loathsomeness. And the men look brutalized. Much I am sure might be done by more

42

use of water, and by carrying on the processes in different rooms instead of all in one. But nothing can prevent it being the most degrading of occupations. I eat vegetarian meals for the rest of the day, and was very glad of a cock-tail half an hour after leaving the works, which Harlan, the reform candidate for the mayoralty, gave me at a Chicago Saloon. On the way to meet Harlan I and my companion began in a car talking about the war. An Irishman, who 'was na' fu' but just had plenty', immediately began a dissertation on the friendship of Americans and Irishmen for England, and on the justice of the war. His patriotic oration did not at all disturb the other occupants of the car. It would have created a revolution in a London omnibus.

At lunch I had a good talk with Harlan, who is son of one of the Supreme Court judges, and a very vigorous fellow rather like an uncultured more human Asquith. We compared notes about London and Chicago reform. In the afternoon I went to some electric telephone works of some interest.

Friday, April 22

The fleet has sailed and war has really begun. Chicago still busily engaged in its ordinary occupations. I visited the City Hall, the corridors of which swarmed with shabby applicants for various forms of municipal favour. I next went to the Exchange, which was very quiet and unexciting, only some fifty business men altogether dealing in stocks. I could not make it out. Then my companion asked me to come on to the Board of Trade. It is a big hall with three large circles in it of steps, which rise and then lower theatre-wise to the centre. One of these was the stock-dealers ring, the other the corn-ring, i.e. Indian corn, the other the wheat ring. There the real business speculation of Chicago was in process. Hundreds of men shouting, gesticulating, waving hands and fingers were buying and selling the corn which is only just sprouting on the plains of South Dakota. I had talk with some leading dealers – all intensely impressed with need of friendship to England.

Then to lunch with Ex-governor Altgeld, the worst abused and most interesting man in Chicago. I had a long talk with him on Democratic politics in America and English Liberalism. He has got an attractive, tired face, very un-American. He has

43

rather a slouch in manner. But is as bright as can be in talk. But he is just the sort of man who gets hated by the great, because he has no presence, but a quiet and unresting power. Next to Roosevelt he is the biggest character I have met yet.

To see some Trade Union leaders and talk about their unions. They are very much the same class and calibre as the leaders in England.

In the evening to a dinner of the Union League Club, started by the Chicago business men and lawyers at the beginning of the war. They had called a special meeting to express their approval of the intervention of the President, and to offer patriotic resolutions on the war. I wish a crowd of telephones could have been turned on to Europe. It would have convinced any one of the real reason of the intervention. Every speech had the same note in it almost, great appreciation of the seriousness of the war, no Jingoism, regret at having to leave their internal development for outside interests; but they could not leave Spain to destroy and devastate within a few hundred miles of their shores without putting a stop to it some day. The most interesting speech was made by W. J. Calhoun, an Illinois lawyer, whom McKinley sent out to find out the real facts for him in Cuba. He, in contrast to the other rather wordy speeches of the evening, spoke in that peculiar unimpassioned simple way that the practical Englishman uses whenever he has a particularly convincing case to present. In twenty minutes he had given us the essence of Spanish rule, a picture of the hopeless depravity of it and the ruin which it had brought on the country. Again I was struck with the superiority of the style of after dinner speech here to that in England, as being less dull. Of course it is hyperbolical often. One lawyer spoke in terms of wild and superstitious loyalty to the President, as a Primrose dame might of royalty. 'Before the angels of heaven – God bless our President.' 'God sent him to save us from the infamy of repudiation; and now' etc. etc. about Spain –

The audience needless to say was Republican mainly. The old general Black who had spoken at the Dutch dinner, made another oration, rather shorter & better than the last. In his peroration however he spoke, comparing the contest for Cuban freedom, of the Scotch who died at 'Snowdon'! There was enough historical knowledge in Chicago to send a puzzled smile or frown over most faces. I came away with a feeling of the fatuity of Spain trying to fight such people. Here a thousand miles from the sea is an enormous Metropolis full of men of the same character and nerve and energy and knowledge as the merchants of Liverpool and Leeds. They have not thought of exerting themselves yet. They are going to send out some 20,000 volunteers in obedience to the President's request. But if there were the least need to summon a hundred thousand they are already at this stage in the quiet, determined, unanimous temper that sent 'three hundred thousand more' to 'Father Abraham'. Again every man I talked to expressed a hope for an English alliance in the future.

Saturday, April 23

Today the war news begins. There are crowds all day of the passers by, who linger for five minutes, before the newspaper offices, where big written posters are announcing the bringing of the first prizes into Key West.

After a short talk with John Dillon's[1] brother, editor here of an Irish paper, down to stay with H. D. Lloyd the anti-trust writer. He lives in a pretty little house ten miles from the City on the shore of the Lake. There, surrounded by his family, he writes his books on economics, most uneconomically feeds tramps who pass by, and watches the tideless waters of Lake Michigan. The shore is rather fine, with sand cliffs, or wooded banks above a short beach of shingle and hard sand, which is pleasant to walk on. Large numbers of tramps make fires on the shore and live behind sand-hills. It is a pathetic sight in this land of freedom. The lake was rather dingy today, but would be very fine in sunlight or storm. It looks a boundless ocean, though Michigan land is visible from high towers on a clear day.

Mrs. Lloyd was very anxious I should tell you how much they appreciate the Life of Macaulay. They had a literary cousin who died recently, who wrote at the time of the book coming out an essay on 'the Torn side of Macaulay', a good title to a criticism which called much notice onto the book. Here I may say that there is the most universal knowledge among all the

[1] (1851–1927). Irish Nationalist politician, supporter of Parnell, with whom he toured America to obtain assistance for the newly formed Land League. M.P. for Tipperary.

educated people of G. O. T.'s writing. He is quite a household word. People are just as delighted as in England at hearing that Fox[1] is to be continued. Many people more delighted, because they appreciate that it means in some sort the history of the American war – an opinion which I do not dispel, though I give no information of course. There is no doubt that there will be a prodigious sale for the new book. For if this is the case in Chicago, it is ten times more so in the East.

A bright dinner with some pretty girls and much story-telling.

Sunday, April 24

After a lake shore walk and talk about Roman Catholic bigotry and misgovernment in Chicago, back to the City. For the rest of the time I am to stay in the neighbourhood of the University, which is eight miles from the centre of the City but still in the City, with Professor Zueblin, who knows England well, and is a lecturer in Economics (very progressive in his views) and on English conditions. He has a very pretty, charming wife. They are some of the nicest people I have met here, and are immensely hospitable. They live very simply, Mrs. Zueblin frequently answering the door and doing a great deal of the household work and being on terms of companionship with her maid. No one thinks it peculiar here, though it is not perhaps general. Still in all households simplicity and self-help are far more general than with us.

I came in for a paper at a Sunday Economic Society on the Webb's book, and of course I had to make a discourse when the paper was finished. It is extraordinary how greedy they are here for speeches. It is not an occasion as in England. But where in England an intelligent set of people would be content with reading, the American likes to be talked to and ask questions. I talk on pretty much what I like, and they drink it in with avidity.

Monday, April 25

An easy day, partly cycling round the handsome parks in this quarter and watching the dainty lady cyclists. They wear very

[1] *The Early History of Charles James Fox* by G. O. T. was eventually continued as Vols. V and VI of his *History of the American Revolution*, called *George III and Charles Fox*.

46

pretty costumes, skirts falling rather below the knee and high boots that nearly reach up to it. In the afternoon I watched a game of baseball. Listen, Cambridge! No man may play for his Varsity who has not attained a reasonable standard of diligence and success in his studies!! An evening among the Varsity dons, who are not up to Jackson and McTaggart, but are not cowboys. They are rather like small college, Pothouse dons, a few of them superior to that.

Tuesday, April 26

Today the doors and windows are hung with banners all. While I write two small boys are laughing, shouting and climbing in the trees outside the window where they have rigged up an American stars and stripes. Their father–a successful Jewish lawyer–has started as a volunteer to Springfield, where the State troops are mobilizing. The favourite doctor of the district is also gone, both as privates! All the streets of the city are hung with stars and stripes. Every block of buildings has a huge flag floating from a mast. Every shop has an arrangement of stars and stripes in it to attract customers. Many people carry little stars and stripes in their button-holes. Coming home this evening we saw sailors walking about accompanied by admiring crowds and sweethearts. Huge crowds have been down to see the soldiers off to Springfield. Certainly the Yankees mean business. It is a great pity that a delegation could not come over from Spain to see what America is before they started defying it. The big policeman is drawing his baton deliberately.

Today I visited a literary and artistic circle. Less said the better. Art won't flourish yet in this commercialism. It reminded me rather of the little literary circle in Ireland, but it was feebler. Only one tiny little woman, Miss Bessie Potter, had done some figures, really natural and beautiful, rather like Tanagra figures. But she was going off to New York.

After to another settlement, the Chicago Commons, run by Professor Graham Taylor. A lot of young men and women at work there. I had to speak to about 200 people about English politics. Afterwards I was heckled as I might be in Leeds or London by Socialists and Anarchists. One old Englishman from Bath said shrewd things in the clumsy English way that the old Chartist, who never saw the inside of Board School, alone can do. He was rather a puzzle to the Americans but I was quite at home with him.

Altogether I believe in the future of this city. Stead has painted its hells, perhaps not too blackly. He has given however none of its hopes. There are bright quarters of the town to set against the dingy. There are well paved streets and well-rolled roads to set against the racketty muddy thoroughfares of the city centre. There is a vigorous and improving education, not deep but very efficient up to a certain stage for the young men and women of the better class, and a fair system of primary education for all, to set against the ignorance of the slums. There is a great public spirit and pride in the City growing, which in the long run must kill corruption. There is a movement among all classes to check the selfish and uncontrolled use of wealth by the great kings of the trusts and corporations. Chicago is not ideal. But it has as noble a future before it as any English city.

Wednesday, April 27

Lunched again with Altgeld and Lloyd. He talked about the celebrated incident of the Anarchists, and of the way in which the Democratic party threw off the money bosses of New York at the Convention which selected Bryan. Altgeld is the brain of the party. I went with him afterwards the tour of some of the State Courts. Justice is a most curious contrast to England, in her shirt-sleeves so to speak, and probably actually so in the summer months. There is no pomp or circumstance at all. The judge sits on a raised dais behind a large desk. On one side on two rows of ordinary cane chairs sit the jury. In a chair between judge and jury sits the witness. On the floor are two tables, at one of which sits the plaintiff and counsel, at the other defendant and counsel. Public sits round or in among the litigants. We first went into Judge Tooley's court, where a divorce case was being tried. The judge rose from his chair to greet us, and, as he did not happen to have a jury to assist him, the examination stopped too while we conversed. Then we went and listened for a bit. But it was too dull and we went on to another court, where we repeated our interruption. I began to get accustomed after a time to delaying justice. But at first it seemed a sacrilege.

Then we went to see the Mayor. While we were waiting for him, a group of officials came and talked to us, one of them the Secretary of the Mayor. With a strong Irish accent he asked me if I were George Otto Trevelyan. I stated the relationship. 'Because, said he, 'your father put me in gaol for three months'. Upon which there was much laughter among all present. He was by name Lahill & had been imprisoned under the Crime's Act in your regime.[1]

Today we had a cycle ride. The roads are splendid, the cycles almost as light as paper. They would not do for Northumberland hills; but do well for flat parks.

So, goodbye, for the present. This is really too much for one letter; but you can take it in doses.

Yours,
Charles Trevelyan

7. SPRINGFIELD AND ST. LOUIS

Bad writing owing to shaking of train between Springfield and St. Louis.

Thursday, April 28

Today every paper in Chicago has got hold of the news of my visit to The City Hall with Altgeld. The cuttings I send show the way American news is worked up. When the English papers choose to be gossipy or sensational it generally makes the same story out of the event all round. Here the little grain of truth gives rise to a variety of anything. The sequel is interesting. While I was out, a gentleman smelling strongly of tobacco and calling himself Fitzgerald appeared at the Zueblin's, said that he was a compatriot of mine, and knew Lord Dunraven. Mrs. Zueblin, in the innocence of American hospitality, asked him to tea. He had the grace to refuse but said he would call again. I

[1] G. O. T. was Chief Secretary in Dublin 1882–1884. He accepted the post immediately after the murder of Lord Frederick Cavendish in Phoenix Park. When G. O. T. went to Ireland, he was known in the House of Commons as 'The Black Man', so raven black was his hair; when he returned from Dublin, his hair was white, so great had been the strain of those two years.

told them at once that anyone who came asking for a sham Lord was a humbug. So–about half an hour after he arrived. He was

John F. Eyre Fitzgerald,
Late of Glin Castle,
Co. Limerick,

no Chicago address vouchsafed. A paper was produced to show that a Fitzgerald had married a daughter of Lord Dunraven. Even this failed to move me. Then came the first request. Would I use my influence with the Mayor to get him a higher place, his own being a very low one in the Chicago Civil Service. When that was politely tolerated as an interesting side-light to local politics, he began to ask for the Almighty dollar, trotting out wife and children. I trotted him out and went back to laugh with the Zueblins. Perhaps the man was more astute than he looked, and thought is just possible that a *real* Lord might be gullible. At any rate that is a Radical interpretation.

I saw again that day Altgeld and Hull House. I bought a patriotic song book. I saw the telephone exchange, 150 girls ceaselessly moving their hands to connect the telephone talkers all over the city. 300,000 messages are talked in the day through the Exchange. All business is done by it. The system is marvellous.

In the evening I went to see a Club of University Students, who were very keen to hear about Cambridge, which I explained and discussed for an hour. They seemed like hard working small college men, but smarter and with no pretensions to literary knowledge, though a keenness about intellectual subjects, and an amused dislike at the idea of doing anything at the Varsity.

At night off by rail to Springfield to see the troops mobilizing. Only just caught the train, and found the sleeping car full of volunteer national officers going to the point of concentration. I made some of their acquaintances and went to bed.

Friday, April 29

After a day at Springfield, I am now nearing St. Louis. I have just caught the first glimpse of the Mississippi, and must stop to look at the lord of new world rivers.

I woke up this morning at Springfield. I had breakfast with a young man, son of a big lawyer in Chicago, who was on General FitzSimons' staff and going down to join his General. He was fresh from ranching in Texas where he had had brushes with Mexicans. But his other military experience was more than nil. He had got the appointment through politics as he confessed with a smile. He was good for rough-riding and would not care for a bullet. But as for military understanding beyond the way to let off a rifle and set teeth to charge – nothing. However, with him I went to camp, to which by the way the Brig. General did not come from his Hotel till eleven o'clock. 9000 men were camped there. It was just such a camp as there must have been hundreds of in 1864. Squads were drilling all over the fields. Some of them were in uniform and with rifles, and could do their evolutions well. They were the old members of the regiments who had seen much drill and even some service against the Chicago strikers. Then there were men half in uniform, half not, drilling for their lives. Then there were small squads of raw recruits marching up and down like the policemen in Birdcage Walk, only that most of them had discarded their coats in the hot sun. They had only been there for two days. And what immediately struck one was that up to a point the officers knew their business, and that as far as drill was concerned the regiments would be in shape in a week, They were fine men all, and working seriously and hard to learn their business, no trifling at drill, though most of the instructors are elected by the companies, not appointed from above. The governor only names the superior officers. These regiments are the pick of Illinois. There are bankers, lawyers, doctors serving in the ranks. Few below the status of clerk are yet enlisted. There are ten applications for every man wanted. There never was such material for an army. In three weeks they will be fit to march. By that time the national Government will have supplied them with uniforms and rifles etc. At present they are getting along with what the State can provide. The only thing that struck me as deficient was the strategic brains at the head. General FitzSimons, who was very cordial, gave me a general pass and made me share the mess with his staff, was in the war. But most of the people round him seemed like my friend Winston, of absolutely no military experience. The government

51

ought to see that they have regular army men to look after the tactics if it comes to fighting.

After leaving Camp Tanner, called after a corrupt politician at present Governor of the State, I went to see Lincoln's tomb and monument, a fine block of stone with a good figure of him. Then on to St. Louis, through a country rather like our flatter eastern counties in spring time, large fields divided by hedges or strong fences, green with springing corn and clumps of trees with fruit blossoms round the bright painted wooden farm-houses. Here all the land seems to be used, and to be prolific, quite different to the past. Landed at the Hotel Lindell, St. Louis. Went to a terrible adaptation and perversion of Zola's Assommoir–'Drink'. Whenever the hero preaches a temperance sermon as he does ten times in the play and gets a dozen workmen to sign his pledge book the prohibition part of the audience cheered loudly. I wondered what Zola would think. An awful scene melodramatically but rather well acted of the man dying of delirium tremens sent the audience into fits of applause. But he did not drum with his feet which is Zola's worst touch in his vivid catastrophe. I sat next a very nice bright young man whose father was in lumber and had come from Yorkshire originally. He was a clerk in a telephone company and spent his evenings mostly at the theatre, not caring, so he said, for society. For that sort of worthy young man the theatre ought to be made educational.

Saturday, April 30

Bicycled round St. Louis with a Mr. Tuckerman, head of a religious settlement here. It is a fine town in many ways, the centre of it dingy and sordid like any great manufacturing city, but outside the parks are fine and the houses of the rich very comfortable. I dined with some pleasant people called Capen to whom Wm. Smith of Halifax had given me an introduction.

Sunday, May 1

An unsatisfactory day. In the morning I went to hear Herron preach at a Congregational Church. There was a wealthy crowd in bright bonnets. The service was very short, the hymns cut down to two verses each. They don't wish to lose time even over devotion. Then Herron gave them the most outspoken sermon on the altruistic side of Christianity, which they took meekly enough. It would do some of our own sleek congregations good.

We lunched with a business man who was a single-taxer. In the afternoon there was a terrific storm of rain, wind and thunder for half an hour, giving one the feeling of being in a tropical country. In the evening I dined with some kindly but dull business people called Bascom. On the whole a poor day.

Monday, May 2

Reports had been floating around yesterday of a victory in the Philippines. Today they are certain, being from Spanish sources. It must be a great victory for the enemy to admit so much. I leave St. Louis tonight after seeing a few more people. It is the least satisfactory town so far. There is no awakening of intelligence and reform as in Chicago. It is a purely material city, caring only for the 'creature comforts' as my clergyman friend said. Perhaps it is partly that they are enervated by the 6 months of great heat, low-lying down by the banks of the muddy Mississippi.

Yours,
Charles Trevelyan

8. GRINNELL COLLEGE, IOWA

May 3, Tuesday

I arrived at Grinnell this morning with Herron after travelling comfortably all night. It is a little University town. But you must put aside your notions of secluded quadrangles and backs and towers. Imagine a rich rolling piece of central or eastern England covered with well-ploughed fields of brown-black soil, cut up by wire rails or low hedges, here and there a little cover with trees, about as old and high as those in Lingey Furlong or Lascombe; and farm-houses of wood, painted white surrounded by blossoming fruit trees. Imagine yourself walking along a road made merely of earth, not a stone visible, quite rough and rutty in its early summer state, passing occasionally a sort of buggy cart on four wheels drawn by two rather raw-boned vigorous horses, driven by a hardy looking, tanned

53

countryman. Then imagine that you begin sliding into a few houses scattered on either side of the road. They are all of wood, with bright verandas and steps leading up to them. There are no flowers, simply grass, generally neglected, growing round, but a great appearance of comfort and neatness. Foot-paths made of wooden planks, broad enough for two people to walk abreast appear on each side of the road—rows of trees, perhaps 40 years old, giving good shade in summer. You pass forty houses of this sort. Then you come to some twenty shops, Post Office, bicycle shop, book shop, grocer's store, tailor etc. which have a raised asphalt pavement in front. This with the railway station is the *town* of Grinnell. The University is some hundred more houses such as I have described where the students board. And on the edge of the town is the campus, a big open grass space, on one side of it four or five of the best wooden houses, where the leading professors live, with close cut grass, as green and bright as any English lawn and as soft to sit on, though nothing is done to it but mowing. On the Campus rise four big stone and brick buildings, about as handsome as the newer Harrow School-houses, and a fifth lower building, which is the girls' gymnasium. The whole place has the most delight-ful seclusion and rusticity. The air is fresh, the whole place is bright green.

I was put by Herron to stay at the house of a Mrs. Rand, who is a great patroness of the college and whose daughter is principal of the women. She is seventy and came to the State as a girl in its infancy, has seen it grow from barrenness to cultivation (of every inch of it.) She is still keen and vigorous. That afternoon I went with Gates, the principal, to see baseball played, and was pitched to by the captain. It is a good game but not half so elaborate or hard to play or good to watch as cricket. While we were playing about 60 other students were drilling in the Campus, under the supervision of a naval officer, sent by the government. They will go out with the *third* call if any Spaniards are left to fight. But it does not look as if Father William would want a hundred thousand more. This evening two or three of the elder professors came to dinner, among them Macey, Bryce's friend, who helped him a good deal in writing the Commonwealth. Gates, the principal, is a very able man. You must remove all idea of the Master,

Warden or Provost. He is not academic, though he is a man of knowledge. He goes about among the students, talks to them or chaffs, as if they were friends. In this land of equality a don cannot be exclusive. But he has a splendid influence over them and I never saw a master or don so obeyed or respected. All the other Professors in different degrees are like him, living on terms of perfect equality–though the students are all uniformly deferential and generally obedient.

There are two or three women professors. There are about 500 students, of whom 200 about are women. There is complete co-education. They all have the same rules. They go to classes together, they walk about together, they have clubs together, parties together. You often see a man and girl walking away from a lecture together, or bicycling together. No restriction whatever is put upon their intercourse. They do not have an immense number of engagements as a result, generally from three to six in the year, though often marriages result from the intimacies later in life. They have hardly ever to warn any student, and they have never had a scandal. The girls are perfectly able to take care of themselves, and the men are civilized by it. There is absolutely no smoking of any kind whatever and as far as I could make out no drinking. The girls take the same subjects. They do uniformly as well as the men, though there is less occasional brilliancy. They all look intensely healthy. Miss Rand looks very carefully after the physique of the girls and trains and watches them as anxiously to give them strong constitutions as wise heads.

Wednesday, May 4

I took it easy today and looked round. In the evening we went to chapel, a big lecture-room, where *all* the students were collected, not compulsorily as at Harrow to hear Stanley.[1] I spoke to them about a future alliance between England & America. Except in approval of some humorous remarks, they listened, as is the American way, with absolute silence; but at the end applauded tremendously.

[1] Probably H. M. Stanley (1841–1904), the explorer, who went out to Central Africa to find Livingstone, whose whereabouts were unknown. Later (1899) M.P. for Lambeth, opposed unsuccessfully by Charles Trevelyan.

Thursday, May 5

I spent the morning in the lecture rooms. The work is half way between the higher English University and the public school. The classical class was like a good VIth form; but some of the older students do very advanced work, but bar much composition. They only begin their classics at about 16 and get on very quickly. The political science class under Macey was a sort of questioning lecture on socialism, helping the students to think it out for themselves.

The education generally is better all-round than the average man gets at an English varsity. But there is not so much specialized and thorough work. But for people drawn from the farming classes mainly, and expecting to go back to the hard work-a-day world it is very broad. They are taught to think more than with us under ordinary circumstances. Neither the students nor professors shirk questions, and they think a frank discussion of modern life to be part of education. They seem to me to be more alive than our people.

In the evening I met the younger Professors, somewhat like the Harrow masters, but with a wonderful liberality of thought on politics and religion.

Friday, May 6

I have had a day's reading. In the morning I went to chapel. The President had been away, and came in late to give his Friday morning address. Imagine Butler. 'My friends, I find it hard to speak to you of righteousness this morning. I have just arrived here by the only means of conveyance which would have enabled me to be here to speak to you this morning, a stolen bicycle'. And I assure you he lost nothing in dignity or his address in its effectiveness by such a commencement. He made a most excellent address on the war, against the military spirit, in favour of alliance with England, and in favour of a noble patriotism. It could not possibly have been delivered in England. Its manner would have been sacreligious in an English chapel & derogatory to a college authority. But it was one of the best & most sensible addresses I have heard given to young people.

In the evening we had a very good concert. A daughter in law of Mrs. Rand played the harp and sang and another lady played. I so far enjoyed it that I was carried back to the Cheviot valley and the ridge of Simonside.

Saturday, May 7

Authentic news of Dewey's victory. Medina Sidonia's[1] reputation is retrieved. *He* killed some Englishmen. In Manila harbour they lose a ship and a half per American wounded.

I have just spent one of the pleasantest days of my life, and all as the result of co-education. It happened to be what they call their field day, a Saturday whole holiday on which the College sports were held. The whole of the students adjourned to a bicycle & running and riding ground a mile out of the town. There was a grand stand, and a small stand, really for judges, capable of holding about 40 people opposite. Each of the four years had divided off and assumed different colours. The seniors, graduating this year, had seized the small stand and decorated it with orange and black. The others had different parts of the grand stand with other colours. When the President and I rode up on *our* bicycles there was a tremendous excitement. 'Praxy' is short and familiar for Mr. President. Each year began raising a lilting yell of 'Ra, ra, ra—we want Praxy—we want Praxy—ra, ra, ra'. The fun is chiefly carried on by the girls. If a man's college were to address their president in that way, it would be disrespectful. But it was obviously harmless when shouted by several score of pretty girls with whom the president was an obvious favourite. Then they began shouting 'We want Trevelyan—ra—ra—ra', I having become a great favourite also it seemed. So I went up into the Seniors stand and spent most of the afternoon there. I never saw a lot of girls enjoying themselves so much, singing their shouting, partisan songs, waving their orange scarfs, cheering and talking. There were a good lot of the men there on perfectly easy terms. But there was not a sign of flirting of a silly sort. I made friends with all of them, but most with a Miss Bartlett, a young professor of Classics from the East, a strong, healthy, handsome girl, the most popular after Miss Rand. During the afternoon a deputation from the sophomores, third year, came to ask me if I would join a 'bum' that evening, which as Miss Rand was going, I supposed it was safe to do. So after the sports were over,

[1] Leader of the Spanish Armada which attacked England in 1588.

57

racing, bicycling, pole-jumping as in England, and we had had supper, about eight o'clock two big hay waggons went round the town, picking up the sophomores, and one or two professors and myself. We all lay down in the hay or sat on the sides of the waggon and started at a sedate walking pace, jerking and jolting over the rutty roads, by the light of the stars. We drove in this way for about an hour, singing songs and talking, the girls' clear pure cries and singing making glad the heart. Then we piled a wood fire and put a hot coffee pot on it, as soon as we had got a good blaze, to get up to boiling point. Meanwhile we danced a Virginia reel, a demure country dance, to the light of the fire upon the President's highway. Then we drank a cup of coffee each and eat a sandwich. Some of the men performed an indian war-whoop in my ear. Then we made our way home again in the waggons by the light of the risen moon, singing solos and choruses, national songs, nigger songs and hymns. I never was with such a healthy, glad-hearted crowd before. It was like going out with the early settlers with the stress off. There was all the health, strength, simplicity, guilelessness of the puritan stock. But they had cast off the old glum determination, now that the Indian is driven back to his last wilderness and the steam-engine has brought in the comforts of the old world so near them. But the fresh heart of a young people was singing there. I shall not soon forget that jolting ride in the hay.

Sunday, May 8

So has ended my University week. This morning I am off very early to get to Lincoln in time to see Bryan this afternoon. All day long I am going through endless stretches of rolling ploughland, which feeds the world. But they have no Cheviots.

Yours ever,
Charles Trevelyan

9. LINCOLN

Sunday, May 8

Reached *Lincoln*, the capital of Nebraska, at about three o'clock. It is only 28 years old. But it is quite a flourishing city now. But you must not imagine a Stratford-on-Avon. The main street is paved with coarse blocks of wood with car lines, of course, down the middle and the side walks are mostly but not uniformly asphalt. All the other streets, except one or two close round the Capitol, are simply dirt roads with trees and footpaths of boards, often rotten, on either side. The houses, except in the shop-street, are each separate, surrounded by grass and trees and very picturesque, standing back several yards from the footpath. The wealthier people make little asphalt footpaths in front of their own doors. At night the frogs sing right in the centre of the town among the grass. But in spite of this crudeness there is a very high standard of effective comfort. The shops have good windows containing all that man needs for his material welfare. Everybody is well dressed, the men in brown suits and billycocks or hats like mine. The women are very neat and smart, though they do not yet at any rate go in for parasols. Both sexes bicycle largely, but the women not with any bloomer costume. There is a University started the same date as the town. The first settlers raised the central building in 1870 as soon as they built their houses and the Capitol.

> And close by every door, John,
> A school-house and a steeple.'

The Capitol is in the centre of the town exactly. It is a massive building, copied as most of the state houses are, from the Washington Capitol. There the state legislature meets once every two years, and there the Governor and officials transact business. There are a good many churches and meeting houses, there is a suburb with a Methodist College, and there is an Episcopalian school. But religion is not prominent. The State University is, of course, utterly undenominational. Almost the first words the Chancellor said when I first met him were in chaff of one of his colleagues who attempted to teach theology. Altogether you must imagine a people quite as civilized as in any of our country towns, though without such a finished condition of living. But they are up to our people in all respects and in keenness and receptiveness ahead of them. They are more independent of the outer world than our farming cities. Nebraska is about the size of England and Scotland I think. And the sense of being an almost independent state makes them

59

self-confident. At present however it is not their State feeling which is predominant. As I came into the town, the roads were full of walkers, bicyclists, buggies, trooping out to see the two regiments which Nebraska is sending to the front. At the hotel they were cleaned out of food. They had had to cater for hundreds of people who had come in for Sunday to see 'the boys', from every corner of the state. Poor Spain! They are sending out about 2000 men from here. There is no reason why 50,000 should not go. They are quite ready if wanted. Every house has half a dozen small stars and stripes. Many are wrapped round with swathes of tricolour dotted with stars. I saw one house so decorated and over the door an old faded design with the motto.

The army of the Republic
1861 – 1866

It had been kept safe in some drawer since the disbanding of the great army. The families of children drill on the grass in front of the houses, imitating their elders. If this war were more serious, it would be a sad thing. As it is, it merely impresses one with the terrific strength of the race and its absolute cohesion. Here, even in this State, settled largely by the disbanded soldiers of the Federation, there is rejoicing at the old rivals fighting side by side today. They are as pleased at the prospect of serving under Fitzhugh Lee as they would be under a Grant.

As soon as I had got settled in my hotel, which is quite as comfortable as commercial hotels at Hexham or Galashiels, I went off to look for Bryan. 'The champion of all the people' lives in a little house with a small veranda. He has one small drawing room in front, a small study, sitting-room and dining-room behind. Above there is one story. He has a wife, a father-in-law, a secretary and three children. It is quite the house for a democratic leader to live in. I had a simple Sunday supper with them of cold meat, salad and jelly. Of course there was no wine. (There has not been any at meals since I crossed the Alleghenies. Salloons are plentiful. But all people comfortably off do without it.) Bryan is a rough simple type of American. He is not very clever; but is a man of very hard work, great conviction and obstinacy. He is too much of a party politician to be a great man. He talks a great deal about the attitude of

60

the Democratic party and not directly enough about the actual problems. He would not take an original line himself. He is not so much of a thinker as a determined advocate of political causes. That is to say generally, he is not the brain of his party, he is their spokesman. Altgeld is the statesman. But after this detraction, I must say that I think him a thoroughly honest and sincere man, and a very long way from being wild or revolutionary in his ideas. He is very deliberate in speech and thought, and is not a man who could be rushed. When he has made up his mind he evidently is slow to change. But he is of an enquiring temperament which is the most saving grace in a man in high position. I had a lot of interesting talk with him about the condition of the farmers, the trusts, the railways and the feeling in the West about England.

Monday, May 9

I went again this morning to see Bryan, and had another long talk. He is going to send me the new edition of his book when it comes out, and I am going to send him G. O. T.'s Life of Macaulay which he has not read. He was very anxious to know what I thought the greatest English oration. I would not give him a single one; but mentioned Macaulay's on Reform as the most readable and lasting. What say you? During our talk Bryan ran out for ten minutes to chase a horse which had escaped from its stable-shed. Everybody here is his own coachman.

I then visited the State University. There are 1,900 students. 1,700 of them are undergraduates. 200 about are graduates and doing theses on special subjects, rather more after the German plan than ours. About one third are girls, who go about perfectly freely with the men. Again, as at Grinnell, the report of their relations is absolutely satisfactory. I was taken round the University by the Professor of Mathematics, Davis, who seemed to be a very able intelligent man, though a little saturnine in appearance. But he looked like an English don. They go in of course largely for science and practically applied mechanics. Their woodwork and electric shops were extensive. They have a good library, the reading room of which was packed with at least a hundred students reading away as hard as they could go – two thirds of them girls. They have got in the Museum some very curious specimens of a fossil found in enormous quantities all over western Nebraska, but only there. It is supposed to be some kind of forest tree; but they have no certain classification for it. Its peculiarity is that it is spiral and very perfectly so. Some of the specimens stood six feet high.

In the evening I dined with the Chancellor, MacClean. I had a pleasant evening, though he had to go off rather early to arrange with the governor about the appointment of officers to the troops that are mobilizing and some 100 of whom are undergraduates. There is a sort of camaraderie among the principals of the different state universities. There are now about eight of them, Ohio, Wisconsin, Michigan, Iowa, Nebraska and three or four others. They are all flourishing. He showed me a photo of the principals collected at their last conference. They are on the whole more likely to prosper than the private Universities, started by wealthy men, such as Chicago Union. *That* was endowed by Rockefeller, and free thought about economics and politics is almost as much banned there as freedom of thought in religion used to be in the old universities. A professor was forced to resign recently because of stray speaking about the trusts. There was a great row and Rockefeller gave a larger endowment. It was said that he was 'pouring Standard Oil upon troubled waters'. In the University chapel his portrait is over the dais, behind the desk from which the principal reads prayers. Grinnell is almost the only private university where free thought on economics may be indulged in by professors. The State universities are in their nature less liable to adopt a persecuting spirit in the interests of the great corporations.

Tuesday, May 10

This morning I paid a visit to the State Farm, which is kept up by the State under the control of the University. It partly enables the university to give education in scientific farming. That however is not largely taken up by the men. The sons of farmers make up quite half the University but they invariably prefer a general course to a special study of agriculture. But the farm affords a really useful opportunity for the scientific experiment by the scientific professors. They want grass terribly in the hot summer, and all kinds of Russian and Asiatic grasses are being tried there. Hog cholera kills thousands of pigs every year. They are experimenting in cholera inoculations. I watched the ploughing. There is not a stone on the land anywhere. The rich black soil seems hardly to resist the plough.

I lunched with Professor Davis who told me a good deal about the Rockies. He has had walking and driving tours there. I shall probably go on his tracks.

I paid a visit to Governor Holcombe, a Populist. He had been elected by the Silver coalition of Democratic and Populists. He was a businesslike man, much like a good Mayor in Yorkshire. He is desperately driven at present, being up at his office till twelve last night, settling the commissions for the two Nebraska regiments. Today matters are complicated. The U.S. doctors will not pass the officers of two companies. The men of the companies swear that it is politics and not ill-health that is excluding them, and refuse to be sworn in as national soldiers, until their officers are. And they are supposed to start for the front the day after tomorrow. It is not all patriotic subserviency in organizing a citizen army.

And now away to *Omaha* on the return track. Omaha is on the Missouri, opposite Council Bluffs. It is the great railway centre of the West, the Carlisle of the new world. On the 1st of June a great Trans-Mississippi Exposition, after the model of the Chicago World's Fair, is to open.

I went at once to see Rosewater, one of the people to whom Bryce introduced me. He is the editor of the Omaha Bee, a leading Nebraska journal. Of course his office is the most substantial building in the town, rivalling the Town Hall and Court House next which it stands. I caught him just leaving. He wished to pass me by. But I muttered the magic name of Bryce, and I was immediately ushered back into his room and discoursed to for an hour. He is a tremendously capable fellow. He does not believe in Silver and had public debates with Bryan and his adherents. But he slashes the railways and has all along advocated nationalizing the telegraph.

This evening I went to a vulgar English Vaudeville, as usual full of respectable young men accompanied by respectable young women.

Wednesday, May 11

Went early to see Rosewater again, and had another long talk with him. He is one of the best men I have met yet.

I went to see the buildings of the Exposition which are a lath and plaster mass, looking like white marble to the uncritical eye of the honest western ploughman, and very bright and decorative to the over-civilized Englishman. In the centre is a Lake half-a-mile long on which gondolas will float in good time. But neither gondolas nor exhibits are there yet.

Then I paid a visit to Burt, the Manager of the Union Pacific. It resulted in an interesting talk and a free pass over the Union Pacific Railroad till next December, which will save me probably about $100. When I return from the north on my way to Denver, he even suggests travelling with me himself, which means luxury. I felt rather wicked. The power that scribbles a signature meaning free travel for me has too often been a death gripe for the small trader and farmer.

But my most instructive visit today has been to the house of a Mr. Lininger. He was born in the East, but came West while a boy. He made a fortune, and in middle life broke down in health. He began to travel and while abroad he got passionately devoted to art. He developed a great taste, he got to know all about it historically, he learnt to tell the painter of every picture by looking at it. Then he began buying a little. Gradually he has increased his collection, till it is now large enough to fill a little gallery he has built onto his house quite full. It is one of the best private collections – under the very great ones – I have seen. He has several old masters – two really good Guido Renis, a cross painted by Velasquez and sent over by Philip IV to the monks of an Augustine Monastery in Mexico. He has a most beautiful picture of a woman by Makovski, one of the most lovely portraits I have ever seen, several very good French and Bavarian pictures, two very fine Scotch landscapes by Hurt, which made my mind fly back to our moors again. Lastly he has found a native painter, Borghun, son of an Omaha doctor, with the highest landscape genius. He has now gone to England. If he goes on as he has begun, he will do big work. The collection is about 250 pictures & busts, almost all worth a good deal, none of them vicious trash. Lininger does not merely collect for his own selfish gratification. He opens his gallery twice a week free to the public, and shows it at other times free to travelling strangers, whom he takes round himself, as he did me. 20,000 people visited it last year. It is the only collection in Nebraska, and to my thinking it is quite as good for a young Ruskin to begin studying in as the Dulwich gallery. He has printed a catalogue with photos of the best pictures which he gives gratis. It is a real work of popular education in the fine arts. Borghun, this new painter, owes his success to him. The man will be memorable. He has shown that the wealth of the new peoples will be spent on art collection and that the new democracies will go to see it as greedily as the old when they get the chance.

I am now on my way back to *Desmoines* where I have some investigations to make into the ways of trusts. Then, with possibly a night at Grinnell, on to St. Paul and the northern farmers.

Yours,
Charles Trevelyan

10. DES MOINES, ST. PAUL AND MINNEAPOLIS

Thursday, May 12

Last night I permitted myself to be interviewed by a lad who had been at Grinnell. We sat in my bedroom and talked for half an hour. The result gave a wonderfully correct representation of what I said, considering that he did not take a single note of what I was saying.

I have spent today in seeing *Des Moines*. It is a dull enough town, but surrounded by pleasant woods, and with the best State Capitol I have seen, a gorgeous building with a gilt dome upon the top of a hill just outside the town. There I spent most of the morning. I saw the Governor, a bright man, but not particularly strong or sage, much bothered by the regimental appointments he is having to make.

I visited the Supreme Court of the State. There is a good deal more ceremonial and dignity about it than the lower courts. Six judges sit side by side on the Bench. When they first come in, the usher shouts 'Gentlemen, the Justices of the Supreme Court of Iowa!' We receive them standing and in silence. They file in and stand for a moment each behind his chair and make a bow before they sit down. They have as much gravity as if they had wigs on their heads. After hearing the arguments, which are delivered by lawyers in turn standing at a desk in front of them, they deliver written judgments. They looked to me to be a most efficient set of men, two or three really weighty men among them. The State is Republican, therefore they are all Republican too, being elective.

I then saw the Treasurer and had a talk about taxes. His son, who was his assistant, was educated at Grinnell. He was very keen to hear about John Morley,[1] of whom he had read everything.

I went down then to see an old chap called Aldrich who has been collecting for ten years an historical museum, and has now got the State to plan and erect a magnificent Art and Historical Museum at the cost of $100,000. There is not enough to fill it yet. But he has himself collected a good deal, especially a splendid and carefully arranged selection of modern autographs. Some time ago he came to G. O. T. and was charmed with his reception. He was then passed on to Aunt Margaret,[2] who gave him a long note of Macaulay's M.S.S. history, also a letter of Macaulay's. He has it all beautifully arranged with pictures of Macaulay, G. O. T., Aunt Margaret in the glass drawer. (Now he has got *my* autograph too!) Aunt Margaret may know that the gift was well bestowed. There is hardly a first-rate Englishman of the century he has not got. He has also got all the Presidents.

As I was coming out I was stopped by a Northumbrian. His name was Hardy, from near the Tweed. He had been in South America some years ago, and had been with some Trevelyan, who died out there, and said he was a cousin of Trevelyan of Hawick. Who might that be? Since then he had been home, and had hobnobbed a good deal with the then Vicar of Embledon, now Archbishop (sic) of London.

The afternoon I spent with a very remarkable man, the Mayor of Des Moines, MacVicars. He has been twice elected on a policy of municipalization. He is first a practical man and came to the conclusion that the corporations would have to be

[1] Viscount Morley (1838–1923), statesman and writer, editor of *Fortnightly Review* for 15 years. He wrote Lives of Cobden, Voltaire, Rousseau, Walpole, and (after 1898) of Gladstone.
[2] G. O. T.'s elder sister, who married Viscount Knutsford.

taken over as a matter of business and justice to the town, before he began dealing in theory. He is now fighting them tooth and nail and is winning. The water and electric light will be in the hands of the people in a few months. He is a man of the highest ability, and withal most genial and pleasant, an obviously ideal popular candidate. He is a very much better man than anyone they have got to do the practical part of reform in Chicago, and would be a great addition to the L.C.C. At a meeting of most of the leading Mayors of the country some months ago, he was elected Chairman on account of a very able paper, which he gave me to read, on municipal ownership. He has taken exactly the right political attitude. He stuck to his party, insisted on having the nomination and then appealed to the people on principle, and got in by the votes of people of all parties. He is the highest type of politician I have met yet here, quite equal to our best. Alas! like all the best men, Roosevelt and others, he swears he will go to the war if there is to be another call. I tried what I could to show him that the post of danger was not always that of duty.

I went with him to see parade at the camp near the city. The troops go in a day or two. They were quite ship-shape now, though I have no doubt a fortnight ago they were as crude as the Illinois boys. In the evening the company from Iowa City was entertained by the leading citizens of Des Moines at our hotel. I went in to hear the speeches, which were made in very good style by the governor, judges & others. The 'boys' were all from 19 to 24 years old. They were as good a type as I ever saw, enjoying themselves quietly and seriously, not drinking a bit too much, not rowdy, but applauding loudly the periods about the cause of the war, and their own responsibility. At the end those who had had fathers in the Civil War stood up. There were 28 out of 78.

Friday, May 13
A slack day. Walked about the town, and in a suburb found 200 people watching a pigeon-shooting match. It is just about rook time at Wallington, is it not?

This evening back to *Grinnell*, and spent a pleasant evening with the Rands, reading Shaw's 'Man of Destiny' to them.

Saturday, May 14

Spent at Grinnell. Watched a tennis match & played bowls. Went to an 'at home' of the Professors, and had a jolly evening with the President and my favourite young ladies of the Faculty, the Modern Language and Classical professors.

Sunday, May 15

A day's journey to *St. Paul*. Country very pleasant and rolling, though rather barer and less finished in quite the north of the State. The Mississippi & Minnesota are very beautiful as you near St. Paul. St. Paul is a great railroad centre. It is very cheerful. There is not much smoke. The streets are wide and generally well-paved. The better houses are on the top of a steep bank, along which runs one of the finest and pleasantest residential avenues I have seen anywhere, with a magnificent view over the river. I am in a very good hotel, the Aberdeen, which Kipling said was the best he stayed in in America.

Monday, May 16

Saw the City, and made calls. Was rather unlucky; but had a good talk to the Editor of the chief newspaper. In the evening I struck oil in a minister of reform tendencies Dr. Smith, professor of Sociology in the Minnesota State University. He took me round calling after dinner, a most excellent social custom which prevails here. He introduced me to several people, especially the Severances, of whom Mrs. Severance is the better half, the intellectual woman of St. Paul, who looks after intelligent visitors. There is a pleasant, musical, rather languid and rather beautiful heiress who lives with her.

Here at night most people sit out in their verandas in rocking chairs, especially the young ladies till about ten o'clock when they all go to bed. The energetic ones bicycle up and down, while the frogs sing in the unbuilt patches and the sides of the hills.

Tuesday, May 17

Went with Dr. Smith to call on Archbishop Ireland, perhaps the leading R.C. in America. He is an Irishman, from among the people, most irrepressibly jovial, the ideal abbot of Glastonbury. He went on a mission to Washington recently to oppose the war in the interests of the Papacy, but now is delighted to be able to advise his flock to fight the Spaniards like mad. He began his career as a military chaplain to the Irish brigade of Minnesota during the war. He is full of keen sense, and has got that layer of intensely capable worldliness under his jovial exterior and clerical garb and dignity which you only get in the great R.Cs. He has done no end of good here as a social reformer and temperance man. Everybody has a good word for him. He is Roman Catholicism up to date, or rather up to the West. He talked most keenly & sensibly about Ireland and English politics, and openly about education, admitting that he could do nothing in Minnesota and was not going seriously to try to get privileges.

I went to see the Labour Dept. here this morning. The Commissioner was not in, but I had a long talk with a capable subordinate.

I spent the evening with the Severances. It was wet.

Wednesday, May 18

Today I spent in seeing the public schools. The St. Paul schools are unusually good, though during the last year they have been suffering from a diminution of funds owing to a rearrangement of taxation. They are managed in much the same way as our good Board Schools, except for details. But there is one enormous difference. The well-to-do people all send their children as a matter of course. There is no social bar as there is in England and somewhat in the East to prevent it. And there was not the organization of excellent private schools as in England or the South before the public school system began. I went into grade VIII (the ex VIIth). There were two rooms of twenty children in each. I looked over some of the exercises. The name of Stickney, one of the railroad kings, caught my eye. It was one of his daughters. All the children looked as if they might be sons or daughters of people living in Summit Avenue, the Belgravia of St. Paul. But more than half were children of artisans. The children of the rich set an example of extra tidiness which is copied by the others, and in return get to know the other children as their equals and are not made into a caste. The work, the teachers say, is very little influenced by the home. The poor do as well as the rich.

69

A beautiful sunset this evening, while another great sun was setting unknown to me.

Thursday, May 19

I did not get the paper for breakfast this morning. I started early for Minneapolis, the twin city of St. Paul, and bought the St. Paul Pioneer Press at a little suburb store, while I was waiting for the car. There was a big portrait of the old man[1] in his chair at Hawarden on the outside page, and I knew what it meant. So I bought a black tie in Minneapolis for the dead King of England.[1]

Minneapolis is a more lively commercial city than St. Paul. It is one of the great milling cities of the world and a great lumber centre. Wood is floated down the river at flood time, and caught as it drifts by ranges of stakes placed across the river opposite the lumber yards. There it is taken out and sawed up for use. Unfortunately I could not see a lumber mill as the water was only just rising enough to enable them to get the wood, and they are not starting work till next week. I went first to see Mr. Charles Pillsbury, the greatest miller in the world in a huge city office with scores of clerks and type-writers. I had some talk with him about England, education, etc. and then went on to the biggest mill in the world, the Pillsbury 'A' Mill. It is run by the water of the Mississippi for all but two months in the winter, when the lakes are frozen and the river runs low. All the processes are wonderful and the saving of labour enormous. I never saw machinery which seemed to require so little attention. The corn is practically unhandled except by crushers, sifters and elevators from the time it arrives in the cars as grain till it is packed as fine meal. There are whole floors with only a couple of men on them.

I lunched with three friends of Mrs. Smith of Halifax, Mr. Alex Campbell, Mr. Frank Nickels & his brother, very nice people, of whom more hereafter.

Three reporters had been after me in my absence.

Friday, May 20

To see the State University of Minnesota, near Minneapolis. I got there about 10.15. The President, to whom I had written

[1] Gladstone.

politely to ask if I might see the University, received me in the most cordial way. Then he announced that the students were assembling for chapel at 10.30 and that he had announced that I was going to address them. Which I promptly had to do, with no little success. Fancy the Master of Trinity collecting George to listen to a speech by young Leiter of Chicago in the middle of morning lectures. I was then taken in hand by Professor Folwell, a very able attractive eastern man, quite like one of our dons, who lectured on Political Science, a good deal better than Hammond I should imagine. He helped me to understand the University better. There are about 2,800 students. There are no fees, except 5 dollars entrance, £1 !! All the rest is paid by the state. In the medical and law depts. there are some extras. Otherwise a penniless man can get education. Lots of the men work for their living, serving at bars, doing household work etc. and so keep themselves for nothing. 1,900 about of the students are doing special courses in Mechanical Engineering and Electricity, Law and Medicine. The 900 in the Academic University proper, a steadily increasing number, have a four years course. Two years of that course is really a continuation of the High School, and is rather like advanced Public School work in England. But the tendency and the aims of educationalists are directed to making the High Schools keep their scholars longer and forcing up the University standard. The last two years are work much like our Tripos for the less good men, a specialised course on generally four subjects which are more or less akin. The better men do special work exactly like our advanced Tripos work during their last year. There is no degree examination, a system disapproved of in the States. Proficiency in the general course of study is the degree qualification. If a man is utterly lazy or utterly incompetent he is just told to go. They are very anxious to make the work more thorough, and are going altogether in the right direction. The history professor deplored to me that there is no means for an American student to come and take an advanced course at Oxford or Cambridge, that they would come in very large numbers to do investigation or study if only they could get the chance.

On my way back I talked with a well-to-do student from Summit Avenue about the social condition of the University.

He says that money does not make a particle of difference. The social life of the Varsities in America is chiefly in what are called Greek Letter societies, cliques of 20 to 50 men who coopt, and live together. It is rather an exclusive system, but better than nothing where the college system does not exist. He belonged to the X Ψ (Xi Psi) Brotherhood. He said they never dreamt of asking what a man's means were when they chose a new member. There are Sororities for the girls, the counterpart of the Brotherhoods, Π Β Φ, Κ Τ, etc.

This evening I was driven out by Miss Fanny, the Severance girl, in a buggy about ten miles, a most beautiful round by the river, which is thickly wooded all along and more beautiful than the North Tyne at Reedsmouth. We dined with the Severances at a country club, which the wealthy people of St. Paul and Minneapolis drive out to in the summer evening to golf, and shoot clay pigeons and eat dinner at.

Saturday, May 21

Had a great talk in the morning with the land commissioner of the Northern Pacific railroad about land development, etc. The railroad have still 38 million acres to sell. Do you want any?

In the afternoon I visited some delightful Westmoreland people, C. Benson & his wife. He is a country gentleman, who has taken to railroad work for part of the year, his wife a Westmoreland lady. Ask Aunt Alice who he is. I want to know. He knows her, and knew grandpapa. His wife is a sweet dignified little English lady, with country house cultivation. He is not as most American business men, but is a man of some capacity.

Dr. Smith took me this evening to see the great railroad magnates, especially J. J. Hill, upon whom I have heard it said that Kipling modelled his railroad king in 'Captains Courageous'. He is just the type.

Sunday, May 22

Breakfasted with Hill, He began as a boy, driving a waggon, when there were 5000 people in St. Paul. Now he has built a great railway, the Great Northern. He controls the Northern Pacific to a great extent. He is the greatest power in the north-west. He has a splendid house, with every imaginable comfort in it, a beautiful picture gallery and a mind packed with information and active for discussion. We had breakfast by ourselves and a good talk on politics etc. He began by showing me with the greatest keenness the record of the Minnesota regiments in the war, and especially the one that lost 80% of its men in the one charge at Gettysburg from the Emetsburg road to protect Sickles' exposed flank. He had not a large library, but Macaulay & G. O. T.'s Life was in it, almost inevitable in every American library of the most moderate size.

After breakfast he showed me his picture gallery, almost all landscapes by Corot, Troyon, Rousseau, Courbet and others like them. They were all good, and about 6, especially the Corots, very beautiful indeed. Unfortunately he is very chary of showing his gallery to the public and does not let the people enjoy or learn from it, as Lininger does at Omaha. Then he took me all over his house, showing me with just as much desire for appreciation his shoots for dirty clothes, and sprinkle-baths. Then we talked some.

This evening I addressed about 600 people in the People's Church, Dr. Smith's, on the Anglo-American alliance. It was a first-rate audience. A good many leading citizens, judges and the like, were there, and at the end there was considerable applause, which they do not usually indulge in there. I have sent you the report. I have now been called

> Lord Trevelyan
> son of Lord Trevelyan
> Sir Trevelyan
> Hon. Trevelyan,

and as a climax, Rev. C. Trevelyan!
I consented to be interviewed by a little Irish girl that had come over from Minneapolis twice to see me and had got wet through in her best dress the second time. So I relented, and after chaffing her for ten minutes, I told her enough to make an interview. She was a niece of Father McFadden of Gweedore.

After my lecture a Scotchman came up who had heard G. O. T. at the time of the Midlothian campaign in Edinburgh market, and an Englishman from Hackney, who had heard

73

him speak for Charles Russell. Both were very keen; but of course the Scotchman was plaintive that I had only used the word 'British' four times – he had carefully reckoned on his fingers – out of my many allusions to the old country. He would not have been so patient in St. Andrews Hall.

Monday, May 23

Spent a delightful day at Lake Minnetonka, the summer resort of the well-to-do people of Minneapolis. Minnesota is a beautiful state, very thickly wooded, with thousands of lakes big and small in it. This Lake is specially beautiful, surrounded entirely by thick woods with bright wooden cottages peeping out from little hilltops. It is all or more than all what our lakes are, except for mountains, of which there are none. Mrs. Smith's cousin, Frank Nickels, entertained me. He has got a house there with two little boys and a pleasant sister-in-law, niece of President Harrison. We had a jolly sail all round the lake with a party of friends, men and women. Tell Mrs. Smith, if you see her, how hospitable they were, and what jolly little boys Frank Nickels has got. I hope to send her a photo of them.

I travelled back with a high school girl a niece of Mr. Nickels. She was very fond of travelling. A little more than a year ago she, 14 years old, and her sister, 16 years old, had travelled for several weeks in Maine, then up by steamer to Montreal and home, *alone*. These defenceless females never dreamt of the necessity of chaperonic protection and were entirely unmolested, and will probably soon repeat the experiment. What fools English mothers are!

It is beginning to get hot now, though there is no need yet for straw-hats. But tonight all sorts of beetles and bugs (Anglice insects) flew in at my window to buzz round my electric light. They evidently have come to the conclusion that summer has come, for they have not been noticeable before.

Tonight I had an interesting talk with a half-caste waiter in our hotel. He was a coloured man of course socially. He had had a University education in New Orleans. He says there are only three things a coloured man can do in the North, be a waiter, a railway porter or attendant, and a barber. In the South he says they can do anything and are beginning to rise

very considerably & carry on business. His brother is a con-
tractor.

Tuesday, May 24

Today I am off from St. Paul northwards to Leech Lake where
I shall see an Indian camp. I am now passing up the Mississippi
which is full of floating timber, all apparently untended. There
are hundreds of logs in sight at this moment. I suppose each of
them is marked and will reach its destination some day, when
the water rises. They are not floating very fast just now. The
country by the river is wooded and very attractive; but a good
deal that we have passed through this morning is bare and flat,
where the farms are new and recently cleared. There is not yet
the richness or settled look of Iowa.

Love to all,
Yours,
Charles Trevelyan

11. LEECH LAKE, MINNESOTA

Walker,
On Leech Lake,

Tuesday, May 24

I have reached the outworks of civilization. You may look in
vain for the town of Walker on any map. The nearest place that
will be marked is Brainerd. From there a new line runs to the
shores of Leech Lake, almost due north. They call it a logging
road, because it is chiefly for the carriage of timber. There is
only one train a day which stops every five miles to drop a car
or waggon by the side track where a little clump of wooden
shanties has risen or timber is to be loaded. The whole country
is forest, rich in oak, birch, and pine. Every two or three miles
are large or small lakes, very beautiful, extremely like Rothley
Lake—only hundreds of them all over the country. The railway
runs close to the shores and logs are drifted across and hauled
onto the cars. We stopped once to let a calf get off the line in
front of us. Walker is a collection of wooden houses, the first of

which was built two years ago. It is a logging town, wood cutters and wood-drivers inhabiting it. An enterprising Michigan man, MacGarry has started an hotel here, counting on the growth of the place commercially and as a possible holiday resort for the town of Minnesota. It is on the shores of a beautiful lake about ten miles long and two broad, which joins another great sea of about fifteen miles across. In every direction there are streams leading to other lakes, which make a network all over the country. The shores are thickly wooded with dark and light foliage. Most of the shores are an Indian reservation, and the loveliness is only broken now and then by a little group of shanties and wigwams clustering on some clearing. The town of Walker consists of two hotels, half a dozen stores, ten saloons, a congregational chapel, three tents, and thirty wooden houses. It has doubled since January. The streets are sand. There are six times as many men as women. They are all in their shirt-sleeves. Half of them seem to have nothing to do except occasionally to fish and deal with the Indians who come in to barter. Almost all the interesting people go to MacGarry's hotel. While I was there there were staying, a commercial traveller with his samples, two young bankers who were thinking of starting a country bank, several engineers engaged on the two new railway lines that are being cut through the forests, the doctor of the town, the national agent sent to look after the forests of the Indian reservation, two people visiting, and two girls, daughters of the chief store-keeper of Walker. His name is Wright and he was a soldier in the war. He has a diary which he kept every day during the war and intends to publish some day. It ought to be very interesting. I talked to him of Gettysburg where he fought on the second day between the Big and Little Round Top, resisting Longstreet. Antietam he said was the worst fight he was in. I told him to send us a copy of his diary if he published it. He has a son and two daughters, the belles of Walker, who keep the store with him. The girls are extremely nice and I made great friends with them, quite smartly dressed but not vain as pretty girls in an English country town would be who got all the attention of all the men, natives and visitors.

This evening we went in a little steamer to the Indian Agency, the chief encampment, of about fifty houses of the Chippewa

76

Indians. They have not got many wigwams left, and live mostly in large wooden shanties. They are dressed generally like shabby Americans, though the women, some of them, wear blankets like a Scotch lassie wears her shawl. Sometimes a man has feathers in his hat and embroidery on his waistcoat. Altogether it looks very like a village in Western Donegal or Mayo, only the people have a darker skin. About a dozen whites live among them, a school-mistress, a goaler, a woman who teaches lace-making and one or two others. We could not stay long as it became dark, and we sailed back over the lake, with the moon dimly lighting up the old woods and shining over the water.

Wednesday, May 25

Today I went for a two hours trip in one of the steamers in the morning, up one of the side creeks where the railway is being built. It was a most wild and beautiful piece of river, yellow wild rice and green rushes growing out into the water, low birch and oak and tall pine crowding the shores, black birds with large scarlet spots on their wings flying across the boat, herons rising out of the reeds, occasionally ducks flighting, and a bald-headed eagle passing across from one pine top to another. In summer the river is overlaid with white water-lilies. As we came back we were blocked for half an hour by a steamer tugging at 200 huge tree-trunks, some of which had got stuck in the shallows. We walked about on the loose logs as safely as on land.

In the afternoon we went a longer expedition into the great lake, a party of about 10, men and women. We had a glorious sunny breezy run about 20 miles and back to Bear Island, where the most primitive Indians of the Reservation live. We passed the place where many years ago a great battle was fought for the possession of the district between the Sioux and Chippewas, ending in the destruction of the Sioux. At Bear Island we were landed by an old man, grey with age, with feathers in his hair. We saw the Wigwams, the babies strapped onto wooden racks, which the mothers carry on their backs, the little patches of ground cultivated by the squaws, the graves made of wooden boxes, looking like large beehives, with holes in the end to pop in food once a year for the dead to eat in the happy hunting grounds. Paths lead through the woods down which you can only walk in Indian file. Horses seem to be the only kind of cattle. The food is some sort of wheat cake, fish, bacon and game. They again reminded me very much of the wilder western Irish, showing how the uncivilization bred of bad laws is much the same as the backwardness of mere savagery. They do not like being photographed at all, and the women run into the houses if you point a camera at them. Some of the women seemed to be entirely in blankets, but there were no men in anything but trousers. They do not put on their finery and their war-paint except for festivals. I have bought two wonderful pieces of Indian bead-work, almost inconceivably beautiful for squaws to work in such surroundings, but undoubtedly genuine. The best piece is a chief's sash, rather like a masonic apron in shape. As we sailed back we drank lemonade and sang songs of all nations while the sun set in glory on the woods.

Thursday, May 26

I could not resist spending one more day here. I suppose I shall never see it again, and it is as good as Killarney or Windermere. Although it lacks the mountains it has finer woods and waters.

I had some fishing, though not successful. Later in the day one party caught 60 pike. It is a great sporting place. You can kill a hundred duck on a good evening in the fall.

I went a canoe ride, in a real Indian birch bark canoe with Miss Wright, who is a better steerer than any practised canoe man on the Cam and a good shot at duck. We got wet through by a storm but enjoyed ourselves vastly playing Indian. In the afternoon we had another trip on the lake, and in the evening sang songs and danced.

Friday, May 27

Today I am on my way back to civilized society, having found that there is simplicity, comfort and law on the American frontiers just as in the Cheviots. There are saloons, but there is no revolver law. Property is a good deal safer than in Chicago. I am sorry to think of never being back here.

Yours,

Charles Trevelyan

12. NORTH DAKOTA AND DOWN TO OMAHA

Webster Hotel,
Fargo,
N. Dak.

Friday, May 27

I got to *Fargo* this evening. I had only time for a short stroll before dark. It is a town of 10,000 on the banks of the Red River. It was burnt down, every stick of it, four years ago. But it was immediately rebuilt by the population and has increased since then. It is on the edge of the State of North Dakota. I walked down to the Red River, the boundary between Dakota and Minnesota. On the other side of the bridge was a group of well-built houses, brightly lighted, with flags gaily flying. They were a group of half a dozen saloons. North Dakota is a prohibition state and therefore the saloon-keepers on the Minnesota side do a roaring trade. All day and night there are four or five wagonettes which perambulate Fargo and take drinkers over the bridge. So Fargo is far from temperate. But they appear to enforce the law pretty well in Dakota. There are at present several druggists with big businesses in goal for several months for selling whiskey for other than medicinal purposes. As I came back I passed a Salvation Army hall, and while I write the Salvation drum is booming.

Saturday, May 28

Today I have made the acquaintance of the prairies. I took a drive of thirty miles through the Red River wheat district, the 'world's bread-basket'. My companion was a Mr. Dawes, with whom I had struck up an acquaintance, a wheat dealer, of English parentage and Canadian birth, who knows the country intimately. The land is absolutely flat. For three hundred miles north and south, and fifty east and west there is not a hillock or an incline. There are no trees except by the streams, and not always there. Here and there a little grove has been planted round a farm house. During the whole day there was only one line of wood by a single river, stretching across the country, to break the view. There are no hedges at all. North, south, east and west stretched an endless green ocean; with wooden farm houses and barns spotted over it like little fishing boats every two miles; occasionally a row of birches or poplars; and lines of telephone posts; and in all directions on the railway lines huge wheat elevators, standing out like three deckers on the main. Gradually you began only to be able to see the tops of the trees and the upper halves of the elevators. You saw the curve of the earth as on the sea. As on the sea everything looked much nearer than it really was. And we often had to drive four miles to a place that looked only two distant. About midday we saw a mirage. Far away west, over the horizon and beyond the last tree tops we saw lines of trees and elevators raised off the ground, and standing in the sky. It was a most marvellous sight. It was a dull grey day that we were driving on, with no bright sun. On sunny days there are immense mirages, which show up all the country for miles behind the horizon.

By the end of the day I had the same oppressed feeling of unutterable waste and sameness one has on the ocean.

Absolutely the whole of the country is under wheat. This year the prices are at least double what they were two years ago, and there is hardly any fallow at all. The soil is quite black, with no grit or stone in it. When oil runs short, they wet the earth and lubricate their wheels with it. Twenty years ago you drove straight across this country, which was bare grass. Now every acre for hundreds of miles is under the plough. What is the use of the Essex farmer trying to plod on with his grain crop?

There is not very much animal life yet, though I suppose when the corn is up, birds must flock into the region. We saw a fox, some blue hares, a huge hawk, and a lot of pretty birds of smaller size, yellow, red and blue. I rather expected sea-gulls.

In harvest time at any rate the *men* increase vastly in numbers. All the refuse of mankind from north, south, east and west flocks to the wheat lands. From Chicago, New Orleans, and Salt Lake they come, crowding the cheap cars and hanging under the freight waggons. They are a terror to the peace loving citizen, these Hobos as they are called. It is better not to go out after dark in Fargo. The goals are full of them. The reason why Dakota is a prohibition state is mainly because the farmers know most of their hands would be drunk when cutting and threshing was to be done, if they could get at liquor.

On the whole Dakota is the very last spot on earth I would

choose to live. Perhaps today's grey sky did not show it at its best. But it would be a weary thing to be always looking out on that unending landscape. Having seen this glimpse of the north-west, I am now off for Colorado, via St. Paul and Omaha.

As I got into the train tonight I got into conversation with a young commercial traveller, 'drummer' as they call them here. He was a dissolute young man who had had to bolt from Omaha to escape an inconvenient marriage, and altogether his morality was rather shaky. He explained to me the best method of cheap travel. You buy a long distance mileage ticket which is gradually torn off. This you present to the conductor if you are going 100 miles with a reasonable sum wrapped up in it. The conductor takes the sum and tears off a few miles, but returns the ticket practically intact. The partial truth contained in it is a side-light on the ways of railway officials.

Sunday, May 29

I am travelling today down to Omaha, a long slow journey but on the whole through pretty country, especially the banks of the Minnesota, which are finely wooded. Most of the popula-tion of the wayside towns, at any rate the male portion, is taking a Sunday lounge in the railway station, as it does in Ireland.

For the last two hours I talked to a lady who has married an English gentleman in business in Omaha. It wiled away the last stages of a long journey. Landed at eleven o'clock at *Omaha*.

Monday, May 30

Went over a great Smelting Works, where they extract from the ore lead, silver and gold. All these metals are mixed in varying quantities in all the rock which is mined for the precious metals. I saw all the processes down to the cooling of the brick of gold which will be sent direct to the Denver mint.

I lunched with the Oldfields, the acquaintance I made last night, and Mrs. O. drove me round afterwards to the park where the veterans of the war were celebrating Decoration Day. In the morning they take flowers to the graves of those who fell. At Gettysburg & other battlefields there are great meetings. It is one of the Bank Holidays of America. On ordinary occasions the National Guard and regular troops parade with the veterans. Today there were only the cadets of the City Academy. All the adult trained soldiers are gone to Cuba or the Philippines. The hearths of Nebraska are guarded only by boys and grey haired men! There were about 150 veterans, looking rather solemn—for the day is to bear record of the 'sacred dead'. Some had the old hats on they wore in the war. A few shouldered their umbrellas as they marched. But they were all in their best Sunday clothes and chiefly showed their military quality by marching in step and obeying a mounted officer who had sometime led them. Nebraska of course is the very outskirts of the civilization of 1863, and there were very few compared to the Eastern cities. They gathered in a dell in the Park, under the trees, with the sun shining brightly through, the school children of the town and brightly dressed girls crowding the hill-sides. There we had to leave them and heard a bull-voiced but not clear-toned orator beginning as we drove away.

I have been sent on my way to Denver with all the honours of the Union Pacific Railroad. I saw Mr. Burt again, and he has given me passes over all their lines and some that are not theirs, so that I shall not apparently have any more travelling expenses, except for sleeping berths, till I get to San Francisco. I was seen off by two or three station-masters and managers. Tomorrow I shall be at Denver.

Tuesday, May 31

Woke up in the midst of the rolling grass prairie, no hedge, tree or green, except the grass, an endless rolling expanse. Lots of little burrowing prairie-dogs, about the size of marmots were playing round their holes; occasionally some lonely looking cattle were grazing. Just before Cheyenne the Rockies came in sight fifty miles away, the higher peaks covered with snow. All the way from Cheyenne to Denver I have been looking out on them rising suddenly out of the flat plain, blue and misty with a white snow line above, gradually fading off north and south. After leaving Cheyenne 50 miles the bare prairie becomes wheat land and potato land with trees and villages, by dint of extensive irrigation.

Yours
Charles Trevelyan

13. DENVER AND BOULDER

Tuesday, May 31

I entered Denver with an old mining speculator who thirty years ago had come across the prairies in an ox-waggon, plodding along for a week within sight of the mountains before he reached their foot. Denver was then a clump of tents and wooden houses on the edge of a little brook. A few years later the town records were sunk in the quicksands of the brook and the town hall washed away. Now there is asphalt paving, electric cars and light, telephones, buildings 13 stories high, five railroads, the Brown Palace Hotel and all the comforts of civilization.

I immediately went to see some people. I was taken off by a worthy young man to see the degrees being given to the girls of a college at the Episcopal Cathedral. Fancy the height of civilization! A well-built church, with artistically ghastly stained glass, gorgeous crucifixes and painted texts, pews duly dealt out to the rich, with little notices in them 'Please respond audibly, and give *SOMETHING* to the offertory', hymns Ancient and Modern, a church full of pretty and very well dressed maidens. This is the modern mining camp. Then a dean ascended a pulpit with a wooden toadstool over his head and delivered a sermon on the authenticity of the Bible, his chief argument being that 'Moule, the cleverest man in Cambridge, had read the Bible 150 times and had only touched the fringe of the subject'. In the middle of his sermon in order to illustrate the excellence of the training given at the College he called upon the girls, who were so prettily dressed in white dresses and white mortar boards with white tassells, to stand up and recite the books of the Bible in order, which they promptly did audibly and presumably correctly from Genesis to Revelation. Then they knelt down before the altar and received their degree diplomas from the hands of a mumbling bishop. Fancy this height of culture in a city only 30 years old. How few English know the real west. I have bought myself a sombrero. But I have not seen a single person like Buffalo Bill, only a bishop's lawn sleeves.

I was not sorry to hear that secular and religious influences have clashed and that probably the college expires this year and starts again on secular premises and foundation.

I spent the evening at the University Club talking.

Wednesday, June 1

Spent all day seeing people, Wolcott's legal partner Vaile, Cuthbert a splendid lawyer, etc. In the evening dined with delightful English family who seem to lead society here, the Pearces. Pearce is British Consul.

Thursday, June 2

Went to see the State University at Boulder. It was Commencement Day when they *end* the term and give degrees. The ceremony was in a Chapel, full of well dressed people, chiefly girls and ladies, about 800 of them. First a horribly stupid lecture was given, the commencement address—sort of Rectorial performance—by an historical professor from the East, Adams. It was on the Historical Decay of Spain—a splendid subject. But I'm derned if the old fellow did not give every reason for Spain's decline except the religious one. He never once referred to the auto-da-fé!

Then about 30 men and maidens received degrees, girls all in white—looking so pretty and happy. After that a dinner to about 300 people. Speeches were all pretty dull until a distinguished Englishman was called upon, who gave them a lively quarter of an hour. It is great fun speaking to Americans. They are much easier than Englishmen generally. By the way one of the degree receivers was John Bunyan. He did not look as if he would sustain the part.

In the evening I went out with a huge party of about 15 girls and 15 men to the Country Club where the wealthy people of Denver golf, dance and eat in summer days. I never saw a drag full of prettier girls, half English, half American. We got back at one o'clock, waking the early sleepers with song and horn. But it was not half as nice as the hay ride at Grinnell. Silks and rustling dresses and sham-flowered hats take away the ease of companionship. We might just as well have been a party

84

driving from the Hotel Metropole to the Star and Garter—
except that there was Long's Peak gleaming white in the moon-
light 15 miles away.

Friday, June 3

Saw various interesting people, late Senator Hill, Mills, a
Populist lawyer etc. Went an evening cycle ride with a party.
Were caught by a terrific storm half way. Had to go into a very
disreputable wayside saloon, where however after they had
huddled away various women and packs of cards—leaving
several queens and aces scattered about the floor—we were
comfortable enough till the storm abated a little. Then we rode
home and got a soaking, but enjoyed it.

Saturday, June 4

Today alas! when I was to have gone for my first walk in the
mountains, the rain still falls. So part of this morning I sang
songs with a fair Engländerin. Now I am going to read Faust.

Yours,

Charles Trevelyan

14. CRIPPLE CREEK, PIKE'S PEAK, COLORADO
SPRINGS AND THROUGH THE ROCKIES

Saturday, June 4

After a dinner at the Denver Club with several good fellows,
one of them an old Harrovian who was very sad about Harrow's
want of recent distinction and glad to hear that an effort was
being made to get more scholarships, started by night for
Cripple Creek with Vaile, Senator Wolcott's legal colleague,
who has interests as well as legal connections in the great gold
district.

Sunday, June 5

Woke up at *Cripple Creek*. It is the most forlorn country. Being
10,000 ft. above sea-level there is no natural vegetation except
pines and short grass. Streaks of snow still line the hills. Every-

85

where for the space of ten miles the hillsides have been bored by prospectors, so that it looks as if some giant rabbits had been at work making a universal warren. Here and there the mounds outside the holes are enormous and buildings and chimneys have risen, where some good find has been made and a company started. Railways circle the bottom of the hills, belching black smoke to scale the up grades. Along the top of the hills runs a cable-car, which yesterday broke loose and entered Cripple Creek at the rate of seventy miles an hour. Only a few were bruised. They all jumped in time. We saw it this morning lying smashed at the end of the main street. A stable-master, from whom we were getting a buggy remarked with some approval that it was the first smash they had had. I asked how long the company had been started, expecting three years or so. It was only 3 months! Cripple Creek only started in '91. It has already been burnt down once. It is still mostly of wood. It looks as if no-one cared for it, and all wanted to leave it as soon as possible. There is no shooting. But the main street is devoted to gambling hells and brothels open to the air. It is just a do-as-you-like town. You can be comfortable if you please in a perfectly respectable hotel.

The better side of the district is the beautiful view you get when you look outside it. Mt. Pisgah, an unruined hill, is rather fine on one side. From some places you see Pike's Peak with its snow-clad ridge. Far away on fine days you can see the Sangre de Cristos Mountains, a long line of giant snow-peaks. But today we had to be content with the dingy surroundings of the gold hills. We spent most of the morning down one of the biggest mines, the Portland. Six years ago or so three men digging in their little claim hit a good vein. They had begun with a dollar. One of them is now living at his ease in the East. Mr. Harman who still manages the mine, and is worth some half million is just like a Northumbrian miner or Elswick engineer, quite simple, unaffected, modest and hard working. How he will use his money, God knows. He won't gamble it; but he does not seem to care for anything different to his present work as mine superintendent. We went through all the workings which already run down 700 ft. The ore is extracted by boring and blasting and is then sold to smelting works where the gold and silver are extracted. Nowhere in Cripple Creek is there any gold left in what they call 'macer' workings, that is loose, that can be washed out of the earth of streams. It has all to be got now out of the rock.

In the afternoon we had another drive round. All the girls ride astride here and look splendid horsewomen. Mr. Vaile showed me some workings of his, which have failed to show a good vein. Almost every man in Denver has sometime tried his luck. In Vaile's case of course it was only tossing away the money of a few briefs and not vital to him.

Monday, June 6

The one American who appears to like walking in the English fashion, named May, came over by the night train from Denver to cross the passes with me to Colorado Springs. We drove the first half of the way on a primitive stage-coach drawn by four rawboned horses. We sang songs all the way, greatly to the delight of our humble fellow-passengers. It was just like a Swiss pass, very bare at the top with snow mountains visible near. Then down into a valley thickly lined with pine trees, sometimes a wooden chalet, less picturesque than in the Neiringen valley as you come down from the Grimsel, but reminding one of Switzerland. The last fifteen miles we walked. The valley for many miles gave us a far distant view of the great plains between rocky gateways. They lie like a still summer sea with the clouds throwing green shadows over them. We issued eventually onto the plain through a gorgeous canyon of red rock.

We dined at Colorado Springs, a cheerful residence town with big streets and avenues of trees, the home of consumptives. Then May left for Denver, and I went on to stay with the Bells at Maniton, five miles nearer Pike's Peak. Dr. Bell had a good deal to do with some of the railways and helped to lay out Colorado Springs. He has a kind but fussy wife, a very charming unmarried daughter, one married in Denver and an Eton boy. They live a good deal at Maniton, otherwise in a Sussex home. At dinner I found a Mr. Thornton who is now a big farmer, once a great protégé of Lady Ashburton, and who talked much of Lady Compton Carlyle and others known of us. It was a most completely English house and English circle.

87

Tuesday, June 7

Up Pike's Peak with the Bells, father, son and daughter. We went up by a cog railway to the top 14,147, where was a house with a nigger beating a gong in front of it to announce lunch, which however we did not take. We had been joined at the bottom by an Englishman called Paget, who turned out to be my fag at Vanity's, and a gawky companion who had a bad headache and did not dare eat lunch owing to the elevation. We had a splendid walk down, with great cloud effects. There were thunder-storms on both sides of us, and when we got back to Maniton we found sand and refuse and tinned-meat cans blocking the car-track. But we got only slightly wet. We got some fine scenery looking over at the Sangre de Cristos, fifty miles away, and in the valleys on the way down. I walked home with the young lady, the others trained the last ten miles.

In the evening a dinner, at which the notable person was President Slocum of the Colorado Springs College. He looked more like a jolly farmer; but is a most efficient guide of the youth.

Wednesday, June 8

Went to see Colorado Springs College. It hardly aspires to be a university, but gives its degrees very stringently to only about ⅓ of the students, so that a very high general standard is maintained. Most of those who take degrees take advanced courses at Eastern universities. Of course it is a mixed College, and the girls mostly live a sort of college life, unlike the State Universities, in a hall of their own; where they sleep, work and eat. They are looked after a little more than in the State Universities, but can talk to the men as they like and go about with them, until gossip begins. Then the Dean of Women sometimes steps in. They never have any real trouble.

Colorado by the way is a woman suffrage state. It is certainly not a failure. The women do not appear to vote as generally as the men on most occasions. But though some men grumble, I do not find any likelihood of reaction. The Conservative elements are rather inclined to approve, because most people think it was the women's vote that threw out the Populist governor, Waite, who seems to have been personally undesirable, though

I am inclined to think his politics were not as black as they are painted. The women are evidently considered a force for emergencies.

In the evening we drove to dinner at General Palmer's through the Garden of the Gods, a beautiful piece of green valley with low shrubs in it, walled in by a line of tremendous red rock, rising out of the earth knife-wise to about 300 ft. Two miles further on the formation crops out again almost as finely, and there Gen. Palmer has built himself a house in one of the finest spots on earth. The general was at Shiloh, Chicamauga, Antietam etc., and in many minor engagements, in the cavalry. He has a family of nice daughters & we had a pleasant evening, and drove home singing songs.

Thursday, June 9

Went a walk over the hills and down into the canyon behind General Palmer's. There was no path and I had to force my way for four miles or so down the narrow gorge through primaeval forest growth. I passed one clearing with a hut and a deserted burrow in the rock, evidently made by someone in search for gold. Otherwise I saw no sign of man. I had to push through tangled brushwood, jump fallen trees, crash through piles of washed down branches, wade to my middle through pools with smooth rocks on either side. I am sure Stanley never had such a job. I came home by the Garden of the Gods, gorgeous in the evening sun-light.

There was a youthful dinner party, among others the son of Walker the economist, who is professor at the College, and a young man who is going out to the Russian Court as one of the U.S.A. attachés. Of course he is appointed by favouritism and not examination. He seemed to me to be quite up to our examined aristocrats however.

Friday, June 10

To Glenwood Springs. An uncomfortable journey. The Pullman was crammed with doctors – of whom there are 1,400 and their families at Denver for a conference – going out to Glenwood Springs etc. I had to get a seat and table in the tourist car, where I had room enough but was horribly jolted and nearly sick.

The first part of the way the view was glorious. The Grand

89

Canyon of the Arkansas and the first near view of the Sangre de Cristos Mountains were superb. Then clouds came down, and a leaden pall appropriately veiled the scenery as we approached Leadville. I am glad I gave up my idea of stopping there. It is Cripple Creek, only older and gloomier. At the station we got out and rushed to the end of the platform, where a man stood whacking a cracked gong under a door marked 'Eating House'. There we gobbled moodily and silently as in Martin Chuzzelwit for ten minutes. On the platform several children were selling specimens of glittering lead ore, like the children who hawk 'boulets' at Waterloo. I played many games of patience and exercised a good deal, till I arrived at this Hotel.

Saturday, June 11

Here is an hotel at *Glenwood Springs* about the size of Bear at Grindelwald and more comfortable. In the garden are hot sulphur springs, whither I go in a few minutes to take a bath at a temperature of '90'. Against the hillside is a vapour bath house.

This morning I scaled the hills, visited a wonderful cave with crystalline formation on roof and sides, and climbed about the rocks, viewing the Eagle River Canyon, & the snowy Elk Mountains. I put up a bird very like a grey hen, which flapped as if wounded to keep me from its brood. I have not got its name yet. I came slithering down the Mountain among the loose stones. The Rockies are as safe and accessible as our mountains at home. But they are much stiffer walking, because there is so much fallen timber and so many loose stones and empty cataracts. There is hardly any water to drink, but thousands of water-courses. The water runs off as fast as it falls.

This Hotel is run by an Englishman called Lyle and a Scotchman called Thompson. Every afternoon they play Polo, Lyle being a first-class player. It is I should think the most beautiful Polo ground in the world. It is in a valley. On two sides are wooded mountains with the mouth of a rocky gorge between. On a third side is a barer mountain, with a cliff of almost scarlet rock. At the other end of the valley, 15 miles away, is to be seen Mt. Sopris, the finest snow peak of the Elk Mountains. After watching a Polo game I had a bath in the hot sulphur water. It is not too enervating if you do not stay in long. But of course most people revel in it, and between 7 and 9 o'clock in the evenings the baths are full of men and women who swim and splash for an hour on end. The place is luridly lit by electric light and with the steam rising from the water, it looks like a picture of some lake in hell.

Sunday, June 12

Climbed the best mountain near with Scotch Thompson, a shrewd interesting man. We talked all the way up and down. Rode with him in the afternoon to see a fruit-ranch and very fine valley. Then went and tried my hand at knocking about a polo ball. I should very soon learn, my chief difficulty being, not to hit the ball straight, but to keep my stick from swinging round onto the pony's nose after the stroke, which naturally the pony is apt to resent. But on the whole he behaved angelically, making every allowance for my incompetence and going slowly whenever it was time to hit the ball. In the evening the Hotel fountain was turned on. It goes to 185 ft. Is that more than the Chatsworth or not? It was very magnificent. Altogether Glenwood Springs is a splendid health and summer resort, and is likely to become celebrated, for dozens of doctors are staying there at this moment, having come on from a medical conference at Denver. Started tonight for Salt Lake City. At once struck an acquaintance with a grey-haired, pleasant Manchester man, who turned out to be brother of our friend Broadfield, the progressive on the School Board, whom I stayed with a while ago.

Monday, June 13

Woke up in the barren Utah deserts, where nothing grows but tufts of broom like grass, except in spots where irrigation has been possible. Passed some fine gorges and hill scenery.

Finally we came down into the valley of the Salt Lake and ran for fifteen miles or so in the middle of a broad plain, rich in orchards, corn fields, snug houses and thick lines of poplar trees, like the best French scenery. But behind was what French scenery has not, a line of mountains, rising straight from the plain, the higher ones still snow-capped. Then we ran into the city of the Mormons, where for the present goodbye.

Yours,

Charles Trevelyan

15. SALT LAKE CITY AND YELLOWSTONE
NATIONAL PARK

Knutsford Hotel,
Salt Lake City

Monday, June 13

I do not think that Uncle Harry's[1] fame had reached to Utah.
But I forgot to ask.

Salt Lake City is one of the most beautiful in the world. Its
situation is splendid. It is just on the edge of a valley, ten miles
broad. The valley is green with grass and wheat and poplar
avenues and orchards. On each side of the valley are mountains, some of them snow-capped rising straight from the plain.
At one end is a pass, the other broadens out into the great Salt
Lake, which lies about five miles away. The Lake looks lonely
and desolate, for no vessels ply on it. But it is grand, with
imposing mountains rising round it, big islands, bare of all but
a little grass, breaking its vastness, which stretches away indefi-
nitely to the north. The city itself is charming. All the streets
are very wide and, except for a few hundred yards in the centre
of the city, they are lined with avenues of poplar trees, which
keep the walks cool by day and are impenetrable to the
abundant electric light by night. Every house, of small and
great, has grass all round it, generally flowers and trees. Except
where the shops are, no one dreams of building houses touching
one another. It is the greatest city of America. The public
buildings too are fine. Utah was lately made a state, much
behind its time, because of its Mormonism. It has not yet been
able to build its capitol, on which all states love to lavish money.
The site is chosen, the gardens are planted, the railings are up.
But no state may build a capitol out of public money for 4
years after becoming a state and Utah has only been inaugu-
rated for two. So it has built itself a magnificent City Hall for
its capital city, which is as fine or finer than Glasgow's. But the
great building of all is the Mormon Temple. The upper part of
the city is the centre of Mormon life and history. At the end of
the main street is a statue of Brigham Young with an imperious

[1] Viscount Knutsford, married G. O. T.'s sister Margaret.

92

glance and a walking stick in his hand. At the back of the monument are the names of the men who came over the pass with him into the promised land. Behind him to the left lie the tithing house, where the farmers bring their tenth parts every market day, and his own dwelling. His house consists of an old part, very simple and comfortable, with an addition in the rear with several separate doors, where the various wives were housed as the establishment enlarged. On the other side of the road is an ugly swell modern building, Amelia house, in which his favourite wife was put to live, apart from his other better fifteenths. Further on is the Eagle gate, a crude steel arch with an eagle on it, and behind it the original Mormon chapel. Several of Young's wives are still alive and inhabit their original dwellings.

Behind the statue to the right are the great Mormon buildings. There are three of them, within a high walled enclosure. The new assembly hall is an uninteresting, large modern building. The Tabernacle, the earliest meeting place of size, looks like an overgrown mushroom. It seats many thousands, and has splendid acoustic properties, splendid at least for a religious audience. An interrupted political meeting would be chaos at once. We heard a man fill the hall when merely talking gently. But we also heard an attendant brushing the floor with a soft broom, who sounded as if he were hammering it vigorously. The Tabernacle is a very big place, but it is entirely dwarfed by the Temple, which is an enormous new building of grey stone with towers and pinnacles, rising far above the poplars and business buildings. The Temple is rather too much closed in by buildings near it and by the wall all round to be able to get a really good view of it. But generally the architecture is impressive. No Gentile, as we are all called, can enter in, nor can any except important Mormons if they are not being baptised or married. But some of the people, who had been allowed through when it had been finished but before it was used, have given me some description. The interior is very gorgeous, evidently the chief purpose being to impress the novice at time of initiation. There is a Holy of Holies. But the chief place is a central hall with a deep pit in it, at the bottom of which are brazen bullocks, bearing a huge porphyry basin. All round are smaller basins. The whole place is for baptism. But as no

93

questions might be asked or answered on that day, the Gentiles had to pass through interested but unenlightened as to the exact uses of each place.

The Mormons are still the most important part of the state. In Ogden, Salt Lake City and the mining camps the Gentiles equal or outnumber them. But in the farming districts the Mormons are a vast majority. The governor is a Mormon, the principal of the State University is son of one of the original settlers. But the great contest is over. The State has been admitted with stringent safeguards against polygamy. The church has given in about it, though it is still taught as the true and ideal doctrine. The old fellows already supplied with more than one wife still go on with the practice quietly. In some out of way parts of the state the farmers are said still to practise it. But generally the younger generation is acquiescing in monogamy. The Church is still very influential however, and the Mormons are still very conservative. They opposed education fiercely because it was likely to oppose their religion. But the Liberal movement succeeded and now there is quite good education from top to bottom. The tithes are still exacted, and almost all the farmers pay a tenth of their cattle, corn and eggs. But many of the better educated Mormons are ceasing to do so, and I found that the University professors, half of whom are Mormon, omit to give a tenth of their salaries. Severe Mormonism is giving way before education, though the wealth and respectability of the Mormon community prevents any real decline in numbers. It is practically the religion of Utah, and on the whole Utah is more religious than most American states

This afternoon I walked about and saw the city, dined with a capital fellow, Mr. Wicks, a land agent, and went to see some pretty girls in the evening, daughters of a judge.

Tuesday, June 14

Saw more of the city. In the afternoon went down with a party to the Salt Lake and had a bathe. You cannot sink. The water is a quarter of it solid, and you flop about on the top. You have to swim on your back, because if you try the other way your legs stick out of the water behind. No one has ever been drowned there, but one man was choked by the Lake water. If you get a drop in your eye it stings horribly. If you get a few drops in your mouth it seems to permeate nostrils and ears and burn the inside of your head out. But except for a few such passing discomforts a bathe is delicious. The water was very warm and I felt better than I ever did before after a dip. The Lake looked very magnificent. Its desertion was impressive. It is very difficult to sail a boat, because it is buoyed up so high out of the water. Therefore there is no sea traffic. So we looked out on a silent sea, glittering in the afternoon sun.

Wednesday, June 15

I began the day by going to the Commencement of Utah University. I had some talk first with the principal and some of the professors. I did not stay very long; but heard a girl recite an essay on the triumph of truth, which wandered from the sinking of the Maine to the education of infants. They must have speechified half the day. But I left them to go a walk in the mountains with two bright girls, one very beautiful and musical, the other very talkative and well-read. We went up a lovely wooded valley, lunched by a babbling brook and walked back over the hill, getting a glorious view of the valley, city, lake and mountains, such as Brigham Young must have had, without the city and the poplars, fifty years or so ago, when he told his followers as they emerged from Emigration Canyon, that here was the promised land.

I on the whole disagree about American girls being better than the men. The men are very friendly and interesting in their own lines. The girls alone have strong literary and artistic interests and therefore at first make better companions. But in the long run, as in England, it is hard to choose.

Tonight I am off for my expedition in the Jackson Lake region. A troop of soldiers has been as far as Ogden on the way to San Francisco with us. A great crowd chiefly of girls came to see them off at Salt Lake, and there was much weeping and some hurrahing. They were only 30 cavalrymen, so there was no universal turn-out to see them off.

Thursday, June 16

The train got into *Monida* two hours and a half late. The town of Monida consists of a station, a restaurant with a Chinese cook, a store with a bar at the back, one house, a few wooden stables and a wooden hotel in course of building. The mail which goes in the direction of Yellowstone had been gone an hour. No arrangements had been made for taking me, in spite of telegrams. I thought I was in for a mountain 'Eden'. There was no train for 24 hours. Suddenly it appeared that a man who was going to run a new line of coaches to the Park was in town. He had no coaches, but all his horses. The sky cleared. On consultation I gave up the plan of going to Jackson's Lake, I arranged to be driven to Henry's Lake as a first stage to Yellowstone, 50 miles, for $15 (£3). I started in a four wheeled cart, drawn by two black carriage horses with long tails, fresh from Nebraska, which would have done credit to Vanderbilt's barouche with a little trimming. They were going to draw coaches in a few days, and it was just as well they had the preliminary experience of driving me. They had never been on a prairie highway before, and were not accustomed to the loose logs with which the creeks (burns) are bridged, or to floundering through marshes. We had a most splendid drive in spite of some physical discomfort. If you can imagine jolting for eight hours on end at a trot over country as rough, though not stony, as the piece of road in front of Epipolae, you will have a conception of the experience. Once I was nearly jerked off the box onto the horses' back, but landed on the shafts. The road is just a double line of ruts, very deep owing to recent wet weather, very hard owing to the present hot sun. We drove down a fine valley about six or eight miles wide, with green sloping hills, like Scotch moors without the heather, on either side. As we got further on they became higher and bore timber and snow. The valley was magnificent rich meadow land, with constant spring streams running down the hill-sides to the river. Here and there were herds of cattle. But in the whole valley for our thirty miles drive along it, there were only about half a dozen ranches. He who says that America is settled up has not seen the Idaho and Montana valleys. We lunched at the ranch of a French Canadian called Shambow, who after much wandering has got a splendid ranch, right under a magnificent cliff. Afterwards we jolted on, under a sky full of white fleecy clouds, such as Northumberland is famed for in July days, past the Red Rock Lake, where a score of wild swans were fishing, over the continental divide, where the Missouri takes its rise, but begins deceitfully flowing towards the Pacific. At evening we got down to Henry's Lake, the source of the Snake River. It is as fine a piece of scenery as you can get anywhere. The Lake is four miles across, full of fish and duck and gulls. Along the north side are fine woods and above them rocky mountains, up which you climb. As you look back on the Lake, you see a range of snow mountains opposite, reflected in the clear water. To the right is the wide, wooded valley of the Snake River and in the distance thirty miles off the tops of the Teton range, all snow except the highest peaks, which like the Matterhorn are too steep to keep much snow on them. In the fall there is very good duck and elk shooting. Today two Englishmen have returned from a three weeks' outing with an elk head, two bears, and one bear-cub (alive). I have put up at the store which is the only possible place. There is a decent body who cooks a good dinner, and Mr. Sherwood is not unlike Handyside. He has a big wooden house. Below he has a huge room full of tinned meats, groceries, fishing tackle, stoves, & God knows what. Above he has a considerable museum of Rocky Mountain animals, stuffed very well indeed by himself, bears, elk, grouse, mountain sheep, beavers, wolves etc.

Friday, June 17
Spent the morning fishing in the outlet of the Snake River from the Lake. I caught 18 trout which weighed 18 lb., several of them were about 3 lb. It was altogether the best fishing I have had. When I got back in the afternoon I found two waggons camped opposite the store, a bearded bronzed man in corduroys putting together a canvas boat, two very nice looking little girls and a homely refined woman all in blue sun-bonnets and rather shabby dresses. They had got comfortable canvas chairs and a cooking stove and looked quite at home. I found that they had started in May 1897 for a two years trip. The man was a Dr. Workman who had found that neither his doctoring nor subsequent ranching had been very profitable, though I do not think it could have been from lack of ability. His wife was a Connecticut lady, who was reading 'Diana of the Crossways', in a cheap American copy, with all the story after the catastrophe in Tonans' sanctum omitted! All last year they had wandered in Colorado, living all the fall on venison, shot by the

97

doctor. The winter months they had spent in Salt Lake City, where the girls had had four months schooling. The eldest, about 16, told me that at school the young Mormons hated to hear their religion talked about, that they were ashamed of it, and that she thought it would break up in the towns in the next generation. Then this May the family have started again for a summer in Idaho, Montana, Yellowstone, etc. and home somehow to Nebraska before winter. They are now on their way to meet their eldest girl who is at College near Boston. Fancy what a country it is where a very nice family can camp out gipsy fashion for two years, live on the meat they shoot or catch, and are not run in for obstructing the highway, trespassing or poaching, and are able for the whole two years to be seeing interesting, new wild country.

Saturday, June 18

I had intended today starting to go up the highest of the mountains near the lake, but cricked my leg again a little jumping over an undrained piece of the main road. So I contented myself with climbing a short way with Mrs. Workman and her girls up the mountain behind the house.

In the afternoon I started with a camp outfit for the Park. I am mounted on a mountain horse with a big ranch saddle, a huge pommel before and great barricade behind to keep the rider on in case of buck-jumping. There are all sorts of mysterious straps to tie on coats and bags. There are huge boot stirrups. I have got a large cowboy hat, and look very much the native, and feel very much the mosstrooper. My palfrey ambles. It cannot trot. It will not canter. And that mysterious motion known to the ancients from the Canterbury pilgrims to Dugal Dalgettie appears still in the primitive west. Behind me, sometimes a few yards, sometimes a few miles, comes my pack train, first the guide, Lat Murray, mounted like myself. Behind him are led two more horses, the first one roped to his hand, the second tied to the tail of the first, both piled with our tent, bedding, multifarious food purchases of canned meat, meal, coffee, bacon etc., cooking utensils and my grip. The pack train walks. It could not go faster, no more than the House of Lords could initiate progressive legislation. But by starting early, it can do about 25 miles a day. This afternoon we crossed a mountain pass to the Madison river basin. We came out upon a wide almost untenanted prairie with rolling hillocks of bare grass, honeycombed by badgers and gophers – All round were pine clad hills with snow peaks behind them. On the other side of the river, three miles away was the primaeval forest. I galloped across the prairie, urging on my unfiery steed, until we nearly came to grief in a badger hole. Then we forded the river and encamped on the forest's edge, 100 yards from the river; as many thousands have done before us, with the fear of the Indian, the wolf and other nameless terrors. We only feared the mosquitoes. Unfortunately we had never thought of mosquito nets and the pleasures of our first camp meal were considerably marred, until we built little smoke fires by our table and half choked ourselves, but kept off the bugs (awful insects.) Then we pitched our tent, picketted our horses and went to sleep to the hum of the mosquitoes, the song of the wind, the occasional cry of the forest bird and the murmurs of the river. I slept pretty fairly, and woke almost with the sun.

Sunday, June 19

Today we spent entirely at this splendid forest lodging. In the morning as I went to bathe heard the wolves or coyotes, a sort of jackal, crying to one another in almost human voices among the hills. All morning I fished and got a fair lot of grayling, white fish and trout. In the afternoon I read and loafed, and made the acquaintance more thoroughly of my guide. He is a young man of 27, who has a ranch, a wife and a young brother. He is very like a Swiss guide, simple, sporting, keen, healthy. He had read some history, and has ideas, such as that Napoleon was a man of great force and much to be admired in spite of his wars. He is keen about the war. I read him a lot of Burns which I had with me. He liked what he could understand greatly. 'My sakes – he's a son of a gun. Gosh! He's a dandy'. The last being the highest form of approval. Since then we have been talking of politics and history. He is much impressed with the absurdity of allowing hereditary legislators, a constitutional expedient which had not been distinctly presented to him before. Altogether I should say *he* is a 'dandy'. In the evening I walked through the forest for three miles, until I came to

99

another and larger river, with brushwood, reeds and pines down
to its very banks, just the place where you feel the wild animals
come to drink and are safe. But sure enough just where I had
sat down to watch the sun-set I picked up two empty rifle
cartridges. Again today we have been damnably plagued with
mosquitoes – I have about 300 bites on hands face and legs.
The beasts even bite through stockings. However they don't
itch for long.

Monday, June 20

Slept excellently and am satisfied with my capacity as a camper-
out. We were up about six and off at eight for Yellowstone. All
morning we made our way up the Madison valley, which as it
closed in became entirely forest. Most of the time we were
passing down winding avenues of tall pine, broken occasionally
by glades, sometimes rising so as to see to the mountain horizon
over the endless tree-tops. There is almost as much timber on
the ground as there is standing, which has fallen and no hand
has come to cart it off. Harwood plantation is Nixon's[1] despair.
I wonder what he would think of this giant litter of charred,
rotting, wasted lumber. Early in the morning we passed the
house of Murray's mother-in-law, who was keeping house for
a man who runs a sort of wayside inn – She fitted me up with a
mosquito net of pink gauze. So I do not expect much further
trouble. At the entrance to the Park there was a soldier's
station. Two troops of cavalry keep order and enforce the rules,
such as extinguishing of fires, hiding of paper and tin cans after
meals, and of course above all the poaching regulations – A
single private of horse received us. His sergeant was away, and
he was much perplexed how to let us in, as according to regulations permits have to be given to pack-trains entering. He was
however a Gloucestershire boy and I very easily got the right
side of him, and he gave me a note to his lieutenant in the park.
He is disappointed at not going to Manila, but likes Yellowstone, because they are usually out in small scouting parties,
and consequently are almost entirely independent of the officers.
Dr. Workman had gone through a few hours before and his
guns had been held up by Private Burdett. All guns are stopped
entirely, except a few privileged ones which get through with

[1] Bailiff for G. O. T. on the Wallington Estate.

official seals, and are confiscated if the seals are broken. After getting past this military terror, and indeed having some of its coffee and apple pie, we entered the park by a splendid canyon about eight miles long, a blue swift flowing river down the centre, thick timber on the sides, except where the steep rocks broke out in red crag formation. I saw some very tame white-tailed deer and big hawks, and little whistling rock-chucks (rather like Swiss marmots but brown.) We made a lovely camp at night, at the end of the valley, looking right down it, where two rivers joined their waters, a great crag towering up above us.

Tuesday, June 21

Rode up a fine valley to the military station, where a Lieut-enant Arnold with a troop of thirty horse was stationed. He gave me the necessary permit to go round the park with my pack-train. Rode on to the first geysers. They make the country hideous. All the plain of the valley is covered by nasty white formations here and there curls of steam rising from the bubbling pools. Most of the pools are of crystal clear water, green in colour, which rises from holes in the centre, unfathom-ably deep. There are what they call 'plant pots' in some places which are cauldrons of bubbling lime, generally white, some-times other colours. It is very marvellous but not attractive. I lunched at the Hotel, where I met Lieut. Arnold again and had a talk.

Then on past the Devil's Acre, a huge geyser which very seldom plays, only once in about 10 years. When it does, it puts out such a volume of scalding water that the fish are killed in the river. What is to be seen now would make the best study possible for a section of hell; a pool, about 20 feet below the ground level, so hot that even at the edge, twenty yards from the bubbling up point you cannot keep your finger in it, sending off stifling fumes with a sulphuric smell, so thick that the pool is darkened when the sun shines brightly. All round are fine wooded hills, but nothing as grand as Henry's Lake or the Madison Valley.

In the evening we got to the great Upper Geyser Basin, where for four or five miles the ground swells with geysers, at least twenty great ones, and countless pools, eternally bubbling.

Every now and then a geyser plays. All the time there are rumblings and spittings. Spouts of steam are always going up from the most restless. There is one that plays every 70 minutes, spouting over 100 ft. They call it Old Faithful. We camped about 100 yards from him and were wet with his spray when the wind was in our direction. For curiosity the geysers are hard to beat. I don't wonder the Indians never come within miles of them. But they are as little an improvement to the scenery as if a factory city using anthracite coal had dumped itself down in the park.

Wednesday, June 22

A long forest ride of twenty miles to the Yellowstone Lake. The woods were endless. Every time we got a view it was over the tops of miles of pines, sometimes a lake breaking the splendid monotony, sometimes a glimpse of the Teton Mts. in the distance. Then we reached the shore of the Yellowstone Lake. It would be hard to beat it. It is about 30 miles long, surrounded by forest, and all along the south and east run ranges of snow mountains, near and far off. On the shores here and there are geysers, sending up their steam. I had a bath under a rock from which fell a cascade of water, just not too hot to scald, fresh from the geyser. This shower with a cold plunge in the Lake after it was as good a bath as you could have. I lunched at a tent restaurant. It is only run during the tourist months. My waiter was a lad from Minneapolis who was going next year to the Minnesota State University, where I was recently. He was working his way by earning a good sum as waiter this summer. He was as nice a boy as I have met. We went five miles further on to camp in a sort of bay, absolutely chock full of trout. I fished for about an hour. I caught 15 big trout, all over a pound. If I had fished carefully I could have got more. They grabbed at every other cast. I never saw anything like it before. You could see them going about in shoals. And weren't they good to eat? Oh no! While I was fishing, several gulls, a pelican, and two bald headed American eagles floated by close to me. The eagle is a good bird, but looks as if he represented the 'unkempt, disreputable, vast' side of America and not the solid greatness. He is not imperial.

Thursday, June 23

Tonight it rained steadily; but we kept quite dry in our tent. This morning it looks like clearing. As we are packing up, several small birds, rather like magpies without long tails, are hopping round within a few yards to see what they can steal. They call them Camp-robbers.

This evening I write with ink at an Hotel. Soon after we had started this morning it began to pour and showered very heavily all day, drenching the ground, so that camping would have been anything but pleasant. In the end I made up my mind to push on to the Hotel at the great Canyon where we now are. The moment I came in, dripping, dishevelled and unshaved the clerk declared he knew me though he could not recall me. And no wonder, for the last time had been when I was addressing the students at Minnesota University. I was at once made very comfortable and he spent some time in telling me about himself and his aspirations. Several of the cooks in the park he says are University students off for vacation.

What we saw today under adverse circumstances was chiefly the splendid wooded valley of the Yellowstone. We passed the mud geysers where the steam of the subterranean kettle keeps flinging up out of a sort of cave a mass of liquid mud, that falls back again in vain attempt to choke the outlet. It is a sort of Eternal Sisyphus struggle of the elements. The last part of the way was through a country very like some broad wild valley in Scotland, so like it that I burst into 'Oh where and oh where'.

Friday, June 24

Today began raining miserably; but the afternoon cleared. I went to see the Grand Canyon with the greatest cattle rancher of the north-west, Wibaux. He has 50,000 cattle in Montana and North Dakota, which he requires 40 men to herd in summer and 6 in winter. He is a Frenchman from Socialist Roubaix. He came over with Viscomte de Morro who took to ranching – but who and what the Viscomte was I have not yet found out. Wibaux is quite western in look and manner, only a little more polite. His heart still yearns Paris ward and his tongue betrays a little. But on horseback in his shirt-sleeves he looks the king of Montana. He comes of an energetic stock. His ancestor, when Napoleon closed the continental ports, rode night and day from

Paris to Marseilles and beat the imperial messengers, and bought up all the tea, sugar, tobacco etc., and then went to bed for two days.

The canyon is indescribably grand. It is enormous. There is in it a fall 300 ft. high over which a large river flows. Its sides are every shade of red, scarlet, purple, yellow & lavender. The top is crowned with fire. It is far the finest thing in the park and quite unlike all other canyons.

Saw a bear grubbing in the garbage heap of the Hotel, which galloped off as fast as a horse can canter when it saw us.

Saturday, June 25

Started again with my pack train through the forest on an ideal day. Climbed Mount Washburn, the most central view and nearly the highest mountain in the Park. Tell Bowen[1] you can see at least 10 miles in every direction from it. All around is forest for many miles until you reach the boundaries of the Park where it is girdled almost entirely with snow ranges, some of them very magnificent. The climb was easy though there was some good rock scrambling that G.[2] would have liked. Then a long ride down a descending ridge looking down on the forest on one side and a green valley with herds of deer grazing on the other.

Towards the end of the day we got into a beautiful open valley, full of good timber on the sides and pools and streams in the middle, with several antelope running about ahead of us and turning round every hundred yards to see if we were following. Here we pitched our tent for the last time and cooked our last camp meal of bacon and coffee, with canned tomatoes and peaches and crusty bread.

Sunday, June 26

Had breakfast at 6.30 and rode off. Passed a place where an old Confederate soldier named Yancey, with long uncombed and unwashed hair and beard, lives out his life and yarns. Then had a beautiful ride across mountains, through passes and over

[1] Master at Harrow. He noted all the hills from which a clear view of 3 miles could be seen in every direction. He wrote many of the famous Harrow School Songs.

[2] His younger brother George Macaulay Trevelyan, the historian.

hilltops, seeing antelope and innumerable chirping chipmunks, 'half bird and half mouse.' Reached Mammoth Hot Springs, where I proceeded to make arrangements for collecting my baggage for leaving the park, until my guide arrived. I intended then to see the springs, which are an enormous geyser formation, like a great coloured lime-kiln heap on the mountain side, hideous and wonderful. But I shall never see the terraces of those springs. The springs is the centre of the military post in the park. All people entering and issuing have to report and register. When Lat Murray, my guide, reported, he was promptly ordered under arrest, and brought my bag from the horse to the Hotel under escort of a soldier with a loaded carabine. He had told me that he had never settled a charge of having hunted in the Park with some 'Andes' as they call all visitors. He had given me his version of the story, which certainly exculpated him pretty completely. But apparently that view is not shared by the officers in charge of the park, and he is to be tried for 'rustling', for which the penalty is 2 years maximum. I think the officer is prejudiced against him; but I talked some time with him and I think he will get a fair trial in the United States Court. I spent most of the rest of my time in despatching the money I owe him to his wife, and in giving him advice as to the evidence he had better get in support of his version of the story. He chiefly relies on the evidence of the Eastern gentlemen whom he took out on the party. It was not a brilliant ending to leave my ten day's companion lying on some sacking on the floor of the guard-house. I spoke as strongly as I could to the officer. He is too good a fellow for a jail-bird. But I suppose the same might have been said of many of the ancestors of Robsons, Nixons, Charltons in the ride and rieve days.[1]

Away on the top of a coach to Cinnabar, discoursing of England and America to a tremendously spread-eagle American, who was very keen and bubbling over with fury at a little German who had been running down our two nations. At Cinnabar station after paying $32 for my ticket to Portland, I was given a letter that was waiting me, in which I found a pass from the Company. So I got back my money, and am £6 the

[1] Refers to the Scottish Border raids. These same families are still to be found on either side of the Border.

richer. At this station, Livingstone, where we are waiting for the west bound mail which is some two hours late, two old fellows came in to my Pullman and hired one berth between them, in which coffin-like crib they are now snoring in chorus. They look as if they had had rougher times in their day.

Monday, June 27

All last night and all this morning we have been travelling through Montana. Today it has been most gorgeous scenery. At first we passed through rich valleys, only half settled, where the rich meadows glowed with blue, white, pink and purple flowers, while the hillsides were covered with pines to the top. In some places irrigation is necessary. But there is plenty of water, and the State is beginning to undertake irrigation works. Then we got into wilder scenery, and all the afternoon we were going down a mountain river, the Missoula, following its windings for 100 miles or so down a splendid valley, with pines on the hill-tops and hill-sides and pines washing their feet in the river. Then we came out on a fine lake in Idaho, which we skirted, and then came out on the plains of Washington. At one moment we heard a man shouting we could not make out from where, until the conductor discovered him hanging on below the train. We stopped the train with difficulty and pulled him out. He was a 'hobo' travelling in their usual style by squatting among the water cisterns and brakes of the cars; but he had somehow got his foot caught and it had been seriously mashed up. We got him on board and put him off at the next biggish town. The distances were so great here that tramps have to take this method of travel, or they would never reach their destinations.

Tuesday, June 28

This morning we have been crossing the Cascade mountains during the early hours, a repetition of the Rockies, except that here there are some monster pines, though most near the railway have been felled. Then we have run down into the plain by the Pacific, through valleys full of corn and hops that rival Kent for richness. We are now just running into Tacoma,

106

where I want to post some of this correspondence. So for the present goodbye.

Yours aff.

Charles Trevelyan

16. PORTLAND, COLUMBIA RIVER.
THE FOURTH OF JULY IN SAN FRANCISCO

Tuesday, June 28

Portland is a beautifully situated city on the Willamette, near the junction with the Columbia River. The better part of the town creeps up the very steep hills that hem the city in on all sides. The streets are all green with avenues of trees. There is a splendid view from the top of the hills. You see right over the valley to the Cascade Mountains, forty miles off, where three wonderful cones, with caps of snow, rise over the dark horizon, Mt. Hood, Mt. Adams and Mt. St. Helens, at intervals along the skyline. They get a special beauty from their symmetry and isolation.

I then went to spend the evening with a lawyer, Mr. Strong, who was born in Oregon and remembers the old days when the fear of the Indians was before all settlers, and the big red box used to be seen in the morning on the tops of the pine trees, having arrived mysteriously in the darkness, the fiery cross of Klickitat chiefs. He has seen Oregon become a very prosperous agricultural state, and Portland the chief town in the Slope next to San Francisco. Besides his business he is an active politician, with no great attachment to political parties, but very active in attacking corruption in the government. In Portland, as elsewhere, they are all waking up to the necessity for honest men. He has two nice young daughters, one of whom is in a great excitement at going off to Bryn Mawr College in the East, where she has just passed her entrance exam, the Newnham of America. I stayed all evening talking.

Wednesday, June 29

Started up the Columbia River on a steamer to Tom Balfour's fruit-ranch. The steamer goes once a day, carrying tourists and

107

long legged farmers, and drummers (angl. commercial travellers) and horses, and carriages, and goods, and Indians and squaws. It stops at little riverside places every five miles up to Dalles, 100 miles up the river. It is about the finest river scenery in the world. It is handsomer and broader than the Rhine and, except for the crown of castles, the crags are as fine. The hills are higher and thickly clad in forest. Down by the shore are willow banks and meadows. Here and there is a yellow wheat crop or vineyard on the hill-side. Half way up Balfour met me and we landed together at his farm. In the casual way they have here, they ran the boat in at a place half a mile further up than usual and left two families on the usual landing stage to wait for twenty-four hours for the next boat. A little while ago they did the same thing to some miners, who sent a rifle bullet through the pilot-box of the retiring steamer. Balfour has the most pleasant farm. He has as partner another Englishman, Magan. They have many acres laid out in all sort of orchards, apricots, plums, blackberries, dew-berries, prunes, cherries, and vines. Lines of shady poplars divide the fields and act as windbreaks. The house is a substantial wooden building with a veranda, shaded by some beautiful willows and ashes and looking down a great reach of the river; in the middle of which is the rocky island on which the Klickitat Indians used to bury their dead, the great river running guard on either side of their cemetery. Balfour likes the life. It is hard work at times, when the fruit is being gathered and there is always enough to do. In the autumn there is bear hunting a few miles away from the river in the Cascade Mountains. The trout are plentiful and the Columbia is a great salmon river, though they can only be trapped or netted. The story goes that in the days when Washington was any man's land, England sent out a Commissioner to report on the value of the territories which we ceded in the Oregon treaty. He happened to be a Scotchman and having tried every fly that ever caught a fish in the Tweed he reported that the Columbia River was worthless as a fish river. Balfour's ranch is very comfortable. A queer ringletted, old fashioned settler's daughter cooks and housekeeps for them. There is a German boy, blue-eyed and flaxen-haired, who lives in the house, who smiles and drives the horses and works on the farm. They all dine together, but there is a spacious parlour, unapproached by any except the masters, with a good simple library and pictures of souls, etc.

Thursday, June 30

Spent the day seeing the ranch, watching Indian squaws picking fruit, climbing hills for views etc.

Friday, July 1

Back to Portland by train with Balfour and Magan. They came in with me because they have determined to celebrate the 4th of July there. We found that it had already begun. All the children were letting off crackers in every direction. It is going clearly to be a phenomenal holiday this year because of the war. I shall see it at San Francisco, where there are still 10,000 troops not yet started for Manila.

In the afternoon we went with Mr. Strong to watch a game of baseball by professionals. We came to the conclusion that it could not compare at all with cricket for skill, variety or interest. It is rather a dull game to watch and it gets duller instead of brighter with good play. It is the opposite of cricket. Perfection here tells against the batsman. There is a great deal of shouting to confuse the bowler, which is amusing, but not edifying.

Saturday, July 2

Spent morning in Portland, not very profitably. Leading citizens are most of them away. Started in the evening for San Francisco. Down the valley of the Willamette between the coast range and the Cascade Mts. A hop and wheat country, very rich wherever there is cultivation.

Sunday, July 3

Woke up still in Oregon, sometimes passing through pineclad mountains, sometimes through mellow wheat fields, and green orchards. An immense country, only sparsely settled and of enormous resources. So easily does the earth yield that much of the wheat is cut for fodder and treated as hay. Then we climbed over a mountain range into California. All the afternoon Mount Shasta was in sight one of the great cone snow-capped mountains of the Slope. I made the acquaintance of the young wife of an old Eastern merchant, who was coming back to see her native west, who knew George Keanan the Siberian traveller. Reports begin to come in of the extermination of Cervera's fleet at Santiago. If it is true, it will be a tremendous July 4 in San Francisco.

Monday, July 4

The Fourth opened for me on the shores of the inland lake which makes the harbour of San Francisco. We were just preparing to cross, train and all, in a large ferry boat over one of the branches, the Estuary of the Sacramento River. A dull pall of mist obscured the view and it was cold, like an October day in Northumberland. San Francisco is a summer resort. Every night there is mist in the summer months. It is often quite cold, and many people fly to it to escape the heat of the inland plains. The shores of the harbour as we saw them were grim sandy tracts, with ugly factories and dirty wooden houses spotted over them, not highly attractive. At Oakland we got off the train and were ferried over in a great steam boat to San Francisco, of which we could only see the docks and nearest slopes of the city.

As I drove up to the Hotel the crackling of squibs told that the Fourth had begun. I found the Webbs at the Hotel. They had already seen enough of the city authorities to procure places in the procession, and had not forgotten me. The procession was chiefly composed of the troops. There are still 12,000 here in camp, which have not yet gone to the Philippines. Besides them there were various city bodies, veteran fireman, health officers, etc. There were the war veterans. There were the Ancient Order of Redmen, a benefit society, dressed up in Indian costume, with tomahawks and wild Indian cries. There was a regiment of Roman Catholic cadets, dressed in white and armed with sabres, all young men, called the League of the Red Cross. Evidently the R.C. Church is wise in its generation; but the priests do not play officer like the English Church clergyman does to the Church army volunteers. Our part of the procession was decidedly different from anything of the kind in England. There were first three or four hired plugs drawn by four horses each, and driven by cabmen in billy cocks or shabby tall hats. The boxes were decorated with a large stars and stripes flag on the left side, and on the right a pole with a little windmill of paper stars and stripes flags at the top, which whirled round unceasingly in the breeze. Each person in the carriage carried a flag, a large flag draped the back of the carriage, the horses were clad in cloth of tricolor. The Mayor who drove in the first fly had white horses. The rest of us had black or brown. The Webbs drove in the fourth fly with the Chief Justice of the Supreme Court. I drove in the one before them with two Judges of the City. My companions were what we should call police magistrates of San Francisco. They are elected of the people every four years. These two men were Irishmen, and regular ward politicians, fat, whiskey drinking, jolly, immoral and ignorant. They possessed a practical shrewdness which made up for the lack of every other quality necessary in England and desirable in America for a position of judicial authority. While waiting in a bye-street to take our place in the procession, we providentially stopped in front of a saloon. Before three minutes had passed the occupants of the three leading carriages were treating each other at the bar. There was of course no great care in the arrangement of the order, so my two companions used their influence with the police to get in the best place, and mightily pleased they were with themselves. All the way along the route they bowed and waved their flags like royalty. They called the police-sergeants by Christian name as they passed them at the corners. They were particularly obsequious to the order of Redmen, who were influential voters. They got plenty of recognition, especially from the baser sort, shabby genteel Irishmen, fat ward politicians, loose women at upper windows, and received their greatest ovations from the doors of the leading saloons in the City. Behind our four-horse flys came flys innumerable, with only two horses, many of them non-official. But there was nothing to prevent private carriages joining provided they added to the brightness of the show by sporting sufficient tricolor drapery. The crowd was very orderly and happy, or rather exultant after Schley's thundering victory. The only part of the town where the people looked stunted and contemptible and poor was in the Italian quarter, where low ignorance and bad health was written legibly in a street long of faces. Next came the placid Chinese, rank on rank of black hats and yellow faces, imperturbable by any Fourth or other spluttering. The rest was mainly ordinary Anglo-Saxon out for a holiday, not noisy, but perpetually waving and sometimes shouting and firing squibs. The troops were as I had seen them before, strong, stalwart, rough from Kentucky, gentlemanly, youthful, healthy from Iowa; but all highly unlikely to run away from Spanish or any other bullets.

In the afternoon we went to a so-called literary entertainment, which consisted first of a long Fourth of July oration, insufferably turgid. How they can stand the fulsomeness of self-flattery I can't understand. A British audience would squirm, in spite of the general truth of the propositions put forward. Then we had the Star Spangled Banner sung by a music-hall singer dressed up as Columbia and dramatically waving the flag. Lastly an impressive lawyer read with profound emphasis, punctuated by cheers, the Declaration of Independence from end to end. It was the most interesting part of the 'Literary Entertainment', in fact the only literary part of it.

Meanwhile throughout the city, in literally every street all afternoon long and far into the night, there went on the bang of squibs, the sputter of crackers, the boom of heavier firework explosives, the crack of blank cartridge pistols. About two thirds was the work of children. But young men and even old ones were responsible for a good deal. It was a universal orgy of noise.

In the evening were extensive public fire-works, which I went to see. They were fairly good, but rather spoilt by the mist, which obscured the brightness of the higher rockets.

After that I went through China town with a guide. It is in the centre of the city, where the original city grew. About 25,000 Chinese are congregated there, though owing to the excluding laws they are gradually diminishing in numbers. They live by washing, boot making, clothes making, keeping of stores etc. They in no way are even beginning to have part or lot with the white men. I went to one of their churches. It is run as a commercial speculation. An upper floor was rented by two Chinamen, who had a little counter at the top of the stairs. There they sit and smoke placidly. The Church is round them. It looks like a shop, but nothing is for sale. There are rows of brass pots and poles with brazen emblems representing various trades, carried in procession on the God's birthday. There are China dogs, there are masks, all sorts of things good to buy. But it is not a shop. They do not make their money that way. At the end of the room is a shrine with the God of war in it, decorated with fans and red tapestry. In front of him are cups of tea to drink if he is thirsty. Beside him is his war horse, a black dollar toy horse on a wooden stand with rollers. In front of this magnificent charger also stands tea. In front of them are ranged flower-pots with little smouldering incense candles stuck into the earth like plants. It is here that the money is made. Every Chinese who comes in to pray buys a packet of candles for 25 cents and offers them, then he prays. If the God is likely to be asleep, there is a bell and gong in the corner which the attendant will whack if need be. After that the worshipper shakes a box of a sort of spilikins till one falls out. Each are numbered, and whatever he happens on is turned up in a book, which describes what sort of luck he is to have in wiving, or trading. The profits of a good God-store are considerable and pay a good percentage on the capital.

Then we saw an opium-den, with two or three men asleep on the beds.

Then we visited the Chinese theatre, which was about the most amusing of all. There is no scenery, only a chair to represent a throne and a curtain which opens and shuts to represent a town-wall and gate. If they mount horses they give a certain wave of the leg and flourish a riding whip. The plays are always historical and continue for several nights sometimes. They do not appear to have a great amount of vivid incident. The one we saw was chiefly the warfare of an Amazonian queen with a king who first conquered her, and then was defeated and captured by her and subsequently beaten with rods. There was a great deal of talking, which may have been Homeric in eloquence, and certainly was in unpracticality. The dresses were rather superb and old-time. But the chief feature was the orchestra. It was on the stage behind the actors. It consisted of a trumpeter, a drummer, and a man who clashed cymbals, and when he was not doing that played on a squeaky stringed instrument. Almost every word was punctuated by a deafening cymbal clash, when there was a change of scene the clatter became continuous, when there was a fight, as there was every ten minutes, the crashing became terrific. As we were on the stage we were glad enough to get away from the fearful row. The audience was made up of several hundred placid yellow faces, all under identically the same sort of hat, all sitting not on the wooden benches provided for their comfort, but with their feet on the benches and seated on the edge of the backs. They showed no emotion during the half-hour that we stayed, but watched every action with unbroken attention. There were about 30 women in a separate gallery.

Tuesday, July 5

Today, after making preparations for departure, I took a walk round by the coast. I had a bathe in a splendid bath-house and saw sea-lions on the rocks outside.

I walked back and got a misty view of the Golden Gate. I saw the soldiers drilling and shooting. It was a Montana regiment, and its practice seemed very good at 300 yards. The distance does not seem much for modern warfare. As I was moving off to see some more of the drilling and to examine the big guns at the harbour entrance, a nice young officer stepped out quietly to me—'Say, stranger, guess you'd better not take that box any further (pointing to my camera.) You know the nation is at war. This is a government reservation. And you will get yourself into trouble.' So I gave up my inspection of the big guns and went home without any more photos.

Wednesday, July 6

Today we spent in seeing people, notably the Chief Justice and Mayor of San Francisco. The Chief Justice, though elected, gives the idea of being all a judge should be, and the pattern of integrity and public spirit. The Mayor, though an Irishman by race, is honest and fighting the corrupter elements, has in fact got into hot water legally by doing it injudiciously.

And now they have come for my baggage; so I bid good-bye to the great new people, and to you my dear home people together,

Yours,
Charles Trevelyan

ACROSS THE PACIFIC,
NEW ZEALAND AND AUSTRALIA

1. BRINGING THE NEWS TO HAWAII

Steamship Coptic.

Thursday, July 7

We have left America. Our ship is British, of the White Star line, but hired by an American Company. We were an hour late in starting, because we were required to carry despatches to Hawaii to announce the Annexation which Congress decreed and the President ratified yesterday. With the despatches have come on board four correspondents from San Francisco papers, full of the importance of their mission – for there is no cable to Honolulu and we shall be the first to announce to the first American colony that Uncle Sam is going to imitate Brother Bull.

The Golden Gate was anything but golden as we passed through today, the same cold cloud, hanging over the city and harbour that has obscured the grandeur of the scenery for us during our stay. The sea outside is choppy and rough, and we none of us feel very happy. It is as cold as the Atlantic in March.

Friday, July 8 till Wednesday, July 13

We have been going at the rate of 340 miles a day to Honolulu. Every day has become pleasanter. Towards the end of the second day it was calm but still cold. But by Sunday we were beginning to put on flannel and duck suits, and on Monday a swimming bath out of a sail was rigged up on the lower deck in which we played water polo. It has turned out the most delightful voyage. I have spent most of my time in reading Faust, the Ring and the Book and Astronomy, and calming down after bustling about America. Mrs. Webb has been writing her diary, which will be the Pepys of the 19th century. Webb has read all the books available on board upon any solid subject.

The company of course is much smaller than on Trans Atlantic steamers, only about 40 first class passengers, and the steerage almost entirely Japs and Chinese. The Chinese do not appear on deck at all until it becomes sultry. They enjoy what at Harrow we called 'fug', and they get herded in an airless cabin, smoking opium and gambling with dice until the thermometer approaches 80. The officers of the 'Coptic' are all English. The crew is entirely Chinese, stokers, waiters, stewards, and sailors. They are very hardworking, attentive and tidy. As waiters I like them far better than the niggers, although they are far less communicative.

The Captain was a Cumbrian from Maryport, a cheerful, capable, well educated man. We sat round him with another Englishman, a shrewd, rather fashionable English merchant at Shanghai, who had a lot to say about our interests in the far East, and expounded the usual creed of the Englishman abroad that everything ought to belong to Great Britain that didn't belong to it, and that the government at home was fast asleep. He also had the aristocratic dislike of America, which we attributed to democratic institutions. Consequently we sometimes differed. There was one other Englishman on board of the Eton Oppidan type. What Bernard Shaw would call a 'chuckle headed' young man, very like the aide-de-camp in the 'Man of Destiny'. He had been sent out to plant coffee in Ceylon and finding it not profitable enough to keep him in sufficient white-shirts was travelling round the world to China to see if he could do better there. His parents were getting tired of backing his bills. He knew very little and nothing of mankind at all. He had been ten days crossing America, and talked to the Americans about all the things he objected to. Consequently he got snubbed, or would have been if he had not been impervious to contempt. Withal he was a good youth, and as the Americans said to me would make a good fellow when he had been knocked about a bit. Like myself, he writes letters home to his people. One day he asked Mrs. Webb, whether that coal they had in the East was called 'anchorite' coal, and how to spell it. And those are the sort of 'business' men that expect to make money in farming. Truly we are a wonderful race.

There were two Russians on board. One, Mr. J. N. Syro-miatnikoff-Signia, was in the cabin with me, a writer for the Novoie Vreyma, of some literary importance in Russia. I had much talk with him. Of course he stood up for Russian government, censorship, imperialism, etc. But this is noticeable – that the Russian has no illusions that his race is yet developed. He looks to the future, and believes that the mute millions are some day to find intelligence and voice, and to equal the Anglo-Saxon. He is quite content at present with what he believes to be his greater solidarity. I talked also to him about Zola. He somewhat justified France, but finally did not try to deny that the English position was a superior one. He believes France to be decadent, the only two forces worth recording being militarism and the money power of the Jews. In fact he believes that the great trouble and struggle in the next century for continental Europe is the Semitic one. Russia is exempt because it keeps the Jews in Poland and overawes them, England because the race is strong enough to dominate them. He was on the whole the most interesting passenger.

The others were inhabitants of Hawaii, etc. The four San Francisco correspondents played poker all day and every day. There was an American consul on board going to Japan, one of a small staff of permanent men whom they have in their consular department. He was a clever rather fast fellow, who had been at Constantinople during the massacres and bore out all the accounts of the atrocity and deliberation of the slaughter, and thinks the deaths were largely underrated officially. We had a good voyage and a really pleasant one. We only passed one ship and that belonging to the same line as ours, with whom we exchanged compliments and gave the news of Cervera's annihilation. Otherwise we saw nothing but the endless blue ocean and a lightly clouded sky, occasional flying-fish, a spouting whale and black sea-gulls always in our wake.

This Wednesday we began about one oclock to see ahead of us the outline of mountains. Presently we drew near to a rocky coast with mountains running up about straight from the sea to over 2000 ft. Here and there there was a plantation nestling at the foot. In one place the sugar-cane was being burnt. It was more like the Cuillins in Skye than anything else I have seen. Then we swung round the Diamond Head, a magnificent extinct crater, and the bay of Honolulu lay before us. The mountains lie three miles or so back from the coast. All the interval is green with rice or banana fields. The town of Honolulu looks like a tropical forest. The pakus and banyans and other tropical trees rise above the houses and conceal most of the buildings. Along the edge you see villas and bathing places, and at one point the harbour and wharves, with a good show of shipping lying there. Behind is the sloping valley running up the middle of the island between the two mountain ranges. But the first thing that drew our attention was an American warship, the Monitor, on its way from San Francisco to join Dewey, with its attendant coal tender, lying at the harbour mouth, with steam up, ready to start as soon as it got word from us. It is the most clumsy looking vessel. It was a comparatively calm day but every wave washed all over the low decks of the ship, upon which we could see the sailors running about in tarpaulins or barelegged. A lieutenant came on board and we gave them a cheer and the news of Cervera's[1] defeat and sent him off undemonstratively chuckling. The sailors meanwhile had begged & obtained a sheaf of Frisco papers describing the victory. Within an hour the ship was out of sight on the way to Manila. We heard afterwards that the Captain had declared that if he met Camara's[2] fleet he intended to take it on single-handed.

We then turned to the harbour. As we were bringing the news of annexation we had decorated our masts with flags, and a signal was flying from the foremast to announce it. The news had been telephoned from Diamond Head when we had first been sighted, and the quay was crowded with several hundred people to receive us. As we approached we could see them waving the American flag and straw-hats and sticks, singing and hurrahing. An American training ship for seamen sent a boat to get news, and as the men signalled news of the annexation but above all of Cervera's destruction, the tars on the rigging of the ship burst out into wild cheering. Meanwhile the artillery of the Hawaiian army were firing salvos in the Square and the people on the quay were getting more and more excited. As we got near a score of brown native boys swam out to us and dived for dimes and nickels that we threw to them, quite as much at home in the water as on land. When we got close to the quay we began throwing newspapers overboard to the frantic crowd, who fought and jostled good-humouredly, and ended by climbing on board by dozens scaling the bulwarks like pirates. Then a band came down and played away a good part of the crowd to the city square, and we got off, left our

[1] Admiral of the Spanish Fleet.
[2] Admiral of the Spanish Reserve Fleet.

luggage to the Hotel man to swindle through the customs, and went off to the Hotel.

So we brought the news to the first American colony that it was part of the great republic.

A hundred and twenty years ago Captain Cook discovered these Sandwich Islands. Or rather he rediscovered them, for there is plenty of proof that not only had sailors been wrecked there as early as 1500, but there are Spanish records of ships having touched there during that great Spanish century. When Captain Cook went there they were a prosperous, advanced savage people, wearing few clothes and boasting little Christian morality. There were two or three hundred thousand of them in the islands. Since that time the natives have become civilized, Christianized and are gradually disappearing. There are now only some 30,000 natives of tolerably pure descent, some 10,000 'half-breeds'. The rest of the population is made up of 21,000 Chinese 24,000 Japanese and 23,000 whites, of whom 2000 are American and 1500 English. I am afraid the disappearance of the natives must be put down largely to the appearance of the Whites, though perhaps in many ways there is not much for which the Whites can be blamed. The Kanakas have shown a great adaptability for civilization. They accepted the missionaries and their religion when they came at the beginning of the century, and the missionaries undoubtedly dealt well with them and they made a happy population. Education spread and commerce came. Merchants came to live there but did not oppress. A native government was maintained though the wiser kings used to take the missionaries as advisers and premiers. But all this time the natives were decreasing. It was partly due to disease introduced by Captain Cook and his sailors, as an evil return for the too generous and barbaric hospitality of the Hawaiian women, partly to the spread of leprosy which is supposed to have come from China with the Chinese immigration. Partly from the wars at the end of the last century when the islands, which had hitherto been governed by separate chiefs were all conquered by Hamehameha, the Hawaiian Napoleon, after devastating wars, which were more bloody owing to the introduction of fire-arms; and finally because of the incapacity of half barbarians to adapt themselves to more civilized ways of living without being at a disadvantage in competition with the yellows and whites who began to mix with them. The natives are a very fine race physically, but they are pleasure-seeking and lazy, happy-go-lucky as compared with whites. If they can get enough to eat and live on they prefer dancing, swimming, decking themselves in wreaths to doing anything more serious. It is owing to their diminishing numbers and to this laziness that they have lost control of their country. As long as they had wise and progressive kings who took the advice of the missionaries all went well. But about 1880 the king began to try to go back to old customs, and the succeeding Queen, the present ex-Queen, began to try to make herself absolute again. Of course a large community of whites, though content with a dark monarch if the government was good, could not stand this. And after some revolutionizing the Republic was set up with the help of United States marines. It is perhaps rather sad that a fine native people should not go on ruling itself successfully, and there may have been some grasping for power by the Americans, but in the long run it is hard to see how a decadent people could go on ruling in the midst of stronger races, where they had ceased even to be a numerical majority. Since then there has been a government of American business men in the Legislature and the 'Missionary gang,' as they are called, in the executive. There is much abuse of the President and his cabinet. It is said that they have brought over their friends and relations from America to fill the offices. But on the whole their government has been good, and they have got as good or better a type of man as official than is normally found in American States. In 1893 they wished to be annexed to the United States, and now they have got their wish. But it is by no means the case that the mass of the population want it. The Americans of course are enthusiastic. The British on the whole approve. Some grumble that we ought to have had it long ago. But our government always avoided interfering, and the residents never made any move in that direction. Now indeed the United States, which takes 85% of the trade, is clearly the most interested of the two nations. The Americans and English formed the crowd which greeted us on our arrival. Perhaps the Portuguese side with the Americans. There are several thousand of them who were originally shipped over for labour from the Cape de Verde Islands. There they were the dregs. Here under happier auspices, they are prospering and good citizens. The Chinese and Japs take no side. They are not citizens under the Hawaiian Republic. They probably will not be under the American. The natives are too easy going to make much protest; but they are all dead against annexation. It is all bare-faced humbug that they wish anything but a return of the monarchy. They took no part in the rejoicings when the news arrived, though they generally are ready to take any excuse for a jollification. All I have talked to have sighed and accepted the inevitable; all regret the good old days. They are a superstitious people, and their bodings have been darkened by the appearance of a great shoal of red mullet, which they say never visit the islands in large quantities unless there is some great misfortune in store for the nation, generally the death of some chief. The present visitation is attributed to the raising of the American flag, and the excellent red mullet is soured to their taste by the thought that it portends their lost independence.

Whether America will govern the place well, heaven knows. One thing of course is certain that the government will be as bad as can be if they appoint a new governor who clears out the whole staff of government whenever there is a Presidential change in Washington. God preserve the Hawaiians from the American politician. Fortunately there is in America a hazy but growing understanding that they have got something to learn from us in the matter of colonial government, and I have no doubt that if McKinley were anything of a strong statesman he could here & at the Philippines and in Cuba establish a reasonable system and a permanent, public-spirited civil service. We shall see.

And here alas! endeth the first lesson. The second must be written on the Pacific of what we did on the Islands of Hawaii, how we fared, how I rode with the dethroned princess in a surfboat, and other wonders.

Yours
Charles Trevelyan

2. THE CHARM OF HONOLULU

Honolulu, my first glimpse of the tropics, is very different to what I expected. I expected sweltering heat, burning sun, necessity for midday siesta etc. But the temperature and climate is one of the best in the world. It is absolutely equal all the year round. It is very rarely over 80° and rarely below 70° Fahr. There is no summer and no winter. There are almost always clouds. In Honolulu you can watch the workings of clouds better than anywhere else. For nine months in the year the Trade winds blow from East to North-East, and the range of mountains along the eastern coast catches the clouds, and there is almost daily rain on the slopes on either side. Not once during our week's stay have we seen the highest peaks. So lowring are the clouds on the hills, that in Scotland you would expect a drenching every time you went out. So did we for the first day, and carried umbrellas. But we soon found that in Honolulu three miles from the mountains there was almost no rain, that on occasions there was a short, warm, gentle, shower, which passed like child's tears into warm sunshine in five minutes, and you were dry again in ten. The mountains to the west of the island catch the clouds, but not so much, and they are not nearly so luxuriant as the eastern mountains. Frost is unknown in Oahu, the island in which Honolulu is placed. An Englishman would need some trip to a cold climate every year. But for a strong warm pleasant place I do not think the islands could be beaten. Oahu is only one of the group. The others are many miles off. So far that we had no chance of going there. On clear days in the dim distance to the south-east, we could see Molokai, where the leper colony is placed. There are still 1000 souls there. The disease is not stamped out, though it is much less virulent. The lepers are secluded on a promontory, six miles long by one in breadth, which is shut off from the rest of the land by a sheer cliff, up which there is but one narrow path, passing through a guard house at the top of the rock, 2000 ft. high. The government spends $100,000 a year on keeping the poor people. There are various sisters of charity who live with them, but do not generally it is said catch the infection as

Father Damien did. Beyond Molokai is another island Maiu as big as Oahu, and beyond that again, 200 miles from Oahu, the largest island of the group, Hawaii itself. Hawaii is one of the finest volcanic countries in the world. The crater is silent now but whenever it is active it is the grandest and most approachable of lava pits. The mountains there are very high, running up to 14,000 ft. and bearing snow. All climates can be found on Hawaii. North-east of Oahu is the other considerable island of the group, Kauai, some eighty miles off. It was the first discovered by Capt. Cook. It is called the garden island from its excessive fertility. But of all these islands in America's new dominion we only saw Oahu, which is and must remain the chief, because it has the only first rate harbour, and will have a quite ideal one when they open out Pearl Harbour, a deep land-locked sea, which has now only a light reef in front of it to prevent the access of large vessels. Congress has already voted the money for cutting it through.

They are a rich little kingdom these islands, and worth having in themselves, apart from their strategic value. There is abundant water. In the hills it is raining ever. There are many streams, though they dry quickly as the hills are very steep indeed. But much of the water accumulates below-ground in the plains; and there is an eternal supply from artesian wells. Wherever water can be got, there the ground will grow luxuriant vegetation, and there is no reason why all the islands, except the steep hillsides, should not blossom with palm trees, fruit, sugar-cane, rice-fields, taro-beds, vegetable gardens, etc. Oahu is about the size of the part of Northumberland between the Tyne and Simonside. Hawaii is far larger, being 90 miles long and 60 broad. And this wonderful domain is thousands of miles from any other land. It has been thrown up by volcanic action, the coral insect having only played a trifling part in making reefs in the bays. The shape of the mountains is very fine. There are several craters near the shore, particularly Diamond Head, an isolated and picturesque monster that guards one end of Honolulu Bay. The main mountains or rocky ridges 3,000 ft. high, with sharp backs and sharp spurs running down to the sea, with lesser sharp shoulders running out from them, all telling of the courses of lava-currents. Now all this hardness is clothed in thick verdure, which you do not mark from a distance. Ferns, mosses, vines, brushwood grow to the very top and conceal the jagged volcanic rudeness. So thick is the clothing that it is almost impossible to climb the mountains except with native guides. From the east they are nearly inaccessible and everywhere it would be difficult to fight through the shrub weed which now covers every vacant space in the island, called Lautauma, – introduced first, like our weed at Wallington, for experimental purposes, and now the curse of all cultivators.

Almost all the tropical palms, bananas, banians, etc. have been introduced, but flourish like natives, and now the cultivated parts of the islands are like any eastern country.

The natives are an attractive race. They are no longer savages. They are a weak civilized people. The missionaries, as I said in my last letter, did their work well. They taught, clothed and housed them. And now to a great extent the natives mix with the Europeans. There are constant inter marriages, besides large numbers of semi-official connections. Many of the leading people on the island are of mixed parentage. The original native is a careless easy-going person, very lazy, never working except to get eonugh to live on, in the country a peasant, in the town a cab-driver or dock-hand, leaving all the hard work on the plantations to be done by Chinamen or Japs. The women dress in a curious garment which the lady missionaries devised for them to hide their nakedness, a robe which flows from the shoulders downwards, waistless and shapeless. The men wear European clothes. It is a curious mixture of population. One moment you pass a little Jap woman raised on her high shoes, shuffling along with the short clumsy gait which her tight picturesque dress allows her. Then you see a Chinese in his blue and black with straw-circle on head and on shoulders his balancing pole bearing merchandise or fruit. Then the native women crosses the road with a neat straw hat, and clean cotton gown, waistless, which blows up enough to show her often bare feet well above the ankles. Then a Yankee passes with 'Remember the Maine' in his button-hole. Then a bright English girl. Then a native man with a garland of flowers round his hat. These garlands or 'leys' are the most attractive of native products. Whenever there is any fun or frolic, the party put garlands round its hats and shoulders. They are made of

READING THE WAR
NEWS IN SAN
FRANCISCO

EATRICE WEBB
RIVING WITH THE
HIEF JUSTICE OF
HE SUPREME COURT
F SAN FRANCISCO IN
HE INDEPENDENCE
AY PROCESSION

SIDNEY AND BEATRICE WEBB IN HONOLULU

BEATRICE WEBB WITH PRINCESS KAIULANI IN HONOLULU

the heads of bright flowers, pinks generally of some kind, or a beautiful little golden flower there is here, so skilfully strung together that you can keep them a whole day, ride with them, bathe in them, and hardly a leaf will fall off. And men and women look twice as happy and picturesque in them.

As I said in my last letter, no one here wants annexation but the Americans, many of whom have been working for it for years. The natives loathe it. They are all royalists, and want the monarchy back. I am sorry for them. But that is impossible and were in any case. The islands have become too cosmopolitan to be ruled by any but a white race. The Japs do not object much. They have been excluded from any share in this Republic and they are hoping for admittance to some political power under the new conditions. The Chinee is placid as usual. The English-man of course thinks Great Britain ought to have taken it thirty years ago; but admits the superior claim of America now. But his attitude is best represented by what happened among the leading Englishmen in Honolulu on the arrival of the news today. 'Hurrah! tomorrow will be a holiday for certain. Let us arrange a cricket-match for tomorrow afternoon! Will you play?'

Thursday, July 14

In the morning we went to see the Chief Justice, Judd, a son of one of the leading missionaries, now a man of substantial wealth with a large and prosperous family. The missionary gang are much abused. But though they serve Mammon some-what now, they seem to me a higher type than the average American politician. The Webbs conclude after investigating that the class of ruler and official in this government is more honest and efficient than in most American states or cities. Certainly they are more externally respectable, those we have met. I cannot judge what the stories are worth against them. I have heard none on very first-rate authority. There is no doubt that the capture of the government from the monarchy was a high-handed proceeding, and naturally the royalists will see no good in them. Later in the day I saw Cleghorn, the father of Princess Kaiulani, who is a heavy browed Scotchman, with a love of that cold misty land, in this warm rich one far away. He is a little soured, and very indignant at the annexation, for his daughter's sake, who would have been Queen. But he generally feels the eventual inevitableness of what has occurred. And though he is furious with the American gang for their usurpation, he does not say that the present government has been corrupt or unjust in its ruling. At midday I saw the 'Coptic' off. All the passengers were decked in garlands, and the Captain and Officers smothered in them, presents from keen Americans who came to see off the ship that had brought news of annexation.

We all had a splendid bathe at Waikiki, two miles out of town. Then I tried to see the princess; but found only her father at home.

Friday, July 15

I was introduced to the Club, which is as hospitable and comfortable as all American Clubs, but has one peculiarity. Liquors may not be sold. So each member who is non-teetotal has a locker in which he keeps his wines and whiskies in the billiard-room.

In the afternoon we first went to see the President, Dole, a very respectable member of the Missionary gang, who will probably be appointed governor by McKinley. From him we went on to see the Princess. She remembered very gratefully being entertained in London by us, and though she likes Honolulu very much, and feels herself more Hawaiian than Scotch – now that her Kingdom has been taken from her, she wishes to be back in Europe. It is a horrid position to be placed in. She is too European, civilized, attractive to marry a native. But in Europe of course she would always be regarded as half-savage. 'Why you don't mean to say she really talks English?' 'I suppose she would like to offer pig sacrifices'. 'What does she wear at home? Surely not petticoats? Oh, I shouldn't have thought it.' In Hawaii there is nothing for her to do. Her predecessors mortgaged their private estates at 60% a month and so got rid of them to sharp Americans. Consequently her means are slender, her father has little or no money, and though as she says the people – annexation or no annexation – look up to them as their natural leaders, she can do nothing by staying among them. It is rather the case of a Macintosh or a Macleod in these anti-tribal days in the highlands. I feel very sorry for her; but not enough so to become a royalist and raise a counter-revolution.

Saturday, July 16

Went to see the Museum which contains old Hawaiian things of great interest. The cloth of fibre, dyed many colours, the excellent canoes, the smooth wooden bowls made by this outlandish people, before Cook came near them, all show what a very ingenious people they were. There is one particularly beautiful art they possessed. They made for their chiefs beautiful shawls of yellow feathers, which they got from birds called 'Oos', black, but with one yellow feather under each wing. These magnificent garments, like velvet gold, were only worn on state occasions and are the grandest robe monarchs ever had, grander than Caesar's purple. Several of them are in the Museum and small ones can still be bought for huge sums. The Princess has a lot of necklaces made of the feathers. The bird is now nearly extinct, and unless they pass game-laws, will be gone forever in a few years.

In the afternoon we went surf-riding with the Princess. You put on bathing-costume and get into a long narrow canoe, with a huge outrigger on one side to steady it. A stern old native fisherman sits at either end with paddle. Paddles are provided for the amateurs to make-believe with. You go out for a quarter mile to where the breakers are on the reef and then paddle homewards till you get caught on a huge wave, which whisks you in at the rate of forty miles an hour. It requires great skill to steady the canoe and it was fine to see the old fellow at the stern with his teeth showing in a grin of keenness and eyes set, keeping the head straight. We had the best men in the island. But even so we once nearly swamped. We swam and bathed and altogether it was a great sport. The princess looked very charming in her bathing dress and black hair all loose, and green garland round her waist. She swam like any mermaiden, and would break the heart of many a merman. With her was the most beautiful little niece, also half-white, with English features and chocolate skin, one of the prettiest little girls I remember seeing. So it was a very pleasant afternoon.

Sunday, July 17

Started on a journey round the island. There is a railway which runs round the western coast, outside the western mountains.

Contrary to the usual practice of young and short lines it goes quickly, and we got round to Waiakua in less than three hours, a distance of more than 50 miles with many stops. We first went through tracts of rice-fields, all under water, with bare legged China-men replanting the rice in careful rows. Mixed with them were the taro-beds of the natives, a big-leaved plant, which grows under water, the root of which they eat in various forms. I thought it unpleasant. But it is said to be very nutritious and palatable with practice. Then we went through the greatest sugar plantation in the islands, a couple of miles through a waving forest of sugar-cane, impenetrable except for paths. For a week they have been unsuccessfully trying to discover a planter's little boy who has wandered off into one of these thick wildernesses. After that we ran along the narrow outer edge of the island between the mountains and the Pacific. These western mountains are rugged like the others and on their ocean side rocky and bare, because the rainfall is very small there. Such rock climbing as they gave promise of! The valleys are less fertile from want of rain, but not unprosperous. Then we swung round and came into a great sugar plantation at the end of the central valley. It was run by an English Manchester family, Halstead, a father and two sons, who entertained me most hospitably at lunch, gave me a horse to go on my way with, and rode with me several miles on my way.

My road lay between the sea and north side of the Eastern mountains. It was mostly desolate and uncultivated. We passed the mouth of a little valley where two English officers were murdered a few years after Capt. Cook, with less justification than that questionable hero. At the northern most point of the island I went through another huge sugar tract, worked entirely by the placid China-man. Close by were the ruins of what had once been a temple of refuge. The Hawaiians had the ancient Jewish and mediaeval escape for criminals[1] until modern Christianity upset it as barbarous. Then I passed through a Mormon colony, so rich is this country in eccentricity. The inhabitants are natives, except the leaders of the church, who are sent out by the heads of the Church in Utah. They were a

[1] Sanctuary, if the escaping murderer could reach a place accepted as such by the community, certain cities in Canaan, and, generally, abbeys or churches in mediaeval times.

prosperous looking set of people, better off materially I think than most of the native peasantry. The stone temple stands out boldly against the mountain scenery. Just about here the grand views of the eastern coast begin, the green, volcanic, inaccessible mountain-side I have described. Late this evening I cantered up to the house of a Dr. Carter, who has married an Hawaiian lady of good parentage and farms the land between the mountains and the sea, at the mouth of one of the most beautiful eastern valleys of Oahu. He has a well-built wooden house, built round a grass court-yard, one story high, with sheds and tents attached for his native and Jap servants. His wife is a stout, handsome, large lipped native. He has seven children, with another expected, who run about bare foot and seem very sharp and intelligent, and are certainly healthy. He himself is somewhat cranky and unpractical, with a good deal of knowledge of men and things; but one of the people who has soured after 40. I had much interesting talk with him about Hawaii and America. He is dreadfully pessimistic about America. He had been in Tammany, and found it worse than he had thought, and had a very poor hope for the politics of his country. He could see nothing but political greed and selfishness in the taking of Hawaii. He gave the worst account of the 'missionary gang', and made the only detailed charges of dishonesty against them that I have heard. He was at bottom defending his marriage, I felt. His attack on American aggression was punctuated by explanations of the excellence of at any rate highly-bred natives. I so far bear him out that I think many of the native ladies very nice, even some whose chief claim to beauty is their stoutness. But Anglo-Saxon damsels are still superior in my eyes. He was all hospitality and I had a very pleasant evening.

Monday, July 18

Got up with the sunrise, a most glorious one, and after a sea-bathe and coffee started before the heat of the day for the valley of the Big Pig, Kamapuaa. We rode for three miles through very stiff brush wood, and then came to the entrance of the valley from which a stream gushes. There we left our horses, and walked through groves of tropical trees, especially Ohias, a tree like a huge laurel, bearing a fruit that looks and tastes like a small but very juicy apple,—unfortunately not yet properly ripe. Both sides of the valley are sheer rock, more than 1000 ft. high, with a stride of 200 ft. After about half a mile you are stopped by a sheer waterfall of 300 ft. up which no one has yet been known to get. The beauty of the place is that all the sides of this gorge are covered with green, ferns, moss, brush-wood, making the most lovely clothing for rock I ever saw. We bathed in the pool, and then sat down, while Dr. Carter told me the legend of the Big Pig, Kamapuaa. It took the local bard two days and several bottles of whiskey to tell him. He dispensed it to me in a shorter time. Some day I will give you the tale, and Bob can make an epic of it. Suffice it here that the Big Pig was the evil demon of the Islands, who could change his form to that of a beautiful hero, Hyde-like—who had adventures with Pele, the benign Venus of the islands, goddess of the Volcano. This was his chief haunt, and to this day no native enters the gorge without tearing off some leaves and putting a stone on them, as an offering to the Big Pig, who otherwise would throw down stones on you from his lofty hiding-places. We imitated the native custom, and therefore came out unscathed.

After dinner, I said goodbye to the seven little brownies and rode off for Honolulu, 30 miles. A finer coast ride there is nowhere. On one side the sea, clear or with white clouds on it. On the other the rugged mountains green and craggy, their tops darkened by showers. Between them, now only a narrow road, and again a broad expanse covered by rice fields, sugar plantations, banana shrubs, pale trees, grass, houses, Chinamen and Hawaiians. Towards evening I passed through a broad plain and up the mountain-pass—which now has an excellently engineered road—the Pali. From the top is one of the views of the world. A sheer drop of 500 feet and general fall of 1,500 to the plain. At the beginning of the century, about the same time that Napoleon was sinking the runaway Austrians and Russians in the Lakes of Austerlitz, Kamehameha, the Hawaiian conqueror, who subdued all the islands under his sway, drove the last army of Oahu that resisted him over this precipice and left their bones to bleach below. There is a glorious view over plain and ocean which cannot easily be forgotten. On the Honolulu side a valley runs down rapidly to the town about 4 miles off – So ended an excellent expedition.

Tuesday, July 19

This day the princess has given a party in our honour. Early this morning we rode out or drove to a house twelve miles down the coast, beyond Diamond Head. There we spent the day talking, eating, bathing, and listening to a choir of four natives who sang to us most beautifully native songs, with very fine voices. The songs were said to be of the broadest – for the Hawaiians are a primitive people. But as no one except the musicians, the Princess and three half-caste young ladies could understand them, they could look demure and it did not matter. Unexpurgated Burns sung to Russian aristocrats! We enjoyed ourselves greatly and then rode home, a funny cavalcade, first the princess driving with her pretty niece and a handsome young American. Then the four musicians singing and twanging hard. Then seven mounted gentlemen and ladies, all astride, caracoling behind, reining in their foaming steeds in order not to pass her royal highness' carriage – All of us had 'leys' of crimson or pink flowers round our hats and necks. After we had seen the princess home, I raced back to town at a gallop down a corral macadam road for three miles with an English doctor.

Wednesday, July 20

Spent the last day in Honolulu, reading Captain Cook in the morning, a blackguard enough story. He only got his deserts when they harpooned him. In the afternoon had another surf-ride with the Princess better fun even than the first. She sent me off with a magnificent present of 3 dozen cocoanuts, which at this moment I had as lief be without. They are somewhat sickly to the much tittupped voyager. The pleasant young lady is coming to England again soon. You will have to be kind to her. But I am not going to marry her any more than an American heiress.

At evening we went on board the Alasveda, with no touch of fear, for latest despatches state that Camara has returned through the canal homewards, as soon as his government have got news of Cervera's annihilation.

133

Thursday, July 21–Sunday, July 24

A doleful record. What do you imagine a tropical, equatorial ocean is like? Glassy, smooth, glittering, no clouds above, only the steadily burning sun quite à la Ancient Mariner,–alternating with violent typhoon, monsoon or some sort of 'oon'? Not at all. But a somewhat unsettled rolling sea, just enough to make the moderate sailor uncomfortable not ill, clouds everywhere, rainstorms often, temperature high enough to make you sweat at once if you take exercise, a damp heat which is only not stifling because of the Trade wind, altogether the most unpleasant combination for liver, stomach, head and body generally that can be devised. We all agree in swearing. We eat very little and do not talk much. I read actively at German and astronomy. But my fond expectations of reading the stars are not being fulfilled. Pah! What's the use of crossing the line unless at least you can see the southern cross winking at the Pole Star–(or at least discover that it cannot so wink?) Our Captain is a fine-looking white-bearded, rather crabbed, taciturn Americanized German. The first officer is Scotch, thank God–'Yes soor–We stop at Samoa just three 'oors whatever'. There is a keen young English business man, Hall, who has factories in Australia and East London, who is soon going to leave Australia and take more exclusively to East London. He is a radical and by way of going into politics, altogether something of a find on a steamer with only a dozen passengers in all, of whom at least eight don't count.

Monday, July 25 to Wednesday, July 27

Weather improved slightly, but it remains deadly dull and unpleasant. On the last night we got a clear view of the stars, and saw the southern Cross splendidly. The pole star was not in sight.

Thursday, July 28

When we got up this morning, it was not yet dawn. We had stopped. The light just showed us the outlines of mountains three miles off. While we were eating a scanty breakfast, the sun rose and showed us the green Samoan mountains with a strip of rain-storm crossing them. In front lay Apia, a lot of bright houses straggling along the sea-front, surrounded by thick palm groves. Above the town rose a thick wooded mountain on the top of which Stevenson lies dreaming of heather. The harbour is a piece of deep water between two coral reefs, a risky anchorage. Ten years ago there were two German warships waiting, it is believed to fire on a recalcitrant native population, if it had not been that two American and one British ship were there to fire on them in turn. But the hand of God was on the deep waters, and the wind rose and the floods came. The ships began to be driven on the reefs. Only one ship, the British Caliope, had engineers that tried her engines to bursting and just made head out of the harbour against the storm at one mile an hour. The others drifted back, merciful and merciless together, to destruction on the reef, the German band on deck playing national airs. Several hundred were lost, with both the German & both the American ships. The hull of one of the German vessels broken and rusty, still rests on the reef, two hundred yards from the spot where Sein Majistätes Schiffe 'Bussard' lies anchored today. Besides this little German war vessel there is only one fair-sized boat, the 'John Williams', celebrated in all English missionary circles as the bearer of the gospel to Polynesian savages. As soon as we had got to anchor half a mile from land, we were surrounded with boats, post office boat, custom's boat, private boat, consular boat, Deutscher Kaiser's boat, and crowds of boats full of natives ready to land us, or sell us cocoanuts, corals, bananas, etc. The Webbs and I got off at once, rowed by two woolly haired youths, with beautiful brown skins, clothed in nothing but the native 'malo', a loin cloth, which is the maximum dress for all the native men and a large part of the native women. When we got on shore the natives were walking and lounging about the well macadamized main street along the sea, the better ones carrying umbrellas to compensate for the lack of heavier garments. The women, who in the town mostly wore dresses had a rather more reasonable costume than the dowdy Hawaiian dames. But the best of them have nothing on their feet. They wear low necks and a mild waist. They look rather winning in the approximately civilized dress.

Very few English or Germans seemed to be up at that early hour, and there were no buggies about. I was determined to see

Stevenson's[1] house. All on the steamer had said 'it was impossible. No time'. It was now 7.45. Steamer was to start at 10 punctually. However I determined to try. My boatman started with me, horrified at the notion of walking it in the time. Seeing I was apparently foolish enough to try, he began to be, and say it was ten miles off. I enquired at the house of an Englishman with a native wife and found it was only three. So I went off at over four miles an hour down a beautiful road through a plantation of tall cocoa nuts varied by banana plantations. My poor native soon began to pant, showing that a stout outdoor savage is not up to a Britisher in good training. He followed trotting and groaning and praising in turns, stopping to chatter to friends for a moment on the record I was doing. Presently we got to the house. It is a two storied wooden house, with verandas up stairs and down, on which wonderful talks must have gone on in the cool evenings. It is a big house, showing that many guests must have stayed, if they chose to come. In front is an open lawn, where he played croquet. Then about a hundred yards off the tropical forest begins. In front all but some very large and magnificent trees, of unknown name to me, higher than our beeches, have been cleared away; and there is a fine vista down to Apia harbour, where we could see the ships and the surf. On one side rises close by the thick woods of the mountain where he is buried. On the other side, tropical forest and palms with a background of mountain. The house is deserted now, Mrs. Stevenson having gone to California. Most of the furniture is gone, only a few books remaining in a single closed room that I could only peep into. It was a comfortable place to write, more so than wierd and lovely Craigenputtock. Then back at the same splitting rate. Saw some native dancing, and talked to an old Cumberland sailor, who now mends yachts and builds boats by the shore, and a woman from Whitby who looks after the reading-room, who gave me coffee with fresh English smiles and greeting. All the British so far away as this come from our stronger stocks in the northern counties or Scotland. You learn here who make modern

[1] Robert Louis Stevenson (1850–1894). Story writer and essayist, author of *Treasure Island*. Lived in Edinburgh, but travelled widely for his health. In 1887 went to America and in 1890 settled in Samoa, where he died.

Greater Britain. Then the whistle sounded, and we went aboard again, and steamed out for Auckland.

Wednesday, July 29–Wednesday, August 3

The less said about this ghastly week the better. At first we had moderate weather. The last two days was informally rough, and we were all ill, our digestions being properly dis-arranged by tropical heat. But this morning we got to Auckland, a beautiful land locked harbour, with a cool north of England breeze blowing. We landed, almost shouting with pleasure at the damp streets, which smelt like England, with big men in macintoshes and Scotch beards going about, and bread and butchers' carts, and pictures of Gladstone crowding the windows, and everything as supremely English as in the home country. The landlord has already regaled me with a disquisition on how the country is going to the dogs under socialistic legislation and overtaxation, as any innkeeper might in his native town of Colchester in the Essex antipodes. It is such a comfort to talk to a real old Tory again, after the flabby politics of America.

And so till our next letter on New Zealand, many blessings to all—

Yours aff.
Charles Trevelyan

4. THE LOSS OF LETTER III. AUCKLAND TO NAPIER

Masonic Hotel,
Napier.

Monday, August 15

Letter III was such a good one. But alas! it is now floating down the Mohaka River, or more probably tossing on the Pacific billows. I have had a fine adventure. New Zealand is not an easy country to travel in yet. Last Monday we left Auckland for Wellington. We reckoned on spending two days at the volcano country and getting here yesterday. From Rotorua you drive the whole way, much of it through moun-

137

tains, of which travel I will try to rewrite an account presently. Suffice it to say that yesterday Sunday we started in pouring rain through a terrifically steep and magnificent range of fern-clad mountains, expecting to get to Napier that evening. At about ten o'clock we drove down to an inn by the side of the Mohaka River. Last year the bridge was washed away, and since then the only means of crossing the river has been a heavy hollowed tree canoe, attached to a steel rope, which is driven across by the action of the water. There is also a rope cage with which sometimes the shepherds pull themselves across hanging and swinging from the rope. When we arrived we were told by the host, who also was the only man responsible for the canoe, that we could not get over. The flood ran too high and would swamp the canoe, he said. There were a lot of shepherds also waiting to cross with their horses. I offered to go with anyone of them to try it. The experienced ones would not dare. The daring ones could not steer. So there was nothing for it but staying till the water fell, and we sadly saw the coach, which waited us on the other bank, toil up the steep bank away. So there we were stranded. The inn was comfortable, and we spent the evening playing chess and reading and chatting on politics with the shepherds who are all keen politicians even as the Cheviot farmers. One indeed was a Geordie from the Tweed. All of them whatever their party and ourselves roundly cursed the government for leaving the main road across the country, one of the mail roads and the chief tourist route, for 18 months with no bridge. Won't we let the Liberal members know our minds when we get to Wellington! Last night it poured and poured and today it was a bit higher. So this morning early I decided, (with due dissuasion from Mrs. Webb, anxious for justification in case I was drowned) to go over by the rope cage and leave them to come on when the floods fell, and to bring on the baggage. The crossing was of course impossible for the unathletic Webb or even the masculine vigour of Mrs. Webb. The difficulty of the situation was first that the rope was fixed to the bank higher at the other end than our end, so that I should have to pull myself uphill so to speak, and secondly that the water was risen so high that, when the rope gave with my weight, I might reach the water; in which case the tearing current would probably make progress impossible. Our host

138

fixed up a board with ropes attached to a pulley to hang only about 2 feet below the rope, the least possible space for me to sit in. My valise with a few clothes, third volume of Wilhelm Meister, the precious Letter III and my excellent razors was tied by a rope to the side of the board. I bade an affectionate farewell to the Webbs wishing them a speedy crossing, and mounted my car. I had about a hundred yards to go across the raging stream swollen high with days of rain. At first I got on easily enough, except that the rush of the water half a foot below me almost made me dizzy with its swiftness. About half way across when it became evident that I should not touch the water, I let go the rope which they had fastened on to drag me back in case I got into difficulties. Then the tug began. For about 40 yards I had to go hand over hand up hill, on a thin wire rope. It was lucky I had done plenty of the 'ladder' in the Harrow gymnasium. With several rests I struggled to the end, where there was a rope ladder hanging down ten feet to the landing, or rather where the landing should have been; for it was now covered by three feet of an eddying backwater. I now undid my valise with some difficulty as my hands were numb with wet and straining. At the last moment the knot slipped, and the valise plumped into the water. I was too fagged to get down quick and I saw it take two or three undecided twists in the shallow water and then shoot off into the current where it was whirled away to the Pacific at the rate of 30 miles an hour. So George may buy himself at my expense a new edition of the red Wilhelm Meister, and I shall have to read vol. III in the original without the crib on calm days in the Indian Ocean. After that I clambered down, floundered for a moment in three feet of muddy water and reached land safely; while the shepherds and Webbs on the other side could not forbear to cheer. I saw them turn back to the inn which must be their prison for 24 hours and may be for a fortnight. Then I tramped up the steep grade towards Napier, most rejoicefully in spite of the fact that it was five minutes before I could straighten out my fingers, obstinately crooked into stiffness by gripping. I soon met my coach coming down to see if we could get over this morning, and he turned back with me to drive me the rest of the 23 miles into Napier. On the way up the five miles of mountain from the river I met a tramp, whom I turned back on representation of what the river was like and how little work there was beyond it. Eventually I drove him back to Napier, and was well repaid. He was an intelligent unskilled workman who had been at the goldfields near Auckland and many other industries. He had voted for Reeves in Christchurch and was sturdy and unembittered in spite of his tramps. He absolutely refused whiskey until the very end of the drive though it was in the buggy with us, and then only when he was nearly freezing with wet and cold. As I neared Napier it began to get a little clearer; but I still have little hopes of the Webbs crossing for a day or two. It gives you an idea of the size of New Zealand & greatness of its mountains and difficulty of communication. If they go back, they have the alternative of going all the way back to Auckland, three days driving and one railway day, and then reaching Wellington by one day's sea and one railway. So they will wait however long it takes. It is a pity they are not on their honeymoon. But they are still sufficiently devoted to enjoy some hours tête à tête a day. But I am afraid the meagre literature of the inn and my bag which Webb will ransack, will hardly fill in the interstices of more than 24 hours. Meanwhile I have been commissioned to get due information about the Harbour Board and Municipality of Napier, which I shall do tomorrow as well as see the great meat-freezing establishments where the millions of sheep are packed for England.

The Hotel here is comfortable, and all the people so deliciously English. Today the chief roadmaker was a Mac something with broad Scotch twang. The river had been renamed the Esk. The wayside innkeeper hailed from the Salisbury plain. All types of English gentlemen, commercial folk, valetudinarians, fathers of families sat down with me to dinner today. But this leads me to begin again my unlucky letter III, which is now in a Pacific grave.

On Wednesday, August 3, we got to Auckland. We landed on a rainy day. But how delightful everything seemed. After a voyage of first rate unpleasantness for a fortnight any land is delightful. But here was a land which was home. I could hardly believe that I could not step into a train to take me in a few hours to Wallington in time for the 12th. All the people were English in gait and dress. In this rainy winter season they carry macintoshes, and the main street of Auckland looks as if it were full of rather townified border shepherds. All the men are tall and strongbuilt. There are no stunted factory hands, no pallid nervous overworked clerks and business men as in America. All look well-fed and contented, rather brighter than in an English Cathedral town. The women are rather plain, but sweet and bright eyed. They are dressed neatly but never with the universal American smartness. They show no taste only common sense and tidiness. There is an utterly English hotel, with a Tory landlord, who stands in his hall with portly belly declaiming against Seddon.[1] 'Why when he came here, no one of quality came to see him. All the riff-raff of the town stood over yonder, waiting to get something out of him. The country is going to the dogs, Sir. We are governed too much. All this socialism. The people are getting lazy'. Most refreshing to hear the genuine stuff again after American personalities. All the more satisfactory as the country is obviously *not* going to the dogs or crows, but in very much the other direction, whether it be in spite of or because of the Reeveses and Seddons. Then the Hotel dining-room. A portrait of Her Majesty in garter band on the wall, attentive English waiters, chicken and bread-sauce, no iced water, knives that cut. In the shops portraits of Gladstone, Robbie Burns, Lord Russell, Cobden–down to the four phases of the boy brightening over Fry's Chocolate and Ally Sloper. The streets are slushy but solid with submerged macadam, instead of slushy without bottom. The first two days in Auckland were about the most simply happy I have ever spent, the sheer delight of being again among the home people. The race is all like enough, and America and we can run side by side. But the British type untinged by Frank or Dutch or Norseman is a little dearer after all.

Today we saw a bright young merchant, Roberton, of Scotch extraction. He took us to see the clerk of the Municipality (for the Webbs to pump) and to the Library, which is free, and is very valuable and remarkable for the fine collection given to it by Sir George Grey,[2] the father of this people, to whom they owe very much of their well-being. Did G. O. T. know the man

[1] Richard John Seddon (18?-1906). Born in Lancashire, Prime Minister 1893–1906 (see Letter 5, p. 151 below).
[2] (1812–1898). Politician and explorer. Governor of New Zealand 1845–1853 and 1861–1868.

before his days of failing? He seems to have had very many of the Gladstone traits in him, universal sympathy, farsighted statesmanship, wide reading and research and deep interest in a great range of subjects, and an experienced command of men unequalled by Gladstone in the executive line. I want to know more of him. Almost every institution and every law owes something to his initiative here.

Thursday, August 4

This morning we spent in seeing the educational side of things. The public schools are like board schools in a provincial town. They are far better than voluntary schools; but have not the modern appliances of the big English boards. We have nothing to learn from them, and Stanley[1] would be very useful for a few weeks, if he rampaged about criticizing. There are no rates, the money coming entirely from government taxes. But the administration and inspection is purely local. It does not work badly, except that no locality can advance beyond the standard of expense sanctioned by the government. There is no room for local energy.

The children of the well-to-do generally go to the public schools. And we were told at the grammar school that the boys who come from the public schools are much better taught than those from private schools. The grammar school has an English master, and they prefer men as masters with an Oxford or Cambridge training. In the same way, almost all the professors of the University of New Zealand, a branch of which is at Auckland, are from England. The University has not the same grip as in America. Here there is rather prevailing the view of the English businessman that his son ought to go early to work. In America the idea of the young men is to get a thorough education before starting.

In the afternoon we drove round the town with Roberton. His brother, who is a doctor in the city, as soon as he heard of our party, said—'I never met Sir George Trevelyan. All I have ever had to do with him is that I got my coat torn off my back and bruises on my head at his Rectorial election.' The town is beautifully situated on a land-locked harbour. It rises gradually

[1] (See note to Letter 8, Series I above.)

ATIAMURI, AN OLD MAORI SETTLEMENT,
BETWEEN ROTORUA AND TAUPO

THE REEVES FAMILY, CHRISTCHURCH

THE CARRINGTON FAMILY, MOMALONG IN THE RIVERINA

THE WOOL STARTS ITS JOURNEY FROM JIMBOUR, QUEENSLAN

STEAM TRAM IN SYDNEY

up to a fine volcanic hill, Mt. Eden, two miles back from the wharves. The streets are wide. The houses mostly of wood, generally built on separate plots with gardens. The suburbs are very straggling, and the idea of elbow-room predominates. Now in the depth of winter there are geraniums flowering in the hedges and that big white lily-like flower with a yellow centre that we prize highly in our hot-houses is growing rank in the ditches. Winter here is like rainy October at home, no colder in the north island. We got a fine view. The country all round is studded with volcanic hills, and the plain cut up into English fields of English grass with wire or gorse hedges.

In the evening we interviewed the two leading members on either side of the Industrial Conciliation Court. In Auckland Reeves' Act has been a splendid success.

Friday, August 5

The morning we spent seeing the industries. We went to the timber yards where they cut up the Kauri tree which grows only in the North Island. It is a tropical pine, with a bole twice as big as our Wallington beeches. In the ground where these trees grow or have grown they dig up Kauri gum, which has exuded in past times and is now hard. Several thousands of men are always employed in digging for it, and they bring up nuggets if they are lucky as in alluvial gold mining. They can earn generally 30/- a week at least, often far more. The gum is used for varnish in England and America. We went afterwards and had a most interesting talk to the Manager of a Steamship Company, who was the only employer in Auckland who had had experience of the compulsory court of the Arbitration. He declared that he was completely in favour of the principle of the Act, and that, although there were some detailed amendments wanted, he would not have it repealed at any price.

In the afternoon I went to visit elementary schools, which further convinced me that we had little or nothing to learn from them. Their worst deficiency is that they do not supply any proper training for the teachers. They go through the mill as PTs and pass a not very severe Government examination and then are qualified. There is no Normal School, and they need not go to college.

Saturday, August 6

This afternoon I went to a football match. It was hardly believable that it was in the Antipodes. The whole male population of Auckland went out the three miles in all the hansoms, buses and trams the city possessed to see Auckland play the team from Canterbury in the South Island. The game was Rugby, the players had the dancing tassel on their heads. They played exactly as at home, only with less attempt at 'chawing' and perfect good humour. The enormous crowd yelped and cheered exactly as at home. I stood next Rawson, the employer whom we had discussed arbitration with yesterday. The Grand Stand was too full for us to get a place. The whole crowd consisted of men with macintoshes and umbrellas. It was quite impossible to distinguish workmen, clerks or employers. Their holiday dress gave the appearance of an even prosperity. They were exactly like an English crowd, down to the swarms of boys who were let in at the last moment without pay as the play began. But with one great difference. They all look healthy and well-fed, and there is an entire absence of the stunted mass that is mixed with the healthy folk at home. I walked back and was passed by an endless stream of vehicles and shaggy horses. Very few walked home. Altogether the afternoon's amusement must have cost the workman 6d each way, bus fare, 1/- entrance, 1/- grand stand, in all 3/-. I don't think they are a very saving population. But they do what is better, spend their money on good food and healthy amusement. One of our drivers subsequently said to me that 'We are not much forwarder than we would be at home on a smaller wage.' And it is true they do not keep money. But in spite of gambling and betting, which are very rife and drinking which is considerable, they make good food, clothes, and houses a first charge, and are on an average far ahead in the custom of necessary comforts than we are on the average at home.

Sunday, August 7

We had another drive round with Leys, editor of the Liberal evening paper and his son. We had a regular north country middle class tea with him in the evening, cold chicken, jam, scones, tea, cream etc., all first rate.

Monday, August 8

We went a long railway journey to Rotorua. The North British is nothing to the New Zealand State railways. We took from 9.30 to 8.30 going 157 miles. The country was much less settled than I expected, after the first 50 miles only a few sheep farms which look prosperous enough. The people at the stations looked healthy, simple and stupid, as in Yorkshire farming districts.

Tuesday, August 9

Rotorua is the centre of the volcanic district of the North Island. It is a valley, rather bare of anything but fern and tea tree, a native shrub, full of geysers and boiling sulphur pools. Every morning and evening you have a natural hot bath, which is very pleasant and unhealthy. The natives sit in the pools a good part of the day. Unlike the Red Indians, who never went to Yellowstone Park for fear of the devils of geysers, the Maoris have always made the hot lake district their home. The geysers are interesting, but as in America they are not beautiful. We had a beautiful ride on the lake Rotorua. The island in the middle is fine and famed in Maori legend. One of the best Maori stories is how Hine-Moa, a new woman on the shores of the lake, who was prevented from marrying her lover on the island, escaped one night, and swam the three or four miles to the island. There she most conveniently found a hot pool close to the shore into which she got to warm herself after her cold swim. There she was presently found by her lover, who immediately took her off home, and they lived happy ever after.

Wednesday, August 10

Today was a great day. I went to see the scene of the great eruption. Thirteen years ago all travellers used to go to see the pink and white terraces on Rotomahana mountain. You drove ten miles through a beautiful country, passing two fine wooded lakes with Maori settlements upon them. At length you reached a pretty settlement of natives and missionaries with an Hotel. At the end of the valley was a splendid blue lake with forests on the sides. At the end of it, ten miles away was the mountain on which the constant playing of the geysers had made a beautiful silica deposit in terrace formation of many acres. Over this the warm water ran into a lake in the centre of the crater. One day or rather night there was a fearful eruption, heard over most of the North Island. For many hours ashes and fireballs were poured up to heaven. All the settlements were destroyed for fifteen miles round, and the only people who escaped were a few who were crowded into a house with a sloping corrugated iron roof that warded off the burning ashes. Fortunately a wind rose which drove most of the cloud of ashes out to sea, thirty miles away. But when people dared to go again to the district it was found that the terraces were gone, that the shape of the mountain was changed, that all the country within ten miles was buried 4 yards deep in ashes and every trace of vegetation destroyed. This was the scene I went to see. I aimed at reaching the mountain. There is now no boat on the Lake and the people scouted the idea that I could reach it by land. I did fail to do so. But I went further than anyone else has gone in trying to get to the mountain by walking. It was the stiffest walk I ever had.

First I rode to Wairoa, past the deserted lakes, which had now lost their blue colour. They are now a sickly white from the enormous deposit of pumice, and their banks are very bare. At Wairoa there are the shattered ruins of houses, huts, and the Hotel, half buried in earth. Over all this land the fern has made its way, a tall strong bracken, which foreruns vegetation all over this country. Then I tied my horse to a tree and proceeded to walk for five hours along the plateau by the lake in the direction of the mountain. I got about four miles and back. The whole land is overlaid with yards of ashes. But of course the ash lies lightly and the rainstorms at once began to wash it away. The whole country is cut up into ridge and furrow. Every two yards is a deep water-course, five feet down, which deepens every shower. The easiest walking is leaping from ridge to ridge, with more incessant exertion than over scotch moss-hags. The falling is soft, so slips do not matter. But every quarter mile is a huge water-course which carries the water down to the lake, cut by the violence of the water for hundreds of feet into the hill. The walls are so steep that it was generally necessary to walk back half a mile in order to get round what you could not get across. At their upper ends these gullies became dangerous because they narrowed down to passages often not more than 2 yards wide but 10 or 20 deep, often hidden by the new growth of fern. For two miles in the direction of the mountain the fern had invaded the whole country. It of course will save the rest of the ash being washed away and will gradually make a mould on which other vegetation can grow. Through this I had to force my way with frightful exertion, avoiding all pitfalls. I then travelled for as far as I could over the desolate ridge and furrow ash plain, jumping, climbing, scrambling, dirtying and tearing myself till I had to give up thought of reaching the mountain. The view though desolate was magnificent, with the silent giant in the background that had done all the ruin. In another two hundred years no doubt the land will have recovered and trees and grass will grow there, and then perhaps there will be another giant eruption. I never felt so near the natural forces as today, more so I should think than would be possible even at Pompeii.

Thursday, August 11

Drove for fifty miles to *Weirakei* near Lake Taupo. We passed through a country absolutely uninhabited by white men, except for one inn. There were a few Maori settlements. But they are the poorest and laziest of the Maoris. The best was a Mormon village. Every Maori is great for his church, if not really religious. A traveller was once asked when he begged for accommodation for the night what Church he was of. He saw that if he made a wrong guess he would not get a lodging for the night. So he answered 'the right Church.' The reply was satisfactory and they gave him bed and dinner.

Friday, August 12

I like looking at geysers, and the geysers of Weirakei are situated on the sides of a beautiful green valley and are picturesque. But I like the neighbourhood of Blackcock Hall[1] better on this date. I was jealous of the party tramping out from Harwood or Greenleighton. This evening we went on to the shores of *Lake Taupo*, a magnificent 25 mile Lake, backed by a fine rough and

[1] Ruined house on the high grouse moors of Wallington Estate in Northumberland.

147

huge snow-clad volcano, the steam of which was unfortunately hid in cloud.

Here we met Brand, son of Lord Hampden, a nice Oxford boy. I was struck with the uselessness of travelling too young. He was incapable of getting any good out of it except the scenery. But as Charlie Buxton is going to meet him probably and go through America with him, he may be enabled to profit somewhat. He seemed to expect to see all America in a fortnight. We disillusioned him. He said that Lord H. was expecting me. So he has got G. O. T's letter.

Saturday, August 13

Today, after a nice spell of sunny but cool weather, we got rain again. We drove 50 miles to *Tarawera*, through an unsettled mountain district, clothed chiefly in fern, tea-tree and flax-plant. It rained hard, and we were pretty uncomfortable.

Sunday, August 14

We started again to drive; and then fell out the events recorded at the beginning of this letter.

SO—I have brought things up to date again. I am afraid this account of N.Z. is not as vivid as what I wrote when it was all fresh. Perhaps the ocean will refund its dead letters. In that case I will send on the original draught as well.

Yours aff.
Charlie Trevelyan

5. THE HOUSE OF REPRESENTATIVES

Government House,
Wellington

Tuesday, August 16

I stayed at *Napier* today. It is the centre of the sheep-grazing district of the East of the North Island. It is built on a sort of rocky promontory, surrounded by inlets and rich alluvial land, which divide the hills from the sea. It is a very bright little town. I made friends with the head of the Freezing Works. He is a

148

Glasgow man, White, exactly like any other Scotch merchant. Scotchmen are very preeminent in these islands. They bear a greater proportion to the population than anywhere else except Scotland. We have met several business men who are Scotch. Plenty of the shepherds are Scotch. Innkeepers are apt to be Scotch. The good-day of half the roadmen is Scotch. The most prominent members of Parliament on both sides are Scotch. Altogether they take a position quite out of proportion to their numbers.

White showed me the Freezing Works, and rode with me out to a rich farm of his a few miles along the coast. I had dinner with him, and we talked of Glasgow people and discussed politics very thoroughly. He is very happy out here, and says that if a man has plenty to do N.Z. is a splendid place. The chief point at issue was whether his sons should go back for an English public school education or only take a University course. His wife, a New Zealander born, had no belief in the superiority of our schools over theirs, and I backed her, because I think schooling ought to be at home, though the best University ought to be looked for wherever it is.

I found the Webbs had got across the Mohaka. The inn-keeper had been induced to ferry them across with fear and trembling by a sheep station manager who swore at him properly. The river had fallen some feet since I crossed; but if it had not been for their local ally they might have been a day longer.

Wednesday, August 17

Travelled to *Wellington* by rail. At first we went through a hilly country, all rich with green sheep-runs, covered with tens of thousands of sheep. Then we passed through a less settled land, where much of the bush was still standing, though recently fires have been sweeping away the greater part of the magnificent New Zealand timber. We were satisfied to find that the last remaining private line in New Zealand goes no quicker than the government railways. We got in late at night to Wellington.

Thursday, August 18

Wellington is most beautifully situated on a very big sea lake, forming a first-rate harbour. All round are hills rising out of the sea, behind are ranges of mountains with snowy tops at this time of year. On clear days you can see from the top of the steep hill above the town, the mountains of the South Island almost 100 miles away. The town is steady-going and prosperous, and the people are English and well-fed as in Auckland.

But there is more life here. For Wellington is the centre of government, and government is not the haphazard thing it is in America. There is even more serious interest in politics here than in England. Party spirit runs high, and questions are really discussed by everyone from the drawing-room lady to the wharf-hand.

Parliament is modelled on England. The Legislative Chamber is sleepy and conservative. It only blocks for a session and then acquiesces in 'revolutionary' legislation. The speakers drone. Seddon appoints his chums and political friends to the Upper House, not always too creditable as men. The Conservatives are very angry. But the ordinary man does not care what the Legislative Council is like, and would prefer that it should be impotent. There are in it several very nice men but no strong ones. The Webbs have gone to stay with one of them, Mr. Oliver, who married Leonard Courtney's sister.

The House of Representatives consists of 75 members. Each man has his seat, and generally the attendance is good. The rules and customs are in all respects based on ours. The Speaker Sir Maurice O'Rorke wears a gown, but no wig. He is first rate as a speaker, and very strong. He has the geniality of the Irish race. I had a talk to him today in his room. But he has a serious failing. Sometimes 'the Speaker has the influenza', and does not appear for two or three days. He is then to be found in the back parlours of public houses, watched by a judicious attendant who interferes if he begins to disclose state secrets. But in spite of this trait which everyone knows and deplores they will not sack him, because he is so popular and so efficient.

The House is divided like ours, and the government sit on the Speaker's right. The side galleries are given up to men. The whole of the end of the house, opposite the Speaker is the Women's Gallery, where they come and listen in large numbers, attentively and quietly, only imitating their French sisters by bringing many of them their sewing, when a long sitting is expected. Oh! you slow-going Anglo-Saxons at home, and is this foreshadowed for you by your precocious children, 'tricoteuses', with no screen in front of them, looking down on your Parliamentary debates! At present there is a row because the reporters and the Speaker band themselves against a certain young lady who wants to get into the reporter's gallery. She is confidently biding her time.

There are two parties. But the Liberals have a strong 'left' wing, which criticize Seddon, and is very much more efficient than the Conservative opposition. The New Zealand Parliament is at present composed of Seddon and the rest. Seddon is Prime Minister. He was a miner and publican. He is self-educated. He never reads a book. He drops a good many of his 'h's' always, and all of them when he is excited. But he is a strong, capable, good-natured, well-meaning, businesslike, dominant character. He rules men partly by their weakness, partly their strength. He is not over-scrupulous, but he is not a bad man. He is loathed by the Conservatives because he is no gentleman. They are never tired of telling you of his vulgarity and reputed jobbery. They most of them fail to see that he is a very competent ruler. He has been Liberal premier since Ballance died. He has had Reeves to give him a Labour policy and McKenzie, a rough Highlander, who has the gloom of crofter memories to drive him on, to carry out a progressive land policy. To a Liberal the Legislation has been extremely good, and continues to be so. They have got Pension and Compensation Bills, etc. still to pass. Seddon has the credit of holding a party and government together to accomplish this. And *that* the N.Z. workman and farmer knows, and is not going to be such a fool as to eject Seddon, in spite of certain shady appointments, to get in return an unsympathetic and very incompetent Conservative ministry.

Since Reeves[1] left, the brains are out of the legislation; but it goes on by force of the original propulsion given it by Ballance[2]

[1] William Pember Reeves. Enthusiast for Education. Entered House in 1887. In charge of Education and Labour in Ballance's 1890 Government. Resigned 1896 on being appointed Agent General in London.

[2] John Ballance (18?–1893). Journalist. Editor of provincial newspaper. Leader of Progressive Party. Prime Minister from 1891 till his death in 1893, when Seddon immediately took his place.

and Reeves. The administration is mainly good. Seddon is a terrific worker and his colleagues mostly industrious, especially the burly genial John McKenzie.

The Conservatives are led by a well-meaning squatter, Capt. Russell, a fine English gentleman, such as South Wilts or North Salop would send to represent obscurely the John Bull farmer for a few years. But he is without power or skill. He has two or three Scotchmen of moderate ability, and one able broad-minded colleague, Rolleston. Unfortunately Rolleston is a wretched speaker. So the opposition don't count much. They have entirely given up the attack upon the socialist and land legislation, say definitely they would not attempt to repeal it if they had power, and begin to grub in Hansard records to show that they voted for one or other of Reeves' bills which they loathed at the time. Their attack is concentrated on the corruption of Seddon's administration. The real foundation of their hatred is Seddon's vulgarity which is indubitable. Seddon does not mind appointing a working man to be J.P. or Legislative Councillor, and does it. Naturally some of the appointments are bad, and then the Conservatives point the finger of rage and scorn. But on the whole it seems to me that the major appointments of Seddon are good. He has certainly made too many small temporary appointments in the Civil Service to political supporters. But that is a thing which could be stopped by constant exposure, which the opposition do not take the trouble to give them.

The most effective men outside the government are the 'left'. The best man is Tommy Taylor of Christchurch, who began as a fanatical prohibitionist and was Reeves' bane when he was member for Christchurch. He is still terribly temperance but is a capable and fundamentally broad-minded man. I had a good deal of talk to him. If he had more communication with experienced politicians of whom of course there are few in N.Z., he would be a valuable man. As it is he is quite on the right tack. He and his friends support Seddon in policy, but attack him for his jobbery. At present he is much too hot and loses his temper. But he will cure of that and will be one of the best men in Parliament. I should be 'left,' if I were here.

The whole of this afternoon and evening I spent at the House.

All parties were eager to talk to us, and make much of us. We occupied seats of distinction on the floor of the house.

Friday, August 19

This morning I spent seeing Civil Servants, especially Tregear, Reeves' right hand in the Labour Dept. and the heads of the Land Office.

In the afternoon I went to see Lord Ranfurly, the Governor. He is from the north of Ireland, owning land round Dingannon. He has married Lord Charlemont's daughter. He is a renowned Orangeman. I naturally thought he would be rather a difficult person for me, probably aristocratic and high Tory. I found him very friendly, and with that sort of shyness which the Viceregal position engenders in rather weak men. He was exactly like Lord Crewe, desire for ease perpetually battling with the consciousness of royal position. He is just the man for the position. He is not strong, but intelligent and hospitable. He is quite sympathetic with people whom he does not agree with. He thoroughly recognizes that he must not interfere with the political action of the colony. He quite appreciates Seddon, and does not intrigue against him as I rather expected to find. His wife is very pleasant, and paints beautifully. The house is half decorated with fine pictures by her of New Zealand scenery. I wish Mama could have a chance of drawing some of the sunsets she has been able to record.

They are surrounded by a nice set of aides-de-camp, 'tame cats' as Miss Wilberforce got in a row for calling them in Ireland. Those here have merely the passive faults of the viceregal hanger-on. They have not the blackguard and bully side of some of their Irish counterparts. Partly I am in a different relation to them no doubt, and they have to behave.

Saturday, August 20

Another morning at the public offices. The higher Civil Servants are a very good class of man, quite as good, in proportion to the size of things, as in England.

In the afternoon we went to see the Justice who now administrates the Arbitration Act. It is unfortunate that the Judge who has hitherto given the awards, and has been recognized as very impartial by both sides, has retired from ill-health. We formed a very low idea of Judge Edward's impartiality and ability. He is an honest man, but stupid. There are hopes however that, as he does not like the job, he may be replaced shortly.

In the afternoon I had a walk and talk with Taylor of Christchurch.

In the evening I dined at the Olivers (where the Webbs are staying.) The most interesting person we met was Sir Robert Stout, probably the ablest of New Zealanders living. He was a leading Liberal politician. But he played his cards badly, and allowed Seddon to get the Premiership. Since then he has sulked. He has a big intellect and wide knowledge. I think he fails in grip of men; but it is a pity he is not in high position. He is one of the men who is injured by disappointment.

Sir Robert told us that during the Penjdeh incident[1] he had been minister, and that the British Government had telegraphed out to the Governor that 'War will be declared with Russia this afternoon'. Can that be correct? He asserts the governor forwarded the wire to him & that he had to hurry back from a tour he was making. What says G. O. T?

Sunday, August 21

This morning I climbed the hill at the back of Wellington and got a glorious view of the mountain locked harbour and the snow ranges in the distance.

I lunched at the Government house. I had tea with Seddon. He is a humorous old boy in private life and told us some good Maori stories. Since then he has sent us some pictures of his expeditions as Premier among the Maoris, with whom he is a great favourite. In one he is sitting in a top hat and a Maori feather cloak all over him, with which they had honoured him.

I dined with Bell, the ablest lawyer in the colony after Sir R.

[1] In 1885, when all attention was centred on the Sudan, where General Gordon had just been killed when Khartoum fell to the Mahdi, Russia seized the opportunity to attack and occupy the village of Penjdeh, some miles inside the Afghan border, thereby seeming to threaten India. Gladstone, then Prime Minister, reacted forcefully, asked the House of Commons for a Vote of Credit of £11m, and said that such aggression would be strongly resisted. The Russians at once withdrew, but there was anxiety for some days, while war seemed imminent.

Stout. He is very much down on the Seddon government, and I had a lot of talk with him.

Monday, August 22

Today I removed into the Viceregal,[1] as I prefer to call it, in memory of Ireland. There are aides-de-camp, and sentries who salute at the lodge gates and sedate English butlers and tall footmen, and Excellency marching in to dinner ahead of us all, Her Excellency following next, and 'Sir'ing as in Ireland, which is all amusing now and unaggravating, when one is no longer part of the system.

Dined with Coates, a strong supporter of the government, almost the only banker who approves of them. As he happens to have a sound bank and big body, voice and temper, he is worth a good many Tory bankers.

I sat up talking for two hours with Capt. Russell, opposition leader, whom Lord Ranfurly had invited to meet me. He is a weak many – but an honourable man – So are they all, all. But Seddon has got the force.

Tuesday, August 23

Scobie Mackenzie, one of the Scotch Conservatives, lunched at the Viceregal today. He too I found ineffective as far as policy went. He pretended to acquiesce in the government policy, and attacked the jobbery. But he could not make a very good case out against them. I am, however, quite convinced by now that it would be a good thing to have some capable criticism of some of the methods of the government. There are no vile political abuses, but many minor delinquencies.

This evening I went again to the House and came in for a scene. A clever but very spiteful Conservative, Hutchinson, made an attack on the government. At the end he raked up an old story against Seddon, practically charging him with having profited in the shady proceedings of a dead relative, who was supposed to have been party to defrauding a public body of which Seddon was member. It was done as nastily and bitterly as possible. It was the most discreditable performance conceivable. After that he brought up a cock and bull story of Seddon

[1] Refers to residence in Viceregal Lodge, Dublin, while G. O. T. was Chief Secretary 1882–1884.

having dealings with Chinamen in the mines in past years. He read a screamingly funny letter from a Chinaman in which Seddon was known by the name of Bun Tuck. The object of the story was to discredit Seddon in the eyes of the workingman. Seddon at once got up, and, dropping all his 'h's' as he does when he is excited, said that it was infamous to accuse his deceased relative and that the guilty parties had been punished, and declared that the Bun Tuck story was a fabrication. Most people felt that whether Hutchinson's stories were true or fake, it was hitting below the belt to introduce them to prejudice the debate. At least it shows that the 'gentlemanly party' is no better than the h.less Premier. It was a low, mean attack, and it failed. Russell, like a feeble leader, as long as he thought the dirt could stick, backed Hutchinson. When his wife, and I, and some of his shrewder and more gentlemanly followers had given our opinion of the proceeding very hostilely, he began to veer round.

Subsequently the Conservative Press has joined the Liberal in pitching into Hutchinson for degrading Parliamentary debate. But the blot will take some washing out of the Conservative toga. Since then the debates have been stormy. Unfortunately the Speaker has had a fit of 'influenza', and a furious repudiation by John MacKenzie in unmeasured terms went on unchecked. Taylor lost his temper and called Ward a 'miserable coward' for which he was named. Several members had to apologize. These sort of small assemblies easily get out of hand. But the ultimate discredit is with the man who laid the train, Hutchinson.

Wednesday, August 24

This morning an old Maori chief from the King Country came to see Lord Ranfurly. He came dressed in the native kilt. Above it, a blue Norfolk jacket, covered with a beautiful Maori rug of feathers of the Kiwi bird, a wingless native. Below it, bare legs, with big boots, obviously hired for the occasion, with white stockings falling round them. The whole surmounted by a brown billycock. He was an old man, tough, wiry and muscular. His face was splendidly tatooed, as you never see them now. Only the older women are now tatooed on the chin, nowhere else. The younger women now are trusting to their unassisted attractiveness. He exchanged compliments through an interpreter, and then he and his four companions, who were in ordinary dress, had a drink of champagne. At the end he took off his Kiwi shawl and put it round Lord Ranfurly's shoulders as a present with great grace of action. No doubt he had been a vigorous fighter and eater of his enemies in the good old days when men might kill each other. Now all the pugilistic Maori can do is to become a football player. He would have made a splendid three-quarter. But he was too old to change his form of sport.

Later he went to see a British man-of-war that is lying in the harbour. He was told he might take his friends with him. 22 Maoris availed themselves of the invitation. They enjoyed themselves enormously, and were only disappointed because the Captain would not allow him to fire off the gun.

I went round the harbour fortifications this morning, with Captain Ward, the best of the aides-de-camp. What I wanted chiefly to see was the way in which mines were laid. I was shown the system very thoroughly. In case of war there would be over a hundred globes of steel full of guncotton, of about 4 feet diameter, floating ten feet below the surface across the entrance to the harbour. Everything looked in splendid order.

This evening we started in the boat for Christchurch, and had a reasonably calm night for the crossing.

Thursday, August 25

Early in the morning we reached Lyttleton harbour, a cleft in a great mountain promontory which runs out into the sea from the Canterbury plain. We got on board a train and were carried through a two mile tunnel cut into the open plain, where the sun was just breaking through a cold morning mist, as it does on some rainy morning in the Eastern English lowlands. The Canterbury plains are a grand flat expanse fifty miles wide and several hundred long, stretching down the eastern coast between the mountains and the sea. They rise about 1000 feet towards the mountains, but the incline is imperceptible to the eye, quite counterbalanced by the earth's curvature. At the edge of the plain rise a beautiful range of mountains stretching the whole length, north and south, in unbroken majesty. In winter they are snow-clad, and now from top to bottom they are glowing white, except where pieces of bush still grow on the slopes to darken them, in sharp contrast to the green and brown plains, where the snow never lies, except for a day or two in winter for a few hours. Christchurch, the centre of the plains is like an English Cathedral city. The houses are not so old, the Cathedral is modern and unfinished, Anglican enthusiasm and monopoly ceasing before more than half the plotted structure had risen. But all is neat, tidy, happy-looking and respectable. There are no unfinished streets, no broken pavements, no squalid suburbs as in a forty year old American city. Order rules here. Each house is cared for by the people in it, and trimmed and decorated with a bright garden. The streets have carefully planted avenues, and the public gardens are delightful. The Avon winds through them, and the willows dip into it, and lines of oak and beech trees back the walks. The football field of Christchurch College, the best public school in N.Z. opens onto the Park. New Zealanders boast it is not unlike the Cam as it goes past Trinity, and though lesser in its kind they are not making an impudent comparison.

I went to stay at the Club, which is very comfortable, the Webbs to a good Hotel.

But here I must stop, as the English mail goes in five minutes, and what we did in Christchurch must be the next story.

Yours aff.

Charles Trevelyan

6. THE CANTERBURY PLAINS

Thursday, August 25

Today we spent in seeing *Christchurch*. In the morning we did the Educational Establishments, with the result that I had to submit to an interview subsequently which I will send you if I can get hold of a copy. I got much the same impression as at Auckland, the only improvement here being that they have a Normal School where they give a year's training to P.T.s. The University is not over well attended. Again the business men prefer to push their sons into business straight, and most of those who profit by the education are teachers, or leisured young ladies. The degree exam. is pretty stiff. The papers being prepared and corrected and marked at home by examiners appointed by the New Zealand University. Last year one of the inconveniences of this loyal arrangement became apparent, when all the papers of all the candidates went down in the Magellan Straits. All the hundreds of unfortunate girls and boys have to submit to a new exam, or go without their degree. There are two good public schools (in our sense) at Christchurch. One is state, the other originally Church. But the Churchiness of Christchurch has considerably moderated since it was founded by the Lyttletons and Godleys, and the School like all institutions, except the Cathedral, is practically secular.

The afternoon I spent seeing Reeves' relations, his mother and sisters, and Mrs. Reeves' mother, sisters and brother. They are all very pleasant people and quite account for Mr. and Mrs. R. Reeves was damnably treated here as a young man for taking up Liberalism. They blackballed him for the Club and snubbed him generally. I don't wonder he fought hard. It must have been considerable pleasure giving them laws they did not like in revenge.

In the evening we went to see the Editor of Reeves' paper the Canterbury Times. The papers here and indeed throughout N.Z. are excessively good. Both Liberal & Conservative here are excellent. In Auckland the Conservative is excellent, the Liberal good. In Wellington both are as good as the 'Leader'. Altogether the class is very high. They also have excellent weekly papers with an elaborate résumé of all the news. But they depend on us entirely for magazines.

In the evening we had representatives of the workingmen in to talk to. They were all as in England, and thoroughly optimistic. One man, who had stood for Christchurch had a bad 20 minutes. He wanted an elective executive. We all three pounced on him.

Friday, August 26

Today I went out to see some of the government settlements in the Canterbury Plains. To the horror of all the big squatters the government passed four years ago a Lands for Settlement Act, which enables the Government to take compulsorily at a valuation the land of any man, which they think is needed for settlement in small farms. You may imagine the howls. The unutterable iniquity of turning away a man who is feeding 10,000 sheep, and making room for 500 men! The world was just coming to an end for poor New Zealand! The government have worked the act very judiciously. So far from creating a business panic, they are annually offered many more estates than they want to purchase. They have taken over above 150,000 acres. Only two large estates have been bought compulsorily, and those from absentee landlords. So far from the transaction being unfair on the owners, the Conservatives are now beginning to complain that too much is being paid by the government in some cases. Almost all this land has been at once taken up by small farmers and allotment holders, who are generally speaking doing very well. Part of the settlement which I went to see was bought from Mr. Wason MHR, brother of Wason of South Ayr. I met him in the House and he gave me an introduction to his manager on his estate. He is a conservative, and yet he parted with 2,000 acres voluntarily to the government.

I had one of Mrs. Reeves' brothers, Mr. Robison, as companion, a very amusing one too. He is a keen Liberal and admirer of Reeves, has been a bank manager and now has a station in the most out of the way district in the north island, where he can only employ Maori labour, and catches wild horses when he wants to ride. We went a two hours ride south by rail. I profited by a free pass which Seddon has given us over the government railways, a privilege which is never bestowed except on very distinguished visitors. They are not chucked broad-cast as in the States. Then we drove for ten miles across the plain. On either side of our road, which was good macadam, was a broad expanse as far as you could see of big fields enclosed by gorse hedges, all yellow with peach scented bloom. Half of the soil was turned to sow the winter wheat. The rest was grazed over by hundreds of sheep. In front of us rose the snow-clad barrier, running unbroken north and south as far as the eye could reach, all clear-cut in the pure air. The Maoris call New Zealand 'The Long White Cloud' from this splendid range. It is a glorious new land for a new race of English yeomen and Lowland farmers. When we got to Wason's place his manager put in another horse and we drove for twelve miles round the settlements which extend over about 6,000 acres.

Most of the land is divided into farms of between one and two hundred acres. When it is settled, a public ballot takes place, and anyone may put in. Between 50 and 150 people put in for each of the plots. They may only take it under stringent conditions of improvement and residence. They pay a fixed perpetual rent to the state. They are practically all of them doing well, and are not grumbling in spite of two very poor years. Most of them have some previous experience of farming; but a fair number were working men previously in quite unagricultural employment. The most interesting man I met was a carpenter, once a colleague of Joseph Arch in promoting the Agricultural Union. He had a large family and was bringing up his son as a farmer. They lived in a wooden house, built by his own hands, and decorated with the pictures of Gladstone you see in the hovels of the village radical at home. But here was a security of prosperity that there would not have been for the old fellow and his smiling old partner in the old country. Another fellow was a north country Irishman with a large family, who thought himself far better off than with Ulster tenant-rights to plague him on his entry. And so on–.

The small settlements of 10 acres, of which there were more than thirty, are not a success at this distance from centres of industry. The quantity of land is too small to make a living alone, and unless a man is able to get some work in the neighbourhood, he is worse off than if he is a permanently employed labourer. I daresay a dozen such settlements could be profitably taken up in this neighbourhood. There are at present too many.

On the way back we had a look into a country school, which was quite as bright as Cambo,[1] though lacking the attention given it by ourselves. All was left to the initiative of the master. But he was very good, and the school was really well-built, neat and smart–far better than our village schools. The master's salary was £140 for about 50 children, whom he taught with an assistant! What a contrast to our voluntary sweating system.

Evidently the schools are managed by the secretary of the Board and the Inspectors, and perhaps the Board members from the city of Christchurch. I cannot say much for the member from Rakaia, the locality, whom I met. He commenced by explaining that his qualification was that he had had

[1] Village on Wallington Estate.

161

no education and therefore knew how much other people wanted it. He ended by recommending that the teachers should learn to box in order to knock down any citizen who resented corporal punishment of his children. A good John Bull Tory farmer, obviously led by the nose by those who *did* understand education.

Saturday, August 27

The morning I spent seeing over a Freezing Works with a Mr. Deans, of Scotch origin again.

The afternoon I spent with the Reeves' relations, and a very pleasant one too. In the evening on board the boat back to Wellington. The Webbs went off in the morning to see Dunedin, another day's journey south. They will see there more Scotchmen, nothing but Scotchmen, and stone houses in the Antipodean Auld Reekie. I am going off to see a Scotchman in another direction.

Sunday, August 28

Reached *Wellington* again in the morning. The liveliest passengers were a football team from Christchurch College coming over for a week's footballing in the North Island, looking much like Jackson, Maclaren and I might have done ten years ago.

Monday, August 29

Among my other introductions here, I had one from Mr. Pearson of Edstone to a James G. Wilson, who is a big farmer in the south west coast of the North Island at a place called *Bulls on the Rangitikei river*—I had no idea that I should find any other connection. When I wrote to him he eagerly asked me to come, saying that he was son of old Wilson of Hawick,[1] carpet manufacturer and quondam supporter of G. O. T., whose words of wisdom he had listened to as a youth before going out to seek his fortune in New Zealand.

So this morning I started for Bulls at 6.30 and got there by midday. The train was full of footballers from Wellington College going to play Wangauri, the best school in the North Island. The number of strong young men is immense here,

[1] Town in Border Boroughs constituency in Scotland, for which G. O. T. was M.P.

brawny cubs, utterly crude, raw, unfinished, but much heartier and healthier than the young American who is a finished product at twenty and consciously a man.

The Wilsons live in a tidy wooden village of 300 souls. They have a very comfortable wooden house, outside unarchitectural, inside very comfortable with all that a sensible simple family can desire, comfortable chairs, open wood fires, shelves of good and well-chosen and well-bound, and well-read books, etc. They have a neat garden with yew bushes and a prolific kitchen garden, a back yard with horses, chickens, etc. Wilson is a bright, sensible, conservative Scotchman, who has been an MHR. and would make a good MP. Mrs. Wilson is Australian born, but just a clever, rather literary, English matron of the best type. She is said to write. They have three sons, all brought up at Wanganui College. All of them work on the farm, taking different departments. They work with a will, and are healthy, strong, unaffected fellows. But they are thoroughly keen on literature, politics, etc., ready to discuss and argue on everything from Old Age Pensions to duck-shooting. There are two very nice girls. The elder one is musical. The younger one, who is very pretty, rides and looks after chickens. They are well educated in the second grade and read a lot with their mother, and are keen about things. If all the families of N.Z. were being brought up in this style they would be the greatest race on earth.

They entertain me just in the best way, all going about their business as usual, and letting me go with them or not, and see and do what I like.

I rode in the afternoon with Wilson to a Maori village, where a chief was just dead. Unfortunately we were a quarter of an hour too late to see the funeral. But there were a great many people about, and they were just going to begin the 'tangi', a sort of glorified wake. All the relatives and connections come from any distance, bringing a certain amount of food with them, for fear the stock of the deceased should run short. Upwards of a hundred had collected for this 'tangi'. They were just beginning to light fires in the farm yard (this Maori settlement being composed of prosperous farmers.) There they cook and eat for some days till the supply of sheep and pigs runs short. Then they go home.

Tuesday, August 30

In the morning I started with Mr. Wilson on horseback to see his farm. It is on the other side of the Rangitikei river. A New Zealand river when it reaches the alluvial plains runs down a broad cutting half or three quarters of a mile wide, which it has cut out in time of flood. When it is impassable. Now it was only a narrow stream through which we waded, tucking our feet up on our saddles. The rest of the flood river-bed was sand, continually blowing up in the strong wind. Before we went up onto the downs we saw a Maori settlement, where they were just preparing to start for the 'tangi' we saw commencing yesterday. They were dressed in good modern clothes, a curious contrast to their hovels. One of the men was a half-caste, but more Maori than English. He had been to Oxford once and whenever he is drunk, he quotes Shakespeare by the yard. But he is generally sober and unpoetical.

We rode all over the farm which is of about 7000 acres, part wheat, part sheep. We saw one of the sons preparing a machine for raking, and another cutting up some cattle he had just slaughtered. They are evidently prosperous as well as industrious.

The evening we spent in talk and singing songs of Schumann, Schubert, John Farmer, Moore, Burns and other great men.

Wednesday, August 31

Today I had a delightful ride with the two girls, who are as good horsewomen as Di Vernon.[1] We galloped over a country wonderfully like Harwood or Elf Hills.[2] We went onto a big station of 50,000 acres owned by an absentee landlord, who neglects it. Wilson who grumbles, like a Scotch theological theorist, at the power the Government has to take his hard-won property, *if it pleases*, would be only too delighted if John MacKenzie would pounce on absentee Moorhouse and settle the 50,000 acres with industrious farmers. Most of the land had been cleared, but was now being recovered by the gorse and coarse grass. The best of it was like our fields, green below but whitened by the long rough grass we know so well. The air was

[1] Heroine of Sir Walter Scott's novel *Guy Mannering*.
[2] On Wallington Estate.

keen and fresh from the sea, and the clouds white and numerous, as in our September days when it is fine. The very gates had rebounding clamps like ours. We got distant views of the hills thirty miles off as we do of Cumberland. Altogether with two bright and pretty girls it was a good day.

At night Mr. Wilson went out into the village to conduct a practice of the 'Trial by Jury', which was to be played next week. One of his sons and the girls are singing in it. The local grocers' assistant is the judge and sings in raucous melody 'When I, young friends, was called to the bar'. The school mistress is the injured plaintiff, with a bend of the head and manner singularly like Miss Richardson.[1] Laundresses, farmers' daughters, etc., make up the Chorus. It was so like a reproduction of the modern rich man or landlord in a north country village – only fortunately he is not landlord.

Thursday, Sept. 1

Had a walk in a piece of New Zealand bush which is condemned to be burnt down this year for sordid pelf by the owner, and the bell-birds and quails will have to find another lodging. The destruction of the fine old timber and its magnificent creepers and undergrowth is very sad.

Then I said goodbye and started back to *Wellington,* and Government House.

Friday, Sept. 2

The A.D.Cs are very 'tame cat' like – I have been very much amused with them today. One of them is preparing a speech to reply to the toast of the army. He came to me to know if three cumbrous but appropriate sentences he had carefully elaborated on paper would serve adequately. I had to decide between the phrases 'I thank you for the courtesy with which you have received this toast' or 'drunk this toast.'

Later I went a walk with a great grandson of the Duke of Wellington.[2] He was a nice boy; but I would have liked to have

---

[1] School mistress at Cambo.
[2] Arthur Charles Wellesley (1876–1941). In 1898 was A.D.C. to Lord Ranfurly, Governor-General of New Zealand. Succeeded as 5th Duke of Wellington in 1934. Lived at Stratfield Saye from 1922–1941.

put him for a few weeks under old Nosy for training. He cant write a letter for his superior to sign half as well as any of the Board School boys Seddon may have jobbed into the Civil Service. He is the heir of the Dukedom, and began grumbling about death duties. I thought a great grandson of the Duke ought to be content to work for his living if necessary and not grumble at the taxes. 'The Queen's Government, sir, must be supported!' So I gave him a little instruction in social radicalism and he did not seem to become less deferential. He is a good youth, and may be worthy to command a regiment in some Waterloo, but never an army. He has not alas! even got the nose.

We went and had a look at a very good football match between Wanganui and Nelson Colleges (public schools.) The boys played really well, and it was a most pretty sight. All the rank and fashion had come to see, and were standing round the ground and above it on the hillside which rises in a steep amphitheatre. The sun was shining warm and bright on this winter day. We sat on the grass for an hour watching–till the sun dipped behind the western hills and the chances of Nelson had sunk also.

This evening I went to see the New Zealand House to say goodbye to the members. Seddon had just brought in an Old Age Pension Bill, a modified scheme on Booth's[1] plan, but quite thorough. It will pass this year, the Tories hardly opposing. He came and talked to me, bluff, swaggering and cheerful, a great contrast to the timid and respectable Russell who came up afterwards. I said goodbye to them all, and came away with a curious feeling at the practical certainty of my never setting foot again in their house, or seeing New Zealand again after tomorrow, in spite of it seeming to me one of the greatest places to live in that the world has got. And all that they do here, football, pension-schemes, pheasant shooting, amateur village theatricals, young ladies reading societies, and all the rest, are a wonderful reproduction of our home world. It is far more truly and completely New England than ever Boston was. Perhaps

[1] Charles Booth (1840–1916). Shipowner, writer on social questions, particularly on conditions of life in London. Advocated old age pensions.

it is because they have got the Scotch. Who knows!

This is the last word from New Zealand.

Yours aff.
Charles Trevelyan

7. TO AUSTRALIA. RACE WEEK IN SYDNEY

Saturday, Sept. 3

This evening we said an eternal and affectionate farewell to New Zealand. It *is* a great country, on the whole I expect ultimately to be the greatest of our colonies from strength health and happiness, which are almost bound to be the inheritance of its people. At present it is certainly England, unmarred by excessive greed, poverty, frost, church prejudice, class folly, and other of our deplorable incidents.

Sir Robert Stout came to see us off, as a last coping to the mass of hospitality which we have enjoyed. Our ship is the Monowai, a good-looking craft. Our destination, Sydney.

This is the only record possible of the next days—

Sunday, September 4
Discomfort.

Monday, September 5
Respite.

Tuesday, September 6
Misery.

Wednesday, September 7
Recovery.

My cabin companion is an able young New Zealand lawyer called Skerrett. I have been arranging with him to make an exchange with the New Zealand Acclimatization Society, which is very active in introducing new kinds of beasts and birds into New Zealand. It is already responsible for the hare, pheasant, fallow deer, red deer, partridge, and mallard. They are at present very anxious to get snipe and blackcock. So Skerret is going to arrange if possible that some of the New Zealand grey duck, a fine shooting and eating bird shall be sent over to me, and I am to send some black and grey over to them. The bargain is more likely I think to be profitable to us, as black are not likely to survive 1,300 miles of sea. Still it would be something to people New Zealand with a Wallington stock. They have an agent in London whom I shall see when I get home.

We had a pleasant day with perfectly smooth water, and as the sun set red in the west, we imagined we began to see the dark line of the fifth continent on the horizon. At any rate shortly after dark the great revolving light outside Sydney harbour began to shine out as bright as Jupiter which was just above it. And about nine we ran into the harbour, twinkling for the four miles between the mouth and the city with countless lights and lamps from villas and suburbs. We landed and drove off in hansoms to the chief hotel, seeing nothing but substantial streets like an English city at midnight.

Thursday, Sept. 8

Sydney is a great contrast to New Zealand. It is the great world again. The shop streets are stone or brick built. Large business houses and fine exchanges adorn the business quarters. There are fine public buildings and government offices. There is rush in the streets, and lots of hansoms. Steam cars rattle along with four carriages to a train. There are finely laid out parks and an ideal botanical garden, overlooking the magnificent harbour, which is all that Sydney folk claim for it. It is full of sailing boats and steam ferries, while in the docks lie quantities of shipping and the great funnels of the Ocean Liners. In the bend of the harbour overlooked by Government House and the public gardens is the British fleet a-lying at anchor, three great cruisers and a gunboat, on a war footing in six hours if necessary. By them is a white Kaiser's cruiser, repairing by permission of Her Majesty within the ring sacred to H.M. warships. The Governor's house is modern Elizabethan and imposing though not highly beautiful. In the centre of the harbour is a little island with a sort of Martello tower on it, the first harbour fortress of convict days, looking now hardly larger than flag-ship Royal Arthur, one shot from which would blow it to fragments. On another little island they used to send and starve recalcitrant convicts. The 'larrikins' still call it Punch-gut. All round the harbour, as far as you can see, are green banks dotted with white houses, till four miles off lie the barrier cliffs which shut out the view and the ocean violence. Sydney you at once feel is a great world. I do not like New Zealand the less for that. Sydney is full grown for good or evil. New Zealand is young and can only yet dimly see its future greatness.

I begin by going straight to Government House, where Lord Hampden received me very kindly. It is race-week in Sydney, and they had a house full and no room for me. For which the lord be thanked, as that would mean being involved in a vice-regal season. But he at once got his aides-de-camp to put me down for the best club in Sydney, where I have settled down during my stay in very comfortable and independent quarters. He also gave me a note to Prime Minister Reid, whom I found sitting in his Parliamentary room in his shirt-sleeves. He received me very jollily and told me to come round with the Webbs just before the House met in the afternoon.

Very shortly the political situation is this. Reid who came in in 1894 as a free-trader, turning out Dibbs a protectionist, is still Premier. Like Seddon in N.Z. he was the only very strong man in Parliament especially after Dibbs' death. He has one strong colleague, Attorney-General Want, in the Legislative Council, Upper House. During his office he has passed some progressive legislation, a factory act, a Civil Service Act, and imposed direct income and land taxes. But he is not very thorough, only a very competent opportunist with popular sympathies. Two years ago Federation came forward. Want is against it. Reid says he is for it; but has been accused all along by Barton, the great promoter of Federation, of insincerity. I do not yet judge him. The Federal scheme did not get the required support of 80,000 votes in New South Wales, and is therefore in abeyance. The Bartonites say Reid damned it with faint praise. At the election two months ago, Barton raised the standard against Reid, and the election turned really on the choice of men. Barton bearded Reid in his own Sydney con-stituency. Barton was beaten; but his party defeated two of

Reid's ministers and reduced Reid's majority to a very small margin, dependent upon a few Independents giving their support. One of Barton's supporters has resigned, in Barton's favour, who will probably be in the House in a day or two. A full dress debate is now on, over a series of resolutions brought forward by the government in which the other colonies are asked to 'reconsider' certain parts of the Federal scheme. The opposition say they agree that the scheme does not quite suit their views and would like a reconsideration with a view to putting it again before the people. But they say there is no need to debate at length, and that Reid only wants delay. Therefore they have proposed a rather clumsy amendment, which we are on the way to hear introduced by Lyne, the opposition leader. Practically it expresses want of confidence in Reid and has been taken by him as a vote of Censure, and is therefore the first stand and fall debate and division of the new Parliament. We are in good luck to come in for it.

At 3.30 we came to the House and Reid at once placed us in the three front seats of a very special reservation to the Speaker's right, where no lady had been known to sit before, except the Governor's wife. The galleries, one of which is reserved for women and not caged, were crowded and the House was full. It is fashioned after the House of Commons, except that the seats curve round to a gangway opposite the Speaker's chair. There are seats enough for all the 125 members. The labour party, really a wing of Reid's party, sits on his side below the gangway. Lyne the leader of the Opposition brought in his amendment. He is utterly incompetent, muddleheaded, dull, stammering, etc. After Reid had listened to him for a bit he came and sat down by us and regaled us with jokes and conversation till the dreary performance was over. He then went back to the table and replied. He is a very fat man, with as good a double chin as Sir William Harcourt.[1] He has light brown hair. He frequently puts an eyeglass in one eye. His expression is rather bright and comic. He made a first-rate debating speech, at least in matter and wording. He shouts tremendously which is a pity, but his argument is so much to the point that it matters little. He ripped up the opposition tactics, and for an able defence nothing could have been better. This does not prejudge

[1] (1827–1904). Liberal statesman, supporter of Gladstone.

the general question of his real sincerity on which all ultimately hinges. In the course of his speech he mercilessly but quite justifiably jeered at Lyne for his incompetence and the certainty that he would be superseded by Barton directly he entered the House. It was somewhat brutal, but much feeble folk ought to be stamped on. It would do Lord George Hamilton[1] and such people good at home. The speech was constantly interrupted by a vulgar, perky little solicitor, called Crick, who was allowed to interject in exactly the way that they do on America, to the destruction of all real debate. Several times the course of the speech was altogether interrupted. But the Speaker, a very respectable but timid knight, did not intervene effectively. At last the House got sick of it, and someone proposed to eject Crick. The Speaker in a miserably pedantic way, quoted precedents to show that he 'could an' if he would,' but did not. I squirmed at the feebleness of authority, which is always so downright at home. However the impudent little cur felt public opinion sufficiently to keep quiet for the rest of the evening. On the whole the Chamber is orderly and the class of member generally respectable. If the Speaker had a grain of tact or force it would be as orderly as at home. I went away when a commonplace speaker began to follow Reid.

Friday, September 9
We went in the morning for a walk in the Park and botanical gardens, which are very beautiful, on the slope down to the harbour where the British fleet is lying. No park at home equals it. There are fine walks, lawns to play on, classic statues to look at, fountains, monuments to Captain Cook and others, tropical and other flowers, shrubs, ferns, trees, various and innumerable.

In the afternoon I went down with Lord and Lady Hampden, one of the Miss Brands and the Minister of Education to Parramatta, an important town of the colony, once the seat of government, to see an athletic display of the children of elementary schools. It was a very jolly scene. They drilled, did dumbells, around the maypole, etc. in all sorts of costumes. I met the Chief Inspector, who rules Education in N.S.W. It is

[1] (1845–1927). Statesman. At that time Secretary of State for India.

entirely centralized, the Government inspectors managing the schools, appointing the teachers, etc. I have still to form an opinion as to the working. But I got well into the confidence of all the Education authorities, and had some good talk with the Parramatta Corporation, a collection of men exactly like the council of any good English town, the red bearded butcher, the solicitor, the fat publican, the non-con minister with white beard and shaven upper lip.

Saturday, September 10

Today I went for a short time to the races. I walked out the three miles, meeting on the way a sturdy, taciturn farmer, rather a dour but well-meaning companion, out of whom I got very little. He got a drink out of me. He came up every year for the races. But life was not very joyful to him. He did not seem to get much out of his farm, but cared less. He was not by way of betting largely. We sat talking on the grass of the flat till the bookees began to shout. Then I went into the paddock. The swells were dressed most absurdly smartly, ladies rustling, men in top hats and frock coats. But the crowd of reasonable people were merely black and billycocked. In front of the swellest part of the stand, I saw sitting on the grass with his hankerchief spread to keep off the damp a nice old bearded fellow, rather like a Cheviot farmer, in shabby brown hat. God knows who he was, perhaps the owner of a sheep-run; but quite at his ease sitting on his hankerchief while the swells were wondering whether they were looking a shade better than their neighbours. I only waited for one race and then came home in the train with two friendly policemen, discussing the relative merits of the Glasgow, London, Dublin, New York, and Sydney police-forces.

In the evening we all dined at Government House, a pleasant viceregal dinner, I sitting next Lady H. who is not clever but has interests. The family are rather delicate, and the daughters feeble but nice. A fellow Harrovian was there, who gave the prodigious news that Welldon[1] is to be Bishop of Calcutta. India *is* in luck. Curzon and Welldon to rule it and convert it. I can't help feeling that Welldon would be better as Governor General. My fellow Harrovian Capt. Vallenge had the same

[1] Head Master of Harrow School.

172

sentiments about modern Harrow as we have. Let G. O. T. look to it that he gets a master who will make 'Harrow as it ought for to be.'

Sunday, Sept. 11

Today we went out on the harbour in a government launch with the Premier, Want, Sir Julian Salomons, a leading lawyer who knows and admires Aunt Margaret, young Brand and Terry, leader of the Independents. The reason of Terry's presence was obvious. He and his votes decide the critical division. So Reid utilized the excuse that we wanted to see all the political people to ask him to a social entertainment, where champagne and good humour flowed free. I think it had a perceptible effect upon friend Terry. We had a very jolly cruise in the harbour, which is a most splendid place. We went up a rather wild arm of it, where the high banks are covered still with bush. There we had a splendid lunch, during which Sir Julian and Reid kept up a torrent of fun for half an hour. Sir Julian is an old man, and has been off his head once or twice, but is immoderately humorous when he gets off, rather like Father Healy without so much preparation. Reid has even subtler humour. I don't wonder he is Premier with his rough and ready wit. Want is a sardonic, big-browed, rather savage looking, full-trained Scotchman, a bad man to have as an enemy. Young Brand has feeble health I should think, but is an earnest soldier. He has been Adjutant of the 10th Hussars for four years and has now come out as his father's aide-de-camp. It was a capital day.

I dined at night with Sir Julian, where the talk was strenuous. He is a Jew and had one intelligent Jewish legal son-in-law, and another intelligent Gentile medical son-in-law-to-be in three days.

Monday, Sept. 12

Today I spent mainly on board H.M.S. Royal Arthur, where I was the guest of Captain Dicken from 11 till 2. Dicken commanded the flag-ship at the bombardment of Alexandria. He showed me everything, and we discussed naval matters, the lessons of the Spanish war, Mahan, big and small guns, the Admiralty, etc. After that I visited the naval stores and works on Garden Island, and saw another ship, made friends with several more officers, and walked from the landing stage with a very capable engineer officer, who explained engineer's grievances to me. It was a very profitable day of instruction in naval affairs. Perhaps nothing makes one feel England so strongly as the tremendous power and perfection of these men, and their ships 12,000 miles away from home.

In the evening I went to a grand ball in the Town Hall, Sydney, given by one of the Clubs. It was very like a Castle[1] ball, except that there were lots of sailors, from the Admiral to the middy, looking far the smartest and jolliest of all the lot. The Sydney girls I did not think as good-looking as Americans or English, and certainly not especially active or lithe. The colonial maiden is on the whole a disappointment. She is by no means modern in the sense of having activities and interests. She is entirely devoted to amusement and marrying. I speak only of the upper ten. The farmer's daughter, etc. works hard and is political and everything a colonial woman should be, at least in N.Z. But the average rich colonial girl is not a patch on the English girl, and not half so good a companion as the American.

Yours aff.
Charles Trevelyan

8. NEW SOUTH WALES EDUCATION

Tuesday, Sept. 13

This morning I had a long talk with the Chief Inspector of schools, practical controller of all the N.S.W. education.

In the afternoon we went to the House again, where the motion of want of confidence was proceeding. The chief speech of the day was by Wise, late member of the 86 Club, a fine cultivated fellow, who has come out here as a lawyer. He has had a considerable influence in politics, was in one of Parkes' administrations, pushed land taxation successfully. He is now Barton's chief ally. He hates and distrusts Reid. Tonight he made a very high-toned speech, which was fairly effective in

[1] Dublin Castle.

spite of being rather academic. He had prepared it carefully, and he had too much of an Oxford manner still. He is altogether a fine fellow; but not quite in easy touch with all manner of men. Reid interrupted him shamefully but very humorously, till the Speaker absolutely stopped him.

A labour man from the Broken Hill Silver mines, who had been imprisoned for strike agitation four years ago, spoke extremely well; and the minister for lands also did pretty well. On the whole the speaking was fairly high class.

Wednesday, Sept. 14

I spent another Education morning, seeing their best school in Sydney, where they have a Normal School, an Elementary school, with an Infant Dept, and about 500 boys and girls doing higher grade work, many of them preparatory to the University. Everything seemed very good to me, except the buildings which were a converted hospital and rather crowded. But the teaching was good and the teachers very nice people.

They excelled us in physical exercises; and the girls have a splendidly complete cookery course, including every sort of simple food an artisan or farmer would require, up to apple fritters, custard, chicken and bread sauce.

Menu being cooked the morning I went.

Oxtail Soup.
Cottage broth.
*
Fried Filets of fish.
*
Roast pork.
Roast Mutton.
Irish Stew.
Stewed Tripe & Onions.
Cutlets sauce piquante.
*
Apple Pie.
Currant Pudding.
Maccaroni Pudding.
Pancakes.

I then went on to see the clergyman who runs the Church organization for religious teaching in the schools. The clergy are allowed an hour to teach children willing to come, and in Sydney diocese great advantage is taken of it. I approve of the system. It seems to allay dissatisfaction and to work smoothly. The clergyman was a long white bearded Englishman, the best type of country clergyman in England. He was exceedingly willing to give me all the information I wanted.

In the evening I went for a short time to a music-hall, which was the Tivoli without the gaudiness. The songs were as inane and vulgar, with occasional sparkles of wit, the dresses and dancing were as indecent, and the tone as imperialist. Miss Britannia, with a Union Jack shield sat at the back, and two girls, wearing stars and stripes frocks, with parasols, Union Jack one side and Stars and Stripes the other, danced skirt dances, and sang how they had come from Frisco 'To see the Colonees.' Upon which the colonial youth cheered and felt he belonged to the Anglo-Saxon brotherhood. If they would never do worse than that!

Thursday, Sept. 15

We went to see the University in state. Reid drove us down in a carriage and pair. The University is of course paid for by the state. So Reid, the uncultured, the popularly humorous, the finely vulgar, is royalty, chancellor, Master of Trinity, and personified endowment rolled into one. All the big-wigs were there to receive us, Principal, and half a dozen professors, mostly in top hats and frock-coats. We were shown round everything and told everything. It was very comic to see Reid, with his queer eye-glass stuck into his eye peering contemptuously at Greek vases or book-shelves.

They have got a fine building, and a very fine hall, like any of our college halls at home. The Professors seemed very good men. But it is not the best way to see a varsity, and I hope to get to see some of the men when I get back from Brisbane. Here men destined for business do not go in for the Varsity as they do in America. There is co-education, about 60 women out of 400 students. There are three boarding colleges, denominational, Church, Wesleyan (or Presbyterian), and Catholic. Except in the Catholic, no one cares about the denomination, and freethinkers think freely at the Church college. There is a girl's college with 15 girls in it. Most of the students board at home or in the town.

In the evening I went to a government house ball. It was very bright, but not very interesting. I only found one girl worth anything, one non-butterfly. She was the daughter of a very wealthy run holder and farmer.

The government got a majority of four, which will carry them on. But if Barton gets in it will be a very ticklish session for them. At least I hope one result from the closeness of the division, that they may be able to make Reid act sincerely for Federation, even if he does not feel sincerely.

Friday, Sept. 16

I spent this morning in the Labour Department and at the Labour Bureau.

In the afternoon I had a walk with a fine young fellow, Bavin, who started a sort of Toynbee Hall here, and still with a few friends runs a Toynbee Society for social reform. He is rather hopeless about the educated Australian. He avers that they will not take things seriously, and that no one studies politics. I think he is too pessimistic. The political thinker has always had a good place in New South Wales. Lowe, Parkes, and now Wise and his friend Ashton (who supports Reid) all owed or owe their position primarily to real political insight. Australia stands half way between America and England, but nearer our English exactingness than American indifference.

Went with Wise to the National Art Gallery, where they have a lot of modern pictures. They have very few good ones, but just one or two quite good. But they have a very good selection of subject pictures, battles, mine disasters, etc., calculated to interest the colonial mind more than Watts or Turner.

Started this evening for Brisbane. I travelled in a Pullman, quite as comfortably as in America, except for more shaking. The Webbs had a compartment to themselves, a present from Reid.

Saturday, Sept. 17

We travelled all day getting in to Brisbane late at night. Most of the time we travelled through an endless forest of gum trees.

In some places the scenery was fine, though not very mountain-ous. All along at intervals there were prosperous looking settle-ments. Many huge tracts had been partially burnt out, the timber gradually rotting off and grass coming instead. There were cattle more or less throughout. There is no reason why in time the whole should not be cleared and make quite as good country as the grass land of Northumberland. After crossing the Queensland boundary we got into the Darling Downs, where the Darling rises that flows out with the Murray waters in South Australia. It is a splendid rich plain, mostly taken up by sheep and cattle runs; but beginning to be partitioned now by the state into smaller farms, which are being sown in wheat. In many places it begins to look like the American wheat states. The people look very comfortable and healthy. There are lots of happy looking children, the little girls all dressed in big brown straw hats that quite cover up the smallest ones. They are very English in look.

We were met at the station by a gentleman, who introduced Webb and myself to the Club before we went to bed.

Sunday, Sept. 18

In the morning I moved over to the Club, where as usual I was invited to stay if I wished. Brisbane is a nice clean city, built with no lack of space round the bends of a fine broad river as wide as the Thames above London. The houses are mostly wood, and almost all detached. The public buildings are in fine stone, rather impressive. They were built when money was plentiful before the hard times of 1893. There is a good botanical garden on the banks of the river. All round for many miles the country is scattered over with suburbs, and in the morning lots of buses and trains run in full of people, while numbers of men bicycle or ride in to their work along the very good roads they have made in strong contrast to America. The people all look healthy, though the girls have not got the fresh red complexion they have in New Zealand.

We were at once taken in hand by a very pleasant young member of the Legislative Assembly, Bell, who is a big station holder in the Darling Downs. He began by arranging a lunch for us in the Botanical Gardens where we met a lot of Educa-tionalists, Flint the head of the Technical School. Then a Miss

Sellars, who runs the Girl's Grammar School, a very bright, exciteable, competent woman, who took her degree the same year as I did in History. The master of the Boy's Grammar School was there too, a Mr. Roe, a very fine cultivated fellow, one of Jowett's men, who would not use his chances in England and become head master of Dulwich and Harrow, because he would not clothe himself in black. So he has come out to this new land where the sectaries are at a discount, and is one of the most respected men in Brisbane. The Education here is good. The primary is all free and secular, though the priest may come in if he can get children to stay after school-hours. There are a fair number of scholarships to the grammar schools, which are very good, thanks to Roe and Miss Sellars. But there are not enough. There is as yet no University, and the better men go to Sydney. The Education Minister is a violent individualist; but the present Premier, Byrnes, is a man who has been through the Education mill, from the lowest by means of state scholarships. And he is going to force on a university.

We went to tea with Sir Samuel Griffith, the Chief Justice, and late premier, who has been much the ablest of the Queensland politicians. If he had been in the government there would probably have been no refusal on the part of Queensland to come into the Federation Conference.

Monday, Sept. 19

We lunched again with Bell today to meet two labour men. Politics here are very dead. There is a government, which does nothing and is very Conservative, opposed by a compact labour party of 20 out of 70 members, which is respectable but quite incompetent. The present party with various ministers has been in power for eight years or so. It has done almost nothing, and is furiously anti-labour. During the shearers' strike of '93 they passed a regular Irish Coercion Law to suppress the strikers. They taboo all social reform. They maintain a bad electoral system, which is far the least popular of any colony. This situation has been brought about partly by the extreme revolutionary socialistic programmes of the labour party in the early '90's. The property people were frightened, and there was no Reeves or Seddon or Turner to come forward and moderate and lead the labour men. So a class cleavage took place, which

179

shows no particular signs of being healed, though the bitterness is out of the contest. The labour party are lead by a Mr. Glassey, who is a Northumberland miner, an admirer of G. O. T., once Burt Election Secretary; but a man who has taken up extreme ideas with not a particle of practical ability. He is like Keir Hardie in genuineness and in competence, with Hardie's eloquence and nobility. He really believes he is going to be Premier. He makes no attempt to conciliate any part of the moderate people and blunders along in Parliament. They never introduce any effective legislation, which they well might do as the government does very little. There is time for discussion. But that time they spend in talking, not about big reform, but on points of order and senseless objections to such motions as the vote of condolence with the Austrian Emperor. The government is very poor material. There are very few squatters in it. But the big squatter bosses the government. The Premier, Byrnes, we did not see, because he had got the measles! The chief reason why the government has a peaceable time is that the land laws are on the whole very good, which is of course the thing of first importance to any of the colonies where settlement is going on rapidly.

In the afternoon I went through the grammar schools with Miss Sellars and Mr. Roe. After tea I went for a jolly row on the river with Roe. As we were coming away, he said that he was going to call on a Mrs. Waugh, a sister of Mrs. Holman Hunt. I went in with him, and found a charming old lady, who had come out with her doctor husband for the sake of his health long ago, when Mrs. Holman Hunt was a girl of 13. She had never been home since, but knew all about everybody, and was enormously interested in hearing about Bell Scott's[1] pictures and Woolner's[1] statue, about which she had heard much. She knew whose head the lady with the child is taken from. I must get the name from her. Woolner was out here for a bit as a young man. There is a statue of Godley by him in Christchurch N.Z., and a fine statue of Cook, a photo of which I think I sent you, in Sydney. It was curious to meet this fine old lady so far away. She and Mr. Roe run a very successful literary society which reads plays and poems etc, and fulfils a need which Australia has for cultivation.

[1] Work of Pre-Raphaelite artists, at Wallington.

Tuesday, Sept. 20

The morning I spent in the public departments, chiefly land and education. I also had a long talk with some of the Editors of the labour newspaper, the Worker.

In the afternoon we went to the House of Representatives, which is a fine chamber in a very effective stone palace. The debate was not worthy of the chamber. For more than an hour the Labour party challenged a ruling of the Speaker. I think he was right. In any case it was absurd waste of time and atrociously bad tactics to attack him, which they did respectfully enough but at enormous length. Two of the government spoke, very tactlessly, and after an hour I went in despair. It comes of their having nothing serious to discuss. They all badly want a commanding man, and then they might do something.

Saw a very able editor, Ward, of the Brisbane 'Courier.' I had a long talk with him, especially about the syndicate to which Joe C.[1] has got monopoly rights of settlement given in New Guinea. The Australians are very angry. I think I shall probably write a letter home about it, unless I have reason to modify my opinion.

Wednesday, Sept. 21

Cycled to a mountain five miles off and got a fine view of Brisbane and its winding river, and the settled country all round, with fine ranges of hills behind, covered by the still uncleared gum-tree. The gum or eucalyptus is not as fine as our forest trees, but it clothes the country well, and gives it a green and comfortable look all the year round. It is evergreen, and in masses is as good as any other foliage, though each separate tree has no grace of form.

Saw the under-secretary of the Home Dept, the best man in the Civil Service, and then to lunch with the Lamingtons. L. (late Baillie-Cochran of St. Pancras Division of London, England) desired to be remembered to G. O. T. He was quite uninteresting, is said to be very fast, as is his A.D.C., has a nice young wife, a Lanark Hozier, and is an altogether useless figurehead for the noble colony of Queensland.

[1] Joseph Chamberlain (1836–1914) Statesman. At that time Secretary of State for the Colonies.

In the afternoon I had a long talk with Griffith, the Chief Justice, and spent the evening at the Waughs, whom I got to like still more. Mind you tell Mrs. Holman Hunt of the meeting. It will interest her.

Thursday, Sept. 22

Having had just about the right amount of Brisbane, I went off with Bell, to stay with him at his home and station on the Darling Downs. He is member for the district, and I accompanied him first to see his constituents. We travelled the best part of the day to Dalby, the chief town of his constituency, which is rather a small one as Queensland constituencies go. It is about 70 miles each way and contained 900 voters. Electioneering is chiefly a matter of personal contact and doing of jobs for the constituents. Bell is upright and honourable. He knows something of politics and leans to Liberalism. But he is not strong enough to have a policy. So he likes the rest wins and keeps his constituency by what he gets done for them. He has just succeeded in getting a house for consumptives built by the government near Dalby, which is expected to bring money into the district and therefore to profit him at election time.

In the evening we went to a Masonic Ball in Dalby. They had rather exclusive prices, so that it was not as representative as it might have been. The most important people were Bell and his station manager, with two Brisbane girls who were staying with them and the manager's wife. The rest were local tradesmen, bank-clerks, daughters of publicans. It was very good fun. Some of the girls were very nice, some extremely silly. One particularly amused me who did her hair in curly bunches on each side of her head like a Miss Austen young lady, and seemed to think that America was a city, did not know what M.C. meant and was generally in a primitive state of culture. But she is not typical of Australia. The entire absence of class feeling was very striking. They all dance very well. It is the passion of Australia. They have ten dances to one that there would be in an English country place.

Friday, Sept. 23

Before starting for Jimbour, Bell's place, I helped him to interview the Dalby Corporation, a solid stupid lot of tradesmen (so absolutely English) with a talkative Irishman who acted as spokesman. One of them had a relation in Halifax of which I made due note. They discussed a local land question, with the same intense practicality and littleness of mind that is usual in vestries. I helped them out by knowing their land laws better than they did. Then we had drinks and I photographed them.

After that we drove off in a four in hand buggy, with the manager's wife and the two young ladies. Most of the way we drove down a road about 300 yards across, railed off from the station. They have their roads this width in order to drive stock the huge distances they have to travel. The road runs quite straight across the plain, and by a curious mirage effect, as it got some miles away the rails on either side and the telegraph posts, seemed raised up from the ground and running along with a big gap between them and the earth.

After a fourteen mile drive we got to the station, which is on the slope of some hills and overlooks the plain. It is a big stone English country house, that might be anywhere in Northumberland and not ashamed of itself. It was built by Bell's father who died recently. He was Agent General for some years, and consequently his sons were educated at Cambridge. The pictures and books in the house show that he was an interesting and cultivated man. But more of the station in my next letter.

Yours aff.
Charles Trevelyan

9. THE DARLING DOWNS: BUSHRANGING

Friday, Sept. 23

In my last letter I got myself to *Jimbour*. First to describe the station itself. It stands on a gentle slope on the edge of the great bare plains. Directly the plains end, the trees begin. They grow about as thickly as in an apple orchard, and all the country, except for a few patches of scrub, feeds sheep and cattle. The station, or houses of the station cover several acres. The buildings are dotted about higgledy piggledy. Here stands the single men's lodging, a long building with several rooms. Here is the blacksmith's shop, the ground round littered with agricultural machinery. Here are two or three neat cottages with bits of garden and untidy hen-coops. Next is the cook's kitchen and dining place for the men. Opposite is the store, full of all necessities, with a reading room at one end, much frequented at night by the older men, at the other end the post office and office of the station. Near by is a large stable with several pens, always tenanted by shaggy coated horses. A little apart is the house of the Manager, a bright little wooden house, with tin roof and clean veranda, with a garden full of flowers and gorgeous shrubs. The manager is a Scotchman who loves Burns, and has a very bright pleasant wife, who reads a good deal and is the life of the station. But she does *not* like Burns. It is her only failing. A little higher up the hill is another very pretty cottage of the overseer, Mr. Cassidy, a very red-faced, white-bearded, jolly, talkative Irishman of 60, with a charming wife of 35 or thereabouts and three pretty healthy children. Cassidy comes from Fermanagh. He might have been a bitter or a cringing and ignorant peasant with a miserable and over-rented 30 acre farm at home, unsuspected of ability to do anything but hoe a potato patch. Here he is a respected and self-respecting compe-tent ranger of tens of thousands of acres. Near by is the school, where is a master, paid well over £100 a year for teaching 25 children. A little further on is the big house, built by Sir J. Bell who first came to the station, who was agent general for Queens-land but is now dead. Lady Bell is a tall rather sad widow, who talks of the good old days rather, but is throughout an English lady. She has a daughter, unfortunately absent visiting a son many hundreds of miles away in the north west, accessible only by a week's journeying by boat, train and buggy. There are two sons at home, my friend, who is member for the county, somewhat pompous but a sterling sort, and a jolly bouncing junior with a cracked voice with which he laughs boisterously, who does nothing but farm and prefers it to everything else. The house is a regular stone country house, with a suite of big rooms on the ground floor, and above huge bedrooms as large as Bob's at Wallington. In the good old days, that Lady Bell deplores, it was a great centre of hospitality. Now they are rather reduced in circumstances. But instead of keeping up a sham and ruinous gentility and the sons doing nothing, they live quite inexpensively and the sons work. The servants consist of a black cook who cooks atrociously, but is soon going to be changed; of Jenice, a dear old Irish retainer, once a nurse, the Booa of the establishment; one nice white boy; and lastly the most delightful little black buttons, called Kar-Kar, who waits at table with perfect gravity, pours out wine most discreetly into glasses that stand the height of his head, and grins beautifully when spoken to. When he is not waiting Thomas becomes Tummas; the buttons fly off, and Kar-Kar runs out to dig in his garden, where he grows 'smartoes' and 'parrowgrass', with bare black legs and sleeves rolled up. Sometimes he goes and captures the horses in the paddock and rides them in bareback, looking like a big fly on their backs. He is quite as nice a boy as any American nigger-boy could be. A few of his hideous compatriots camp in bark tents behind the house; but they are no good to anyone and just live and let live. This is the community where I have lived for a week. It is as civilized as any country village in England. It is not a wild, outlandish place. There is a daily post, and a yesterdaily paper, a telegraph, a fortnightly man of God, a better school than the average English country school, a reading room and novel library, a good modern library at the hall, poets and current literature at Taylor's the manager's. We dress for dinner, and discourse after dinner on every modern topic from Cuba to state regulation of breeding. The main differences between this Queensland country house and a Northumberland one are – first, that the country gentlemen are not only rent-receivers, but ride out in the morning in their shirt-sleeves; and secondly, that, instead of 14,000 acres, the estate consists of 150,000.

This evening I went to see two men shearing the rams. They do it slowly and carefully compared with the hurried way in which the great mass are shorn. The fathers of the flock, who have horns something like those of McCracken's prize winners, must not be cut by hurried slipping shears.

Saturday, Sept. 24

This morning I rode out with Bell to look at some horses of his in a big paddock about the size of Harwood. We had a grand gallop. First we went through an open plain of very Northumbrian looking white grass. Then we went into the bush, still grass land, but with the apple-orchard arrangement of gum trees. As we went along four kangaroos jumped up 150 yards in front. I gave chase, but as the ground was rough, they soon got far away with their tremendous hops. In a piece of scrub, or thick undergrowth, we saw a lot of wallabies, a small kind of Kangaroo, and several white screeching cockatoos.

We had out with us a nice lad who looked after the horses. Directly after we got home, the alarm was given, and we found him lying with his leg broken near the house. He had been exercising a half-broken horse that had bolted and bashed him against a tree. We all turned out, and the station cook most successfully set his leg and tied it up, and he was driven off to Dalby hospital, 16 miles off. Next day we heard that the job had been so well done by the cook that the doctors did not need to do more than put on splints.

Sunday, Sept. 25

Went a ride of twenty miles with Bell and Cassidy away from the plain. We rode some miles through the bush, and then came out into an open valley about six miles long, at the back of which the mountains began rising up to about 3,000 ft. It is a very fine scene. The valley is full of prosperous small settlers, with farms from 300 to 2000 acres. We saw an intelligent, well-read old Irishman, who had quite a political library and roasted Macaulay for unfairness to the heroes of the unsuccessful party at the Boyne River. He again might have stayed at Fermanagh; where, if he had not become a Parnellite member, he would certainly have shot his landlord in 1881. As it was he was a slightly cantankerous, thoroughly valuable citizen. There were several other Irishmen doing really well on the land. There was a good little school. We had a cold lunch and tea, which is the drink here at every meal, at one of the settler's houses, by the side of a beautiful tree-girt plain with blue mountains in the distance. Then we rode homewards and met Taylor and the ladies and had tea by the last rays of the sun, after boiling the 'billy' in the open air. Then we rode home by the moon's pale light. Soon after we got in there was a tremendous thunderstorm. All the evening long the lightning flashed gloriously over the plain. The godly attended church, where the

Presbyterian minister had a short word. The ungodly read Lecky's Rationalism.

Monday, Sept. 26

So much rain had fallen in the night, that there would be several inches of mud to drive through on the plains. So I made it my excuse to the Webbs for not going to the Blue Mountains, and I stayed here. Most of the work of the station was stopped by the wet, so I went out with Taylor to shoot a plain turkey. The turkey is as big as a capercailzie and as wary as a black-cock. There are no hedges in the plains to stalk him by and he has to be approached on horseback or by buggy. So we went out with our guns on our saddle-bows, or poised like the carbines of cavalry scouts. We failed of our wild turkeys. But we attacked the pigeons of the farm, as we used to do after a Blackcock shoot. I slew six pigeons, the only slaying I have done this year.

Tuesday, Sept. 27

I went in early to see the school, and heard the usual things that are being taught to Anglo-Saxon children whether in Popham Road or Maida Hill bush-school. The sun never sets on the mental arithmetic class.

Then I rode off eleven miles with the jolly, farming brother to a distant paddock to muster cattle, which he was going to sell. He expected two men to help him; but as they did not turn up, I had to help him. It was glorious fun herding 250 bullocks and cutting out the cows from the herd. I got highly commended and shall apply for a post of stock-driver if all else fails. I rode home after we had mustered, leaving Oswald Bell to sleep the night out in a ruined cabin covered with bark. He told me afterwards that the men turned up who should have helped us, and that one Cameron from Scotland was bitterly disappointed at missing me. He had been expecting to have a bit of argument on politics, my fame being pretty widely spread apparently, through newspapers and other agencies.

On the way back I met Bell senior and two of the ladies riding. They had just killed a snake. We rode back by moon-light. I spent the evening at Taylor's, where Mrs. Taylor was very charming and lively. We ended up with auld Scotch drink.

187

Wednesday, Sept. 28

Today we spent collecting horses. I went out with Bell and two ladies. We got into a huge paddock, half of it bush, as large as Greenleighton or larger. We separated into couples and went after horses to drive them to a trysting place. It was the greatest sport. Directly you found a herd and began to drive them, they would start off at a canter for the nearest bush and you had to tear off at a gallop and head them out of the wood, repeating the experiment half a dozen times. Finally we selected and drove six of them home. I came to the conclusion that I handled them more delicately than Bell. I think I am a gifted drover.

Thursday, Sept. 29

Got up early and shot a cockatoo for Miss McIlwraith. They infest the fields in hundreds like flocks of rooks. They are white with yellow wings and crests. After breakfast I drove off with Oswald Bell to Dalby. Near there I saw a big shearing going on. About 20 shearers were employed, with attendant 'rouse-abouts,' as they are called, men who collect the wool, etc. It is wonderful to see them at work. The best man in the shed shears about 140 a day. The slower men do as low as 80. I timed the best doing one in $3\frac{1}{2}$ minutes. They cut the sheep a good deal in doing it, though Bell says not more than usual. A boy stands ready with a pot of tar to dab on any specially bad wound. On one side of the shed is a sorter who stands at a table and receives the fleece and classifies it according to its thickness and cleanliness. The men are mostly selectors, or small farmers, who shear for some months and farm the rest. In the wilder west they are a rougher more wandering lot. They are strongly organised and there have been great strikes. Things are not yet what they should be. But they looked a fine prosperous lot of men, and they *did* work. They are paid by the piece, 4/- a score of sheep shorn. So they earn from 16/- to 28/- a day.

There I saw the last of Queensland station life. For I took the train from the station, getting into a single carriage at the end of a long luggage train, entirely composed of waggons packed with wool coming from the furthest west. We went very slowly, at North British pace. Tonight I am at *Toowoomba*, a prosperous farming and railway centre of Queensland. A very good week it has been.

Yours aff.
Charles Trevelyan

10. BACK IN SYDNEY

Friday, Sept. 30

I have not got an exciting letter this time. So do not let expectation rise too high, my family. I have come back to the sober monotony of a capital city after bushranging. I had a prosaic journey back to Sydney. But – by the way – before I left Toowoomba I went to see an Australian poet, who as a reward for his poetry has been given a registry of Births, Deaths and Marriages. Mr. Essex Evans and I talked about the future of Australian literature. At present there are only a few minor poets, who have the merit of simplicity. They try to paint bush life. They are unimaginative but fairly true and do not strain themselves by trying dramas or epics or anything which budding intellect is apt to try imitatively. A couple of Gordon's poems are all that really are worth reading except for the Literary student who is watching the development of colonial intellect. Bolderwood is the best of their writers. I am reading all his books, and in Australia they seem even better than at home. Again there is no play of imagination. A school-boy could invent the stories and incidents. But the picture of Australia is literal and loving. 'The Colonial Reformer' is not the best story, but every 'new chum' ought to read it before landing. Essex Evans and I parted with a promise of his works to me on his part, and of Bob's poems to him on mine.

Byrnes Premier of Queensland has died, an Irish Catholic by descent and Catholic still by religion. He was Premier at 38 with no jealousy of older men. He was, all say, a big man, whom certainly among the horde of very insignificant men they have got in Parliament they can hardly afford to lose.

Saturday, Oct. 1

Got back to Sydney.

Sunday, Oct. 2

Moved to Government House, where everything is very hospitable. Hampden is ready to talk. He is anxious to become Liberal again, and thinks he can do so if Home Rule is dropped. I do not discourage him, but if it were not for the marvellous capacity of our public-spirited country gentlemen to accept tendencies they utterly distrust, I should have no hope. He is a Tory for me and my efforts. Trade Unionism, Payment of Members, State Regulation, and Death Duties are all the risky tendencies of modern Radicalism. And yet numbers of these men, such is their public-spirit and final broad-mindedness, shall learn to rejoice in these heresies. I am slowly learning to treat these very tender babes of progress judiciously. But it irks. With an opponent one can boldly state fundamentals and fight for them. With a half friend one has to graft the new ideas onto the old. Here of course no one supposes he is anything but a Tory. My God, what a man Gladstone was to keep shoals of these excellent fellows trotting at the heels of his revolutions!

Monday, Oct. 3

Today is Eight Hours Day, a public bank holiday by law. The trades march in procession from the Trades' hall to the Agricultural ground. They have a lunch for the secretaries and committees, where the leaders of political parties come and make non-committal speeches. Then in the afternoon there are sports. It sounds very wonderful and awful to reactionary ears that the state should recognize the triumph of Eight Hours. But the individualist takes heart when he finds that it has all been by so-called 'voluntary effort,' which I heard explained with gusto by Lord Hampden. I was so well satisfied with this evidence of the strength of democracy in Australia when it chooses to rise and shake its mane, that I did not trouble to point out that said 'voluntary effort' still left busmen on the box-seat, and shop-assistants behind the counter, and barmaids at the bar 12 and 15 hours a day; that there was grumbling among lots of the keener workmen that the day ought to be used to preach eight hours instead of sitting contented with half-measures. The truth is they are not so very well forward here. The Sydney Unionists are a rather poor lot. They have only just got a

190

Factory Act, enforced in only one district. They have only just got a Miner's Regulation Act, which is permissive instead of compulsory, and the enforcement of one of the clauses of which is probably going immediately to result in a big lock-out at Newcastle. However an Eight Hours Day is a fine sign. It bodes more for the future than many Factory clauses. The Webbs complain that these people are not really progressive. They have the efficiency of expert inspectors too much on the brain. They do not reckon the small power of resistance there is in the Tory classes when there is a real crisis. If the people had wanted factory laws as much as land laws, they would be far ahead of any other country. The land laws, which in early stages were all in the interests of the 'fat man,' i.e. the big squatter, are now in New Zealand, Queensland and New South Wales, proofs of the deep and wise democracy of the government. In the last ten years each colony has codified its land laws, all tending to helping the small man, to discouraging speculation, to keeping the land in the hands of the state, to turning large runs into populous settlements. The more I look into them, the more proud I am of the political talent of our countrymen out here in the question of most vital interest to them. That the Trade Unions celebrate Eight Hour's Day, organize Sports as popular as the races, and get His Excellency Lord Hampden, Queen's representative and head of squatter and other 'fat' society to patronize them, makes it clear that if needful they will codify factory law as rigorously as the laws of land selection, whenever the worker ceases to be as lethargic as he is apt to be at present. I had a long talk to a Newcastle socialist, with the usual hot eye and contemptuous lip known in Halifax and Glasgow, who had refused to drink the Queen's health at the lunch among his too complaisant fellow-working men. As I expected, when stroked the way the bristles lay, he turned out to be reasonable enough. He would be quite loyal to any New South Wales Reeves who came along but had a little too much iron in his soul to appreciate what I was rejoicing in; the happy greedy children and laughing well-dressed girls and prosperous parents who were crowding the ring, and showing the real reason why a social reformer had got to wait a bit before he could get his leverage.

On my way home I went to see a pleasant family called Garron, the father a wise old politician in the legislative council, the son an intelligent fellow, who has written much on Federation, and been in the thick, in secretarial capacity, of the Federal Conventions. There I talked considerably. I do not feel moved to discourse on Federation here. It is not in a picturesque stage, very much practical. They are squaring existing interests. They are all agreed on the ultimate advantage and theoretic grandeur.

Tuesday, Oct. 4

Walked in the morning in the botanical gardens with Ashton, most promising of young N.S.W. politicians. Smoking is forbidden, presumably for fear of cigar-ends. So we bought twelve oranges for sixpence and littered the ground with twelve skins, discussing land, labour and federation meanwhile.

In the afternoon I went to the University with Bourin, and saw the Colleges, two halls one Presbyterian and the other Episcopalian, containing some 15 students each, out of the total 250. They do not demand subscription to the 39 articles very strictly or the Auld Kirk equivalent, as they have so many rooms still untenanted. The men are simple and hard-working. But they do not understand Universities as well as the Americans.

In the evening I went with Lord Hampden to see an Exhibition of old books and N.S. Wales papers, etc. at a Conversation of a Free Library convention, a creditable collection and gathering.

Wednesday, Oct. 5

I went to see the annual Art Gallery of Sydney. It is exactly like the poems and the novels. They love their country and try with varying success to paint it faithfully. There is no imagination, no religion. There was hardly a single subject picture. It was all bush or coast scenery. The flights of imagination where they were attempted were appalling. 'The Australian Artist dreaming of Europe –' a young man in a faultless black-coat sitting in front of his easel, sleeping stiffly on his arm. Round him hovered two hideous phantoms of a Raphael mother and Murillo's virgin, while Cologne Cathedral towered behind. Two or three artists had real merit, and chiefly as reminiscence I have bought for 10 guineas a little picture by Gordon Gouths which is a very true representation of the bush. It was the best but one in the gallery, and the other was beyond my means. It will bring back to me the hanging gum trees when I am at home. I am shipping it to Grosvenor Crescent.

I dined with the Garrans and talked.

Thursday, Oct. 6

Talked with the Giffen of Australia, Coglan, Government statistician, chiefly about the finance of federation.

Lunched with the literature professor of the University and three others, mostly Scotch, and talked of American Universities. Had tea with a fine young engineer, who practically bosses the repairing yard for the Australian fleet. Dined with the officers of the 'Katoomba' at mess, said 'Chin-chin' before I drank and talked Santiago.

In the evening I went to hear a censure motion at the House against Reid for sending down his minister of Works to influence the election, where Barton, the Federation leader, was returned, by promises of public works. I there met Barton, and heard him speak. He reminds me very much of Bryan. But more of him when I have seen more of him. He did not speak specially well. Reid was as usual gorgeously humorous. He drew a beautiful picture of Barton surrounded by his 'perspiring parasites' on election day, excitedly reporting exaggerations of what the Work's minister had said. The House sat till nine this morning, when it divided. They copy the vices as well as the virtues of the mother of Parliaments. They have not yet found that she now goes to bed at reasonable hours, so they are still loyal to the practices of the baneful years of the Irish obstruction.

Friday, Oct. 7

Loafed.

Saturday, Oct. 8

Today I lunched with Barton, the great hero of federation and spent the afternoon with him till past six o'clock, talking politics. He is a fine sort of man, much more of a statesman than Reid. He is quite fit to be the first Premier of Australia, if that is his fate. He is somewhat Conservative in mind. He would not

193

be a driving force for big social changes. But he has large sympathies and would in England be a Liberal. His manner is rather heavy and I should not have guessed him eloquent. But he is keen to learn and discuss. He is very modest, though ambitious for his cause. He is the best Colonial politician I have met except Reeves, and would take a place among our home people. As we were coming back from a walk in the gardens an oldish man stopped him and congratulated him on his return to Parliament. The oldish man was son of 'non mi ricordo.'[1] An odd ancestry to be famous because of.

Yours aff.
Charles Trevelyan

11. LIFE ON A STATION

Sunday, Oct. 9

I gave a farewell party to three or four of my Sydney friends. I got a launch from the government trustees of the National Park, which is a large forest reserve, round a river inlet ten miles south of Sydney. Ashton, the most promising of young N.S.W. politicians arranged it and got a feed prepared at the Trustees cottage. We went down by train, passing Botany Bay. We sailed about all day in a little oil launch, fished unsuccessfully, talked, and looked at the scenery, which was very fine, wooded hillsides rising straight from the water. In the evening we left for the Riverina, the district between the Murray and Murrinbridgee on the other side of the Blue Mountains. I branched off from the main line at Junee Junction in the early morning of

Monday, Oct. 10

We travelled all day, we being myself, a local solicitor from Berrigan, a bank-manager, Lysaght, of considerable ability, Mr. Horsfall, the largest squatter of district and others. All day long we were going through interminable bush country, that is to say fields, scattered over more or less thickly with gum-trees.

[1] (I do not remember). The unvarying answer of the Italian courier at Queen Caroline's trial in 1820.

In large tracts the trees are dead, having been ring-barked or chipped all round with an axe so as to stop the sap reaching the branches. As time goes on they get burnt, or rot away or are eaten out by the white-ant. Part of the country has been completely cleared where they are growing wheat. But all of it now is settled. It is going to be one of the great granaries of the world, although it is subject to periodic droughts, of which this year is the worst on record. When we had passed Narrandera, the grass began to look more and more parched, looking much like the space in Hyde Park opposite the cavalry barracks when at its barest and hottest in July or August. Mr. Horsfall was selling several thousand sheep, and was satisfied that he could now tide over the worst possible summer, even if it did not rain again till March.

In the evening we arrived at Berrigan, a small country town, composed of a shop street, three Hotels, two chapels, an R. C. church, the only brick building finished, an Art School and Library in brick just rising, and a few other houses. Everything looked clean and prosperous. The Hotel we went to was quite excellent, like the best English country Inn. There were three quite good billiard tables in the town. The people were thoroughly alive and intelligent. There was a travelling company acting the adventures of Bushranger Kelly in the town hall. We heard volleys at intervals, which showed that a most realistic melodrama was in progress. He is at present the only national hero who has become mythical. He will gradually become a Robin Hood I expect. Almost every bush town claims that it was the scene of some of his chief exploits. The only objection to Berrigan is an insufficient water-supply. There are baths but no water. Already they are fetching water by train from Narrandera for many of the houses! They had to do so for two months last year and will probably have to do it for four this year.

The most important people in the town are the Hotel keepers. The Australian is not a temperance man. At the stations there is no drinking allowed. Tea is the universal drink in the bush. Each man 'boils his billy' over the wood fire three or four times a day and drinks two or three mug fulls of tea. Beer or whiskey do not go into the bush. But when the shearer gets his cheque for £15 for a fortnight's shearing, or the station hand gets his quarterly wage, he goes off to the nearest town, hands the cheque to the publican, and gets gloriously drunk, till the publican thinks he has had enough for his money. Then he is kicked out, and goes back to the station or onto the next wool-shed, a sadder if not wiser man for another bout of sobriety.

This habit is not yet breaking much, though there are a few more sober ones than in early days. But the custom has its advantages over the old world habit of permanent boozing. Most of a man's life is spent in strenuous and sober work. Some-times he must relax. There is nothing that offers but drink. Life is so dull in the bush. If only however the better man could be shown ways of improvement and amusement there is a far better chance of a sober custom prevailing, where everyone is trained to an enforced sobriety during three quarters of the year or more. The English aristocracy, a century ago the most daring drunkards of history are now the most sober set ever in high places. Change conditions and opinion somewhat, and there is a good chance for the bushman.

Tuesday, Oct. 11

Lysaght took me a drive round Berrigan among the farmers. It is an awful year. Most of the crops will absolutely fail from want of water. But no one grumbled hopelessly like the British farmer. They are so certain of recouping their losses in a good year that they do not despair even in this third year of drought. We had lunch with two fine English fellows from Clifton, who were working away in the bush on a farm of 3000 acres. They had a comfortable three roomed wooden house with a corru-gated iron roof. The walls were hung with public-schools groups, the mantlepiece loaded with family photos and selec-tions of pipes. They were quite happy in their life. Occasionally they go off to some tennis tournament or party at a large station, where they play and dance and talk about Sydney and England, and perhaps get married. The big, healthy, muscular giants are far better off than as hard-ground clerks or un-successful lawyers or vulgar stockbrokers in London. They would have pleased MacTaggart these big Cliftonians.

In the afternoon I drove out to the station where Carrington, brother of Lord C., lives. It is a curious fate for a swell Whig M.P. But he seems to like it. He has married a nice but common,

196

fashionable little woman, daughter of Horsfall the great local squatter. He has settled on one of the Horsfall stations and looks after its 30,000 acres. He has got a comfortable wooden and corrugated-iron house. He seems perfectly content riding about buying and selling sheep, looking after wheat-fields, etc. He is very anxious to be remembered to you G. O. T. His liveliest interest is in English politics. He has a way of grumbling at everybody especially Gladstone. He is an arrant Whig, rather of the Hartington sort, caring chiefly about Whips and party management, dislikes Gladstone for splitting the party not for bringing in Home Rule. He reads French memoirs and argues everything. There is one boy whom they spoil. For some weeks in the year they live in Sydney or Melbourne, which she lives for, though he is less enthusiastic. But he allows himself to be led about to parties. Somehow this country life is very ennobling, making contented simple fellows out of the biggest of swells.

Wednesday, Oct. 12

Spent the day driving and riding about the station. A large part of the land is let to what they call 'halves-men', yearly tenants who have half the seed given them, and provide the rest of the plant, and then give half the produce to the landlord. It is a sort of metayer system. I don't much like it. It will not create as independent a set as the freehold or state selector. Carrington is far from being a mere rent-collector yet. But it is the beginning of our plan, which there is no need to introduce, with all its disadvantages, here. The crops are hopeless this year. Most of them are already parched and yellow only six inches from the ground. Here and there a few ears will show if they have some rain which is not likely. They will turn the sheep onto the corn within three weeks and give up the crop altogether. I had never seen the desolation of drought before. There is enough grass just to keep the sheep going through the next four summer months. But all the ponds are dry, and they are now pumping up every drop of water from wells which Carrington wisely sunk last year. All night the sheep feed. Early in the morning they trot off to the troughs or ponds which are filled from the wells, drink their fill and lie down in any available shade till the heat of the day is past, then go off again to their feeding-grounds.

In good years the grass comes up to your knees at this time of year. Now there is none in some paddocks and only an inch in the best.

My companion was a young Australian, book-keeper for Carrington. He was taking to reading. But he could only get novels, and was reading 'Gerard Eversley', Welldon's production!! He thought it got rather religious at the end, and I advised him to get through it quickly. I gave him some advice as to a course of history reading. In America he would have been to a University.

The clergyman of the Berrigan church came to lunch with Mrs. Carrington. He might have come from Hampton Lucy or Weston Zoyland. He was a pompous religious ass, who said he had always been loyal to the Primrose League, who had plans for raffles to raise money for his church, which he discussed with Mrs. C. He might have walked out of the Austen drawing-room. And the fellow was in the Australian bush, among the new, common-sense, emancipated, Anglo-Saxon. They'll tolerate him all right. But poor dunder-headed old church of England, discussing raffles in the bush! The book-keeper and I had a good laugh at him as we galloped off after lunch.

Thursday, Oct. 13

Did nothing. It was the hottest day I have ever suffered. It was 92 in the shade. There was a hot wind blowing, like a breath from one of Keith's hot-houses. No it was more scorching than that. May I never be condemned to live on Australian plains. But I suppose three months of such weather, especially if you have plenty to do, are not worse for a man than three months of unremitting frost.

Friday, Oct. 14

In the morning there was thunder, which cleared the air, and a little rain. It made the drive in to *Yaurawonga*, 32 miles, quite pleasant. As the sun was setting I crossed the Murray, a beautiful wooded stream (about the size of the Thames at Oxford), flowing lazily down its earlier courses. Very comfortable hotel, managed by an excellent Irish family. I beat the marker and a commercial traveller at billiards. The table would not have dissatisfied Roberts.

Friday, Oct. 14

Up very early. Breakfasted after three hours railway at Benalla on the main line, where I met the Webbs again, who had been at other stations, near Wagga-Wagga. In to Melbourne, reading 'Son Excellence Eugene Roryon', long recommended to me by G. O. T. Nothing can beat the scene of Roryon in his Cabinet transacting public business.

Of Melbourne–hereafter.

Yours aff.
Charles Trevelyan

12. LIFE IN MELBOURNE

Saturday, October 15

Melbourne is like an American city, with broad streets running all at right angles, with cable cars whirring up and down, with towering business houses and giant banks. But the people are British. I am staying at this Club which is reputed to be the best in Australia. It is almost as luxurious as Brooks's, there are almost the same proportion of old fogies; but there are enough men of vigour to keep the place alive, and you can hear the approach of a waiter on the not too Turkey carpet. Still no Unionist peer could fail to recognize the ideal comfort of the Melbourne Club.

I was immediately met by Moore, late of King's and the Eighty Club, protégé of the OB,[1] Historical Society man, etc. He is law professor at the University, and has made himself a considerable position here, being very able and wise and humorous to boot. He is taking any amount of trouble to apprize people of my arrival, and to explain things to me.

This afternoon I went to see a cricket match, with an aristocratic Roman Catholic swell, son of a legislator. The cricket was first-rate. But except on very great occasions, such as test matches with English teams, they only play every Saturday,

[1] Oscar Browning (1837–1923). Schoolmaster at Eton, Fellow of King's College, Cambridge, historian and educationist. A man of wide friendships and practical philanthropy.

beginning about three o'clock. There are hardly any professionals, and there is no large leisured class. My aristocratic R.C. friend said that last year he played a match. His side won the toss on Dec. 5. Their batsmen stuck, and he got his innings on about January 8. I was surprised how few people were looking on, only a scattered hundred or so. But they love racing even more than cricket, and there were races today. The whole town is convulsed this evening with the news that in the chief race, seven horses fell in a heap, one jockey was killed outright and three taken to the hospital.

Sunday, Oct. 16

I lunched today with the Weigalls. I recognized Annie Hamilton at once. She has just the same snub-nose and bright little face, she is very happy, has three jolly little girls, and a very good husband. He is one of the three or four leading young Victorian lawyers, certain to be a judge in the course of time. He is an excellent specimen of young Australia. He has never been home, and is rather cock-sure and argumentative. But he is a thoroughly sound thinking fellow and keen to learn. Altogether the lawyers here are very good. The leading men would take a position at home, and they are many of them cultivated and bright-minded gentlemen. I went on next to the house of Thomas a' Beckett! His Honor is a descendant of – we will not say the martyr, but of the great archbishop's near relations. He is a judge of the high court, and is going to be Moore's father in law.

In the evening I had a long talk to H.H. Champion, late a labour agitator in England. Now he has come into money; and is a sort of swell out here, with some popular proclivities but no enthusiasm. He is not a man of great wisdom, but quite clever. He gave me an admirable résumé of recent Victorian history. Bah! I am afraid this is rather uninteresting. But I am going to stay a fortnight in Melbourne seeing people. There will not be events to record, and I cannot give you all the conversations at length.

Monday, Oct. 17

This evening I went to a public meeting of the Anti-Sweating league. There has been some very valuable and stringent legislation against sweating here in the last two years. Boards have been appointed to settle a minimum wage in five of the worst trades, boots, furniture, men's clothing, women's clothing, and baking. This they have done, and sweating is being beaten out. Now there is an agitation to include a lot of other trades.

The meeting was exactly like a Liberal meeting in Yorkshire or Glasgow. It was a long hall with galleries. The hall became full about 8.30. The front row of the galleries was lined. The first four rows were occupied chiefly by old men, who might have been Chartists, and had probably attended every Radical meeting since they were boys. Two of the chief speakers were non-con clergy. Then came a series of trade-union secretaries, who stated their case in practical, unpoetical English, then Trenwith, a big, capable labour M.P., then Deakin, the Liberal M.P., a cultivated oratorical man, most anxious to be remembered to G. O. T., who was courteous to him in London. The audience cheered, laughed and applauded exactly as they do in England. They allowed themselves to be bored to exactly the same point. There was exactly the same mixture of pomposity, practicality, eloquence, exaggeration, pathos and absurdity in the speeches. I am glad to say that Anti-sweating league (which the working men pronounce with a very long i) has general sympathy. But the 'Argus' and the 'Age', the two leading papers support further legislation. There is hardly any a priori theoretical objection to state regulation. The Webbs attribute it to the Protectionist politics of the colony, that laissez-faire notions have never caught tight hold. I attribute it more to a general absence of effective conservatism throughout society. When anybody can show that there is a damnable abuse, people are inclined to say that it is better to blunder a bit in finding the remedy than sit indifferent and inactive. In England the Conservatives harden their hearts, until the remedy has almost proved itself effective. Here they do not hate change.

Tuesday, Oct. 18

Went to see the University. We went over all the medical, science and engineering schools. The great smash of '93 injured them as it did Sydney University, and the numbers are only now beginning to recover. It is modelled on English Universities to a great extent. The people at large do not regard it as their institution as in America. The state only pays a small sum to supplement the endowment, and reduced it by two-thirds in the bad times. However they are doing good work. Some of the professors are very good men. We lunched with Masson, a son of the man whom G. O. T made historiographer of Scotland.

In the afternoon I went to the Legislative Assembly, where the House was in Committee over a Land Act Amendment Bill, very technical. I was introduced to everybody by Deakin, to the Premier Sir G. Turner, a good financier, who saved the colony from complete collapse, but otherwise unnotable; to Duffy, son of Gavan; and to the Speaker. The Speaker escorted me round the Parliament buildings and grounds in company with the Sergeant at Arms. The Speaker was pompous, stupid and bibulous. Four successive times in half an hour he asked me to drink with him. I refused. At last out of compassion the Sergeant at Arms drank a thimble-full to justify his superior in taking a wine-glass. We perambulated all the buildings. They are very imposing, though as yet unfinished. Something like a million has already been spent. Outside are gardens, with tennis-courts, bowling greens, bath-houses, shrubberies for the members to enjoy themselves in. There are two billiard tables, almost always occupied by the labour members. The Speaker turned electric lights on and off, tested the telephones, presented me with a button-hole, put me to sit in the chair used by Manners Sutton in the first reform Parliament as Speaker, gave me some of the Victorian Parliament notepaper as a souvenir, and asked me again to drink. Altogether I felt highly honoured, and I figured in the papers next morning.

Victorian politics are generally rather dull now. Federation is the only critical issue and all the other colonies are waiting for New South Wales. The Turner Government saved the country from financial wreck and are going on chiefly on their prestige. They are improving the land act, and are attending to the labour party enough to enter upon the Anti-Sweating legislation of which I have spoken. There is a good deal of ability in Parliament, but most of it is on the government side. So they will probably continue to hold office. Isaacs, the Attorney-General, a Jew, is probably the ablest man. Higgins is another very strong Liberal lawyer, Deakin is a cultivated eloquent

Liberal. There are one or two other lawyers, Irvine and Moule, who are rather Conservative whom I like much. They are industrious and well-meaning. But there is no great political activity.

I dined at the House with Duffy and met several of those I have mentioned on both sides. Gillies the leader of the opposition seemed rather a stupid old boy.

After dinner I saw a deputation of about 200 workingmen and their spokesmen meet the Chief (Home) Secretary, to discuss improvement in the Anti-Sweating law. They stated their case very well, turn by turn in trades. Then Peacock answered them in an admirable way, outspoken, sympathetic and strong.

Wednesday, Oct. 19

Today I saw the land minister and spent most of the day at public offices. In the evening Syme, the Editor of the 'Age', gave a dinner to Webb and myself. Deakin, the Attorney-General, Hoare and Windsor the two chief sub-editors, Champion and two more were the guests beside ourselves. We had much political talk. Syme is a silent, strong, shrewd man, who through his paper is probably more powerful than the Prime Minister. He is said to have selected Turner and put him in office at the critical time, when all the recognized politicians were failing to meet the crisis. At the end of dinner Windsor, who writes most of the leaders, said that he, as a young man, had sent an article to Macaulay to ask if it would do for the Edinburgh. He still keeps Macaulay's reply, which is laudatory, but tells him he would not publish it, if he judged it nine years hence (some Horatian quotation). This, said Windsor, was such encouragement, that he pursued literature and journalism, till here he was the leading journalist in Australasia.

Thursday, Oct. 20

Lunched in a basement lunching room with a set of young men, half of them Hebrew, who have collected round Max Hirsch. Max Hirsch is a single-taxer, and rather a remarkable person. He has raised a great interest in economics, and brought together a great many people to think and discuss. He is disappointed in his hope to convert the masses to single-tax views, but he has brought the idea of land taxation much to the front and attacked protection very strongly. But perhaps his best work has really been making a lot of people think about economics. We talked taxation questions all lunch time and there was a great deal of good political education shown by the company.

I dined with the Weigalls and argued much with the very combative young lawyer.

Friday, Oct. 21

Spent all the morning interviewing secretaries, factory inspectors, etc. Lunched at the lawyer's club, the Bohemians. Dined with Hall, a cheerful Radical English business man, and went to the Red Robe, a detestable representation of that moderately historical play. A large and uncritical audience of well-dressed playgoers watched it with intense appreciation. Then I went home and read myself to sleep over Son Excellence Eugene Roryon, a real picture of a ruler of France.

Saturday, Oct. 22

Did nothing much except see some more of the town. Melbourne spreads over an enormous area. And the houses are built far apart along very wide streets. The suburbs are quite infinite. It is immensely overbuilt for the population, owing to the land boom before the smash. The result is that now in walking through the Hackneys and Kenningtons of Melbourne, you see large numbers of quite good houses untenanted, or occupied by people who are clearly unable to pay a remunerative rent for the original outlay.

Brassey has today got back from England, and has at once invited me to dinner. He is curiously unpopular here. He partly bores people. The Bulletin, the scathing Sydney critic of Australasia, has a tremendous dislike to him. I enclose a specimen. They say that when a reporter goes to interview him, he puts his back against the door and proses for an hour and a half, and prevents the escape of the unfortunate reporter. He is accused also of giving cheap champagne – a far worse offence in the eyes of the 'push', i.e. people who are asked or would like to be asked to Government House. I think however he really tries to do his duty better than most Governors, having tried to associate with the intellectual people. The sporting society governor, Hopetown, who preceded him, was the most popular they say they ever had.

Municipal Melbourne is in considerable excitement over a unification project. Webb has arrived at exactly the right moment. London of 1885 is exactly reproduced in miniature, ten small rather incompetent municipalities, and a central, unrepresentative, questionably honest Metropolitan Board of Works for some of the necessarily central functions. They are going to unify. Webb advises no local bodies analogous to vestries. But they are sure to retain them for some purposes.

Sunday, Oct. 23

Lunched with Duffy and several politicians and their wives. There is a bright Miss Duffy, enthusiastic, at present, about Dizzy. Had tea with Higgins the democratic enthusiast of Parliament. Dined in legal company with MacKinnons.

Monday, Oct. 24

Very unremunerative day for news. Went to law courts as the only event. Fine buildings, and astoundingly like England. Judges in wigs and red robes, barristers in wig and gown, witnesses lying and sweating, courts the same shape, law the same, everything the same.

Tuesday, Oct. 25

Went to National Gallery. They have a few modern pictures that are good. They have best Peter Graham I have seen. It is Glencoe after the massacre, the huts dimly burning in the bottom of the slack, and flying women dimly cursing the unseen red-coats. But the mist is absolutely moving upon the canvas, driving out the last gleam of sunshine. With such places to walk in, I do not want to wander again to the Rockies or New Zealand. 'My heart's in the Highlands.' They have got Lady Butler's Quatre Bras Square there too.

In the afternoon I went down with the head of the Defence Department to see the Victorian navy, which consists of five torpedo boats and one turret-ship, the Cerberus, for harbour defence, inside the five forts at the entrance of the bay. It is a clumsy arrangement having a separate and inefficient defence force, about which I am getting some ideas. While I was on the Cerberus, the flag-ship of our Australian squadron sailed down the harbour. I think it was as good a sight, gliding along moved by an unseen power, with the admiral's gay double balls and Union Jack flying, as any old three-decker. We and another cruiser in port fired 13 guns each in salute. I am afraid the French stand a very poor chance if they fight.

Now I must close this letter. It is a very poor one. But talk and not events is marking my stay in Melbourne. It is decidedly the most intellectual society I have been in outside England, whether in America or the colonies. The lawyers and politicians are decidedly well cultivated, with far less provincialism than elsewhere. The University is making a fool of itself by sacking Professor Hall for irreligion. But that is part of the Toryism of culture, the price that must sometimes be paid.

Love to all,

Yours aff,
Charles Trevelyan

13. MEETING PEOPLE

Tuesday, Oct. 25

I am afraid that this letter will not be an exciting one, my Family. I am becoming part of this southern Anglo-Saxon community, in order to understand and appreciate it. They make much of me, and I see the best of them. But I have chiefly to record conversations. I ended the day at Parliament, dining with a Conservative lawyer, Provine. In the lower house they began discussing resumption of land by the state for closer settlement. The opposition did not dare oppose it directly on principle, but tried red herrings. But below their breath they swore, and at the club, which is the home of the squatters, there was much anger. In the upper house there was a pedantic debate on proportional representation. A worthy but academic gentleman called Sir H. Wrixon proposed it, in a dull in-effective speech, much applauded by his colleagues. It is curious to find these old fogies dreaming Hare's systems still, which we discarded as meritorious but unpractical thirty years ago. The power of the upper house is very serious here. It is elected by a high qualification constituency and so can plead a sort of popular mandate against the lower house. The power of creating councillors, which saved the situation in New Zealand, is impossible here. There has already been one great crisis. Payment of Members was rejected twice, the second time when tacked onto the Appropriation Bill. There was a strong, rough Premier, Berry, who was ready to fight. He discussed every Civil Servant connected with any councillor, and gave notice that the police, army and railwaymen were going to be disbanded if the money bill was not passed entire. The Council gave in. Since then they are constantly affecting legislation injuriously and frequently rejecting it. There is the chance of a graver situation here than in any other colony some day in the future. There is hardly any ability in the Council; they are thoroughly respectable and thoroughly stupid.

Wednesday, Oct. 26

I spent the morning with the secretary in charge of the State System of boarding out neglected children. It is a very valuable experiment, which is succeeding. All children committed by the magistrate to the care of the public for neglect are no longer shut up in industrial schools, but are boarded out with respectable people who bring them up as their children. A careful supervision is kept over them by committees of ladies and a staff of inspectors. The state pays 5/- a week to the foster parent. *All* children are now so boarded out, and the state saves about 4/- a head per week compared with the old barrack system. I went round to see the homes, where nice homely mothers, mostly women who had brought up children of their own, were looking after little families of two or three state children, who were clean, happy, well-educated at the nearest school, and free from both bars and taint of pauperism. Sometimes at a later time the foster parents kept them on, instead of letting them go to other service, when the time has expired.

I dined with Brassey, who was friendly, but rather ponderous. Afterwards we went in state to a concert in the town hall, which I greatly enjoyed, partly for the good singing, partly for the humour of the bad.

Thursday, Oct. 27

Had a long cycle ride being much in need of exercise. Dined with Masson, son of the historiographer, at the University.

There was a very charming, intelligent, Miss Lambert there, a graduate who was working at biology, and has already exposed a blunder by a leading English specialist. Her strength is in leeches! She is the best girl I have met in Australia. She recently acted in a Greek play here, without knowing Greek. But so excellently did she act that even the classical professors were in ecstasies.

Friday, Oct. 28

I breakfasted with the Weigalls and photographed Annie's charming family. After that I went to see a married sister of W. P. Reeves, with whom I had a very pleasant talk about friends and politics.

I lunched with Morris, the Professor of literature at the Varsity, whom I told all about G. O. T.'s book.[1] With him I went to see the national library, which is free and very well-used, and open till 9 or 10. But sabbatarianism still closes it on Sundays. I was asked to write my name in the book of distinguished visitors. I was on the third page since 1879, and was in company with Governors and J. A. Froude. The Art Gallery was very fair, much like the Sydney one, only with some pictures that were stronger. Still the clear characteristic of Australian painting is faithfulness to the nature they see, and no imagination.

Dined with His Honour Thomas a' Beckett, with several lawyers. I gave them beans about Professor Hall.

Saturday, Oct. 29

Nothing notable except a dinner with Wrixon, the promoter of proportional representation. It was exactly like an English party in a third-rank politician's house in London. The best people were two or three bearded Scotchmen, exactly like Provost Bell's commercial colleagues on the Glasgow corporation.

Sunday, Oct. 30

Talked all day. Went a walk with Higgins in the morning, lunched with Irvine, tea with Mrs. Carrington, and dined with Buckleys. Buckley is a tradesman, who with British shrewdness

[1] *Life and Letters of Lord Macaulay.*

and snobbishness fought his way some years ago into society. Now Governor's sons and daughters dine with him, and now he has the pick of the visitors in Cup week. He is President of the Victoria Racing Club, the greatest institution in the land. He is a polo player. His daughter whom I sat next to is one of the chief heiresses of Australia. It is astonishing how exactly English society is reproduced. We are all sorry to notice how very little the women do, if they get money. They are lazier and more fashionable than in England, except that of course there are fewer of them in proportion, and fortunes are more precarious. But the rich girl does absolutely nothing, the moderately rich nothing but some of her own dressmaking.

Monday, Oct. 31

I have not mentioned yet that I have with great good luck fallen on the best moment to visit Melbourne. 'The Cup' is the greatest annual event in Australia. On the first Tuesday in November the great race comes off at Flemington Racecourse in the Melbourne suburbs. All Australia that can pay the railway fare flocks to Melbourne. All the Governors are here except Gormanston from Hobart. The Admiral of the Australian squadron happened to sail into Melbourne harbour for his annual inspection three days ago. This club is full of squatters and such English visitors as there are, to whom the cup is often the only sight worth visiting Australia to see. 'By Jove, they do that well. By Gad, it whips Ascot!' The main streets are full of smartly dressed women and men in top hats in the afternoon. Every young business man or squatter buys a new frock coat or hat. Every lady who can by a year's parsimony collect the price of a new and fashionable gown appears for these few days to enjoy herself and be criticized. There are balls every night. There are theatre parties, when some popular squatter asks 150 people to the theatre. There are luncheons and picnics. There is betting and flirting and drinking and merrymaking, most of it decently and in order, though sometimes uproarious.

I went to see Syme again this morning and told him about G. O. T's book, and promised to send him a copy.

In the morning I went round two of the public schools of Melbourne. Victoria is far the worst colony in Elementary

Education. Only one or two young inspectors know how inferior their teaching is. The department is clogged by red-tape and fossilized ideas. They still pay by results. They promote by seniority, not merit. They have no training college. They have no extra subjects. They have enormous classes. They have three or four pupil teachers to each assistant. I am either going to write to the 'Age' about it, or have a talk to the Minister. It is sheer stupidity most of it.

Max Hirsch gave a dinner to the Webbs and myself, where we met some of the political young men whom he has got round him. I walked away with a young man very like Hirst both in mind and appearance.

I ended up at the Governor's Ball. It was St. Patrick's Hall over again, but rather brighter than the Castle. To make it more like Ireland I danced chiefly with Annie Hamilton (Weigall) and the fair granddaughter of Gavan Duffy, who would not go to supper till 12.30 for fear of the priest. For Oct. 31 was All Soul's Day.

Tuesday, Nov. 1

Breakfasted with the Weigalls. Rode on a bicycle to a suburban cottage to see a fine old settler called *Scott*, who now has a farm and vineyard in west Victoria, where he has raised a happy family, and where he is the leading politician on the various local bodies. The last letter he received before he left England as a boy of 14 was from Maria Macaulay, sister of Zachary, aunt of T.B. He was a pet of hers. It is a clear, good, pious, confident letter, in correct, forcible English, bidding him remember his prayers and his duty, and not 'go on the water for pleasure on Sundays', a habit he apparently had indulged in with the sons of the faithless somewhere within Maria's ken. Sunday was not a day of 'forms and ceremonies' but of godly contemplation or some such phrase. Altogether a most good and sensible letter, a treasure now to the boy whose hair is grey and who has brought up a healthy and worthy family in the new land. He is going to present me with two pictures by him of the dry mallee country where he lives. The pictures are nought, but they have a tinge of Australian colour in them.

Then I went back to the Club, put on respectable clothes and went off to the great Australian event 'the Cup'. I expected to be bored, but went out of duty. I never saw such a sight. There must have been several hundred thousand people there. 'The Flat' is the least select, where the workingmen, youths, thimble-riggers and farmers' picnic parties congregate. On the other side is 'the Stand', an enormous enclosure with lawns and stands and paddocks. Above it is 'the Hill' the middle place socially, from which you get the most magnificent panorama of the whole course and the crowd. I went to the Stand. It was like Lords only fifty times more so. The whole place, lawns, parades and stands, was bristling with smartly dressed ladies with parasols. I could never have believed that Australia could have produced such a crowd. Everybody was there, Governors, premiers, Speakers, lawyers, professors (even the father of the University who says he ought to have been in the Beagle instead of Darwin!) down to the smallest man or woman who could afford the minimum 13/6 for entry. Mrs. Webb was personally conducted by the Secretary of the Victorian Racing Club (to such honour do socialists attain in these parts!) What pleased me most was the physique of the crowd. They represented all the Australians who had any money at all to spare. They were all tall and big. All the girls looked strong and healthy, with an extraordinarily high average of good looks and best of all good colour. It is very disappointing to find that they will go back from simplicity of life the moment they get the chance, and the universal rage for racing is a pity. But it is all more than cancelled by satisfaction at this better set of animals than we have got at home, who at least know how to enjoy themselves, though barbarously. I think they would know how to die too if necessary. But let them at present be light-hearted and add a cubit to the stature of the people by good feeding and living such as never been so universally known before.

I went to a very smart luncheon and tea with Mrs. Carrington, and watched the great event at the railings with pretty Miss Duffy. The favourite did not win, and the excitement was not very wild. But there was a tremendous inarticulate roar as the race closed from a hundred thousand throats. I walked about the Hill and Flat afterwards, and saw small boys throwing away their threepenny-pieces and the horny handed his hardwon shillings on various swindling games of chance. I walked back with the common crowd down a road lined with people watching the carriages with the swells in them passing. Most of the swells have not carriages and go by train. But there are enough to make it a sight, especially as Brassey drives past with a company of grey Victorian cavalry prancing on their bush-trained horses. I ended up in a tram car where a long argument was going on over some abtruse piece of racing history in a group of workingmen. The chief arguer had of course a strong Scotch accent.

I dined in the evening with Sanderson, one of the nice Harrow brothers, one of whom was at Bojons with Bob.

So ended the Cup Day and all Cup Days for

Yours aff.
Charles Trevelyan

14. LABOUR COLONY AT LEONGATHA

Wednesday, Nov. 2

Today was my last day in Melbourne, which I spent to a great extent in saying goodbye to people. I have made a lot of very good friends, especially among the politicians, lawyers and university people. The fashionable people are more uninteresting than at home. Mrs. Webb is terribly contemptuous today about the dress and figure of the women at the 'Cup' yesterday. But she has to admit that they are well fed if not distinguished.

This evening I started with Moore to see the labour colony at *Leongatha*. It is about 80 miles from Melbourne in a district which is only just being opened up by the railway, until recently all bush. We had a four hours journey to reach it. The superintendent, Col. Goldstein travelled down with us. We stayed at a comfortable village Hotel for the night, kept by an Irishman of course, leading local politician, very effusive and friendly to me.

Thursday, Nov. 3

Spent the day in seeing the colony. It was started in 1893 to relieve the pressure of unemployment by private enterprise.

When subscriptions fell off the government offered to subsidize it and Goldstein offered to superintend it without a salary. He is an ideal man for the job, enthusiastic and practical. They have had since the start an average of about 150 men, varying with the state of the labour market. Now there are about 100 as times are rather good. Entrance to the colony is purely voluntary. No one goes who does not really want to work steadily, because if he does not work, out he goes. No one goes who can get work elsewhere, because the wage is below the market wage in practically all trades in Australia. It is intended as a place of honourable labour for men who are temporarily out of employment. They are housed and fed gratis and have a small wage put aside for them weekly, which averages 2/6 a head, but can rise to 4/-. They may not have it to spend while at the colony, except to pay for a new suit of clothes or boots. When they leave they take the accumulated wage to help them to start and find work. The work they do is clearing the bush. The government gave Goldstein 800 acres to carry on his operations upon. It was originally entirely bush, that is, huge gum-trees taller than our beeches with thick undergrowth and beautiful clumps of tree-ferns. He has now cleared several hundred acres entirely by his labour-colonists. When it is cleared he uses it for farming. The farm has no direct connexion with the colony, is not subsidized, and has to pay itself. He has skilled ploughmen, etc. But so good a farmer is he that, if it had not been for a terrible bush-fire last year which swept the country and destroyed half the buildings, the farm would now not only be paying itself but supporting the colony without any government contribution. The men come there mostly as a stage to better things. Hardly any loafers come. They know the graft is too hard. Goldstein says he frequently gets men so hungry that they are ill for two days from greedy overeating on their arrival. These men work until they have earned enough to carry them over a few weeks of search for work, or until there is a busy season, and then go off, independent and self-respecting and in capital training, instead of despairing, starved and debauched by begging, loafing or drinking. I found exactly the right temper in all the men. They thought their treatment very good, they praised the food; but all spoke of going off directly for work. One fine young fellow who was acting as

213

'ganger' to seven other men who were clearing out stumps of felled trees, was tall and brawny and red-haired, recognizeably Northumbrian. I went and spoke to him. He was from Riding Mill on the Tyne and could not get permanent work in his batching trade. He was as brave and independent as Taylor or Hedley but down in his luck. There was nothing of the pauper at all about him. They were all men who had had bad luck, a few gone down through drink, but all intensely anxious and through the colony mostly able to retrieve their position. More than half were emigrants from Great Britain and Ireland, which speaks well for the new stock. For the proportion of emigrants is far below half now in the whole population. There is a bureau attached which attempts to find work for the men when they leave. But the labour bureau system is not developed as it is in New South Wales. Altogether the colony is an admirable success. It does not profess to find work for all the enemployed, but only for those who are really ready to work. It offers no inducement as against other employment, very much the reverse. This is quite right, because it is not work which the government would undertake except as a matter of wise charity. It may pay the government in the end. But it is doubtfully remunerative. What it does do, is to keep men well-fed, self-respecting and laborious for periods when at home they would be begging or starving. It does not solve the difficulty of fluctuations of employment. But it does test to a great extent the bona fide desire for work in large numbers of unemployed. It proves that there are hundreds who do not fail from want of will, only from want of right opportunities. And it performs the true duty of the state in not only keeping these men alive, but in keeping their self-respect alive and their muscles in training, without offering employment which would draw men away from the necessary industries which are more certainly productive. It is an experiment well worth imitating in England.

In the afternoon I had a look at a cattle mart, where a set of brawny farmers were dealing. One man was like red-haired Brodie, another had the grizzled beard of Handyside, the auctioneer who strutted up and down in the pen was the image of Henderson of the Gap. And they looked and digested slowly the qualities of the cows and calves and passed slow remarks exactly as they do at Rothbury sales.

We got back to Melbourne late at night, having the company of a very noisy, good-natured, ignorant Australian young man, type of beef-eating self-sufficient Anglo Saxondom. He was very strong indeed about the importance of keeping close to England and uniting with America. The Australian no longer looks forward to living his last days in England, he is promoting Australian nationality by federation, he has started an Australian Natives Association which is a great political force. But this movement which is the young men's movement is thoroughly and healthily imperialist. So strongly is the feeling growing, that the Bulletin, which three years ago was violently anti-British, has had to cease its attacks and urge federation as a part of the solidification of the race.

Friday, Nov. 4

Off at 6.30 for Ballarat. I found myself next a stout, red-faced, good-humoured personage with a strong Irish accent. He turned out to be the Mayor of the Town of Ballarat East, the original camp, as distinguished from the now greater City of Ballarat, which is divided from the town by a creek. He is a member for the locality and had heard me talked about by his colleagues in the Assembly. So he immediately became very friendly. He was the regular ward politician of America, kept in check by a British public opinion which demands outward respectability and honesty. He told me he had had a brother who had begun a political career in Pittsburg at the same moment that he had begun in Ballarat. I have not the least doubt that if Mr. Murphy U.S.A. had been elected Ward Alderman for the Irish quarter between the Allegheny and Monongahela, he would have been as great a rascal as any Pittsburg boodler. His brother had since died and had the 'greatest funeral in all Pittsburg.'

When we arrived at Ballarat we went to the City Hall to present my introduction from the Chief Secretary to the Mayor of the City. The Mayor was a stout, vulgar Australian, exactly like the Mayor of an English watering-place. The two rival Mayors were great friends, and began at once chaffing about their respective domains. They soon determined to drive me round the place, and solemnized the determination by the first drink of the day, whiskey and soda.

We drove first to the School of Mines, where 400 students from different parts of Australia and Africa are learning all necessary for mining engineering, assaying, smelting, crushing, etc. We then saw the crushing machines of a great mine. Almost all the mining here is now quartz. There are deep pits, more than 1000 ft. down. The gold is found in quartz rock which has to be blasted. The remains of alluvial mining is visible everywhere, huge cuttings and irregular quarry heaps, where the early miners delved. Now only big companies with expensive shafts and machinery, wage-earners and Mines Regulation Acts can get out the gold. The alluvial miners have moved on to Kalgoorlie and Klondike.

We then had a second drink at an Irish pub, this time of beer.

We then went to see the municipal enterprise of Ballarat. It is a charming, bright city, well-built and regular. The streets are excellently paved; fir, oak, lime avenues are rising already to the height of the roofs of the two-story house. Well-dressed girls trip through the streets to the School of Arts. There are fine stone churches. There is a bad statue of Burns, facing a worse statue of Moore in the market-place. It is indeed far different from wretched Cripple Creek, where discomfort, boredom and vice are the order, and all including man is vile. The latest improvement, which we went to see was a municipal football, cricket and sports ground with a fine pavilion. Close by was a fine municipal lake and park and beautiful gardens, decorated by abominable statuary, but meritorious in intention. Murphy was particularly anxious to make me appreciate a statue of 'Modesty.' In the gardens too they had a place for breeding trout, which are distributed gratis to anyone who wants to stock his river or pond. Ballarat folk are wonderfully proud of their city and rightly so. We then drove to the Hall of the *Town* of Ballarat East. We had another drink in the antechamber. Then ten minutes of business was gone through, mostly found. They agreed to accept an invitation to lunch. The Mayor was congratulated on having obtained from the government the expenditure of £1,000 on a new bridge, one of the 'many benefits he has conferred on the community.' The Mayor having suitably replied, we retired to the ante-chamber with the reporters, and had another drink. The Mayor proposed the health of their distinguished visitor and I replied in suitable terms. (I may say that my speech *was* articulate, not because I could stand as much as Mr. Murphy, but because there had been on the last two occasions a temperance alternative to whiskey and soda.)

We then drove off to see a mine. It was much as coal-mines are, except for want of gas and black dirt. The boring machines are American like those used at Cripple Creek. Murphy did not go down. The Mayor of the City lost several pounds weight and nearly died of the exertion. Murphy would have had to be carried out.

We then visited an orphan asylum, on the whole a pretty good institution externally. We inspected it for twenty minutes and drank for another ten.

We drove past the Eureka Stockade, which to Victorians is their Bannockburn or Naseby. For though the rebel miners were defeated, government had to recognize miners' wrongs and rights, as a result of the battle, and the slaughter of some dozen heroes. In the market place stands a monument of a Speaker of the Legislative Assembly. He has only one arm. He lost the other at the Eureka Stockade, and no doubt owed his position as president of law-makers to having once resisted the law at a time when the people thought it dangerous to their freedom.

Finally we saw an engineering shop, owned by one Cowley, who was once the foreman of Laird's at Birkenhead, and had built the boilers of the Alabama,[1] 35 years ago. We then returned to the Hotel, where we had a parting glass for 'auld lang syne'.

Saturday, Nov. 5

Yesterday I had made the acquaintance of a very able engineer called Anderson, who took me in hand this morning. I went with him over an engineering works and to a woollen mill. The woollen mill was a real going concern, with large modern machinery, up to date and active in every way. The manager was a Leeds man, trained in the greatest manufacturing school of the world, a splendid type of north countryman who had built up the mill, practically unaided. I had a lot of interesting talk with him.

In the afternoon I photographed the monument of the Eureka

[1] Confederate cruiser in the American Civil War, built in England. Sunk off Cherbourg by the Union ship *Kearsarge* in 1863.

Stockade. I then saw the small municipal picture gallery, which contains very few bad pictures and some half dozen really good landscapes by Peter Graham, Leader, etc. Over the door is the royal proclamation of the day of the Eureka Stockade, beginning 'wheras a large body of evil-disposed persons of various nations.' They hang it up to remind them that they lost only to win.

This night I took the express for Adelaide in company with the Webbs, and had a good night journey, waking up on

Sunday, Nov. 6

in the dry plains of eastern South Australia, as yet useless for cultivation or pasture.

Before midday we got to Adelaide, and I was at once housed at the Club in great comfort. The President is Sir Richard Baker who was at college with G. O. T. and therefore very anxious to do all he can for me.

Adelaide is the best situated of any of the great Australian cities. Sydney has finer water to recommend it. But Adelaide has mountains. It is very like Dublin. About four miles away a very fine range of hills stretches north and south, partly bare grass downs, partly thickly wooded hill-tops. The ground is rolling and from some places which have generally been picked for residence there are really fine views. The houses are much more substantial than in most other Australian cities. Much more brick, and a great deal of very fine stone is used instead of wood. The public buildings are effective. Parliament House is unfinished, but what is built is in white marble. The University is a good building on the main street and they are putting up what promises to be an artistic Conservatorium of Music. The roads are quite excellent. Everybody bicycles. Young men in straw hats are even more omnipresent than in other Australian cities. The city covers an enormous space of ground, thanks to cheapness of land, which gives all suburban cottages a little space round them.

Government House unfortunately is empty. But Capt. Wallington, the Buxton's secretary, has immediately taken me in hand. The Buxtons are very much respected here. Everybody thinks Sir Fowell a good old boy, and they all say that Lady V has done a great deal of good by her philanthropy and godliness. The Buxtons are not unpopular like Brassey. But Sir F. does not interest them, and they are rather irritated at the extent to which the clergy have been specially entertained at Government House. A clergyman was at lunch almost every day, so says Wallington exaggeratively. Wallington, while thoroughly loyal, would have preferred a supporting or political man or two sometimes. Guise, the A.D.C. who was godly is known as 'the Church,' Wallington as 'the World.' At the Government House balls the clergy in affection for their governor used to come and dance with their daughters. The clergy are wild in their enthusiasm. Others would rather have another governor, but are not angry. Charlie Buxton and V[1] were both very much liked where they got known. In the photograph shop windows are many photos of the two serious, handsome, contemplative faces of our two friends. V very energetically ran a reading society for young men and girls which was evidently a good deal of a success, as it is going on in her absence to read, write upon and debate the Renaissance this year, a subject which apparently none of them as yet know aught of.

Wallington took me to see the Bishop, who is young and vigorous and sensible, very sensible for a bishop. Mrs. Bip is a cousin of Lady H. Somerset and Haldane, (a Miss Somers-Cox) and very pleasant. After that we went to see Chief Justice Way, the factotum of S. Australia. He is a first rate lawyer, enormously read in a superficial way, knowing everyone and everything, and at present acting governor in Sir Fowell's absence. Moore described him as the Australian O.B. It is a good comparison, except that he is not always off the mark.

Monday, Nov. 7

The ruler of South Australia is Kingston, who has been Premier now for six years and apparently has got an indefinite lease of power. He is generally a Liberal and his opponents are generally conservative, though party divisions are not very marked. He is a very strong, capable, businesslike man, very much after the type of New Zealand's premier, Seddon. But he has not as much public spirit as Seddon, and is more of an opportunist. His

[1] Children of Sir Fowell Buxton. Charlie became a Member of Parliament and an early member of the Labour Party, with Charles. V. married Lothar de Bunsen.

private life is rather shady, and he has done one or two acts of administration of a very high-handed and blameworthy sort. But here again as in the other colonies, the administration is competent, and the legislation is bold in the direction of democratic experiment. I spent the morning with the Treasurer, Holder, the most thinking man in the government, who rose as a Wesleyan preacher, and with the Land minister who is a practical farmer.

I lunched at the House with Kingston and met several of the leading politicians. After lunch we smoked with the Labour party who were just going to have a caucus. They support Kingston generally, but act independently. On the whole they are the best labour men in Australia. But again they want leading badly. Kingston's sympathies are quite vague and he only does what he thinks will pay in the way of legislation. Still something gets done. We had a lot of talk and discussion. The least effective of them but most talkative is a stumpy Londoner called Archibold, who shook me by the hand for a minute or so, on the ground that Macaulay was the greatest man who ever lived. He quotes Macaulay and Carlyle at length in his speeches. He is very proud of having worked in '71 to get Lyulph and Haxley in for Marylebone on the first School Board. Another oddity was King O'Malley a wild red-haired American Irishman, (in appearance rather like that Irish whip whose name I forget). He brings in many bills and makes wild speeches. Otherwise the people I met were sensible solid British folk, who smoked their pipes and discoursed seriously about Compulsory Arbitration and the prospects of war.

Tuesday, Nov. 8

Had another talk with Kingston. Saw the Factory Inspector and found that the Factory Act is most inadequate and feebly administered. Apparently Kingston is afraid of some of the employers. I have advised the labour men to look after the Inspector who is willing enough but not very competent. I then saw the Education minister and arranged to visit the schools, which are very good here I believe, as they have only just lost the best school inspector in Australia.

In the afternoon I went to the House, again a facsimile of the House of Commons, wigged Speaker, gowned clerks, ministerial bench, time-honoured procedure all in due order. A very businesslike, well-conducted Committee discussion was going on over a law reform bill. I saw several people, and had tea with Sir John Downer, the opposition leader who was premier before the Kingston regime began.

In the evening I had a delightful cycle ride into the mountains, up a valley, with green fields, and cottages overhung with trees, and stone public-houses that reminded me more of England than anything I have seen here yet. From the top I got a very fine extensive view.

Wednesday, Nov. 9

This morning I spent driving round the city with the Land Minister and one of the Labour Members, Price, looking at a sort of allotment settlements, where the government have placed working men in order to give them comfortable permanent houses with a little land to help them as a supplement to wages. It is a splendid success, and financially satisfactory to the government. Many of the settlers have built themselves substantial stone and brick houses and planted fruit gardens. There are upwards of a thousand families so settled round Adelaide.

In the afternoon I went again to the House.

In the evening I dined with the Bishop at a pleasant party. I talked most of the evening to a great friend of V. Buxton's Miss Andrews, an enthusiastic member of the reading circle.

And now, my Family, I must abruptly conclude. I am off to visit schools.

Love to all.

Yours aff.
Charles Trevelyan

15. LAST LETTER. STARTING FOR HOME

*On board
R.M.S. Ormus
between Adelaide and
Colombo.*

This letter will possibly procede me by a few hours, so I shall post it at Marseilles. (Naples, as it turns out.) I sent the last on

Thursday, Nov. 10

That day I went over several Adelaide Schools with the Education Minister, Mr. Butler. They are the best in the colonies that I have seen. The reason is that they have only just lost a very fine inspector, called Hartley, who for years had controlled, and stimulated the system. The deficiency of most of the colonies is in initiative. They have most of them gone along the lines of 15 years ago, with inspectors trained then and with the same ideas predominant still in their minds. They have watched the modern developments in England and America very little. The system is everywhere, except in New Zealand, so centralized that all depends on the inspectors. A constant level of high but unprogressive efficiency has been maintained. Here in South Australia, owing to one man, they have got bright schools, full of modern appliances, with a careful system of choosing teachers, as good as in the best boards. It is greatly to their credit.

In the afternoon I rode up into the hills to stay the night at a vineyard belonging to a very energetic Etonian called Cholmondeley. He makes light clarets, which will in time get a good market. At present South Australia is under the disadvantage of not having large enough vineyards to provide the mass of wine necessary if it ever becomes popular at home. But their wine is good and will prosper in time. We spent about an hour tasting wines which is not the attractive, bibulous process which it sounds to be. It consists of taking mouthfuls of wine and spitting them out into a sort of milk-can, and then rinsing out your mouth with water in the vain hope that your confused palate will be ready for a taste of the next vintage.

Friday, Nov. 11

Rode in for 13 miles against a strong hot wind, the most swelteringly hot piece of exercise I ever had. I had to race in order to get in time to go down with the Education Minister to see the government freezing works and export department at Port Adelaide. It is a perfectly successful socialistic experiment which they have undertaken. No private firm would start the export of frozen mutton, so the state has undertaken it and is now doing a considerable trade.

Saturday, Nov. 12

Watched cricket, Melbourne v Adelaide. Dined with Sir John Downer, leader of the opposition, a good-natured, vulgar, stupid lawyer, quite without knowledge or grip of politics. I don't know in which of the colonies the Conservative opposition is most incompetent. It is rather a pity it is not better here, for Kingston has done some shady things, which there is no critical and formidable force to protest against.

Sunday Nov. 13

Went out to stay with Mr. Barr Smith, a rich squatter, who lives up in the hills. He has a pleasant house in a village, with a pretty garden. The house is furnished by Morris, all the papers were well known blue and yellow patterns with suitable chintzes and curtains. He is a fine old fellow with very sane ideas and very moderate. He and his rather invalid wife are great readers of all modern literature, and I had a very pleasant day with them and the only unmarried son remaining of a large family.

Monday Nov. 14

In the morning we went to the village sports, running, bicycling, riding etc. But the most original attraction was a competition wood-cutting. Thirteen large logs were fixed firmly upright in the ground standing up about 7 feet. For many miles round the best woodmen of the hills flocked to the contest. At a given signal they all began. The diameter of each log was about 2 feet. They hacked, the crowd cheered, I took photos. At last in 4 mins. 25 secs. the first tree fell. It was a splendid game. (Have we enough woodmen at Wallington to introduce it for the countryside at our next industrial exhibition? Ask Nixon.)

This evening I drove over to the house of a Professor Bensley, a very fine fellow who is doing work in the University. I had a pleasant evening with him and his English wife.

Tuesday and Wednesday Nov. 15, 16

My two last days on Australian soil were spent in making final investigations, seeing some more of the Bishop and Chief Justice, saying goodbye and making preparations. So ends the diary of Australia, tapering rather at the end into dullness, owing to my having left it three weeks nearly before writing it up. Still there it is as a record.

Thursday Nov. 17

Several friends came down to see us off, particularly Captain Wallington and Mrs. Bip. We put out on a steamer at Largs Bay and went out to the 'Ormus', which lay a mile away in deep waters. We settled down in most comfortable cabins on the side of the ship, where there will be most air in the tropics.

Friday Nov. 18–Wednesday Nov. 30

At last we are enjoying a voyage. The first two days were unpleasant but not nearly as bad as usual in the Australian Bight. We stopped a few hours at Albany, a bleak, desolate looking shore. Since then we have had the most perfect weather. By the third day everybody was quite well. There has been a good breeze most of the time. Except for a hot night or two when there was just enough motion to require our ports to be closed we have had ideal comfort. The food is excellent, and we are really enjoying ourselves. Our only trouble is that Webb has already got through all the books we have brought, all those belonging to other passengers and all in the by no means despicable library, those at least which he wants to read or has not already digested. And it now appears that there are no second-hand book-shops in Colombo, which we reach tomorrow.

We have got very pleasant travelling companions. It is the empty time of year. Sometimes there are 150 first salooners. This time there are 32. The most notable man is Mr. MacEachern, the greatest shipowner in Australia, a man of great force, very Conservative but broad-minded. He sits at the Captain's table opposite the Webbs and great are the discussions and chaff and information that pass between them. Captain Veale is a most delightful youngish man, with considerable intellectual interests, who greatly enjoys his company. Judge Stephen of Sydney sits near us, one of the great legal clan. He is not interesting, being rather slow-witted, but a fine conscientious character. On one side of me sits a Mrs. Bear Crawford, wife of a Victorian squatter, who was once a new woman in England, and hopes to meet Mrs. Amos in Cairo on her way home, There is a party of silly young ladies, one of them very pretty, who flirts with the officers; all of whom are young, gentlemanly, and companionable fellows. There is a Miss Hawke, sister of Lord Hawke, and a Yorkshire friend, Miss Brooksbank, who are sensible, mildly fashionable, country-house girls. There is an Indian Civil Servant who knows Hubert Watson. There is a young man who was in the Matabele war, and who swears that Rhodesia can never pay and that the gold is nought.

My day consists of a hour's exercise and walk and an hour's German before breakfast. Then I read Wilhelm Meister with Mrs. Bear Crawford till lunch at one. I am rapidly getting to read it easily, and hope by the time I get home to find I have broken the back of the language. In the afternoon we generally play deck-cricket, which is great fun and very good exercise. I find myself an adept. The rest of the day is spent in playing chess, reading Zola's Paris or other books. Tomorrow we reach Colombo, and shall be glad of a run on dry land, though we are all so well we do not need it.

Wednesday Nov. 30

We found ourselves this morning with sunrise entering Colombo harbour. It was full of great ocean liners, big merchant tramps and small coasting junks. We had hardly anchored when swarms of boats surrounded us and dozens of brown skinned half-naked Singlalese or sedater turbaned Mahomedans clambered up by any loose rope or chain to sell to us their bright silks or thin silver ornaments. A dozen huge coal-barges followed, piled with sacks of coal on the top of which clustered picturesque groups of coolies in all imaginable colours and variation of head-dress and clothing. We left the silk-sellers and coal-boats as soon as we had got our letters and learnt that we were not at war with France. I went straight to Government House to see the Governor, Sir West Ridgeway, who was Under Secretary when I was in Ireland. I was escorted there by one old man walking in front of me who wished to act as guide, who constantly turned round and gesticulated vehemently. Beside me on the footpath ran a rickshaw. In the road parrallel drove a buggy, equally anxious for my patronage, and behind stalked a younger and official guide. I left them all disconsolate at the gate and was received by four magnificent native servants in gorgeous and artistic liveries of an older pattern than Belgravian, with large combs on their heads. I found that Ridgeway's secretary was an old Harrovian contemporary, Wyndham, in Welldon's House. I had breakfast with Lady W. but did not see the governor who was not down yet. After breakfast I was trotted round in a rickshaw through the native town. Everybody walks down the middle of the road. The rickshaw man goes straight on and shouts to every man, woman or child to make room and they have to jump aside, even the staid turbaned or combed, long clothed man of caste and position who saunters along with a big umbrella over him. It is only when the meanest member of the ruling race happens to be in the way. Him the rickshaw goes round. The native town was very interesting to see for the first time, with the good English road, the frequent English water taps, the slovenly native houses, the priest, the barbers shaving the heads of their customers, the naked brown babies, the slow-labouring talkative road gangs, the high-caste women going in carriages, the walkers watching everybody that passed, the pale faces in swift rickshaws watching nobody, the strong native policeman, the dry old women, the horrible deformity of the beggars, the bright colours of the turbans and clothes, the seeming lassitude and satisfaction of the people, the boys bathing in hundreds, the white coated mustachioed British Officer with pith-helmet and native servant behind rushing along in his swift gig.

I found a great gay crowd outside the R. C. Cathedral, where a new bishop was being consecrated. Rome seems to have made its adherents dress and wash better than the average to judge by the crowd. My camera collected an immense concourse. After that I went to an Hotel where I took a buggy to drive out to Mt. Lavinia, a favourite resort six miles away. I took with me three disconsolate silly young lady passengers, who had no swain and would have had to lounge in the Hotel all day. We drove along a smooth English road, with stout steel English bridges, through groves of palms, children running after us and begging, shouting—'You're my father, you're my aunt, you're my grandfather, you're my grandmother', and as climax 'you're my mother-in-law'. At Mt. Lavinia we had lunch. It was a sufficiently dull sea side Hotel, interesting enough no doubt to distract the hard-worked, banished Englishman when he wants company. We brought things from vendors, and the young lady who flirts with the officers is making me two green sashes out of silk which I bought. Unfortunately, as we discovered afterwards, one of my three young ladies had her pocket picked of their sovereigns; but as I had stood them lunch and their drive, they were not much the losers, only the gainers of an adventure. We drove back in tropical rain and thunder. I afterwards went to the Club, where much whiskey was drunk under punkas. I dined with MacEachern, Mayor of Melbourne, who goes home from here, in whom we lose our most interesting passenger. We raced down to the landing stage in 13 rickshaws. I beat the Captain by a length having carefully chosen a strong-looking man. Then on board and away to the ocean again into the night, having had at least a twelve hour's glimpse of our Eastern Empire.

Thursday Dec. 1–Monday Dec. 5

A beautiful calm voyage, entirely uneventful. I go on with my German and play cricket in the afternoons, gradually taking the lead owing to energy and skill. We have got an officer of the Blues on board, who has been on a voyage to cure him of the gout. He is a blasé youngish man, clever enough to have done something in any but a swell regiment. As it is he does not know enough of military history to say if Marengo is in Germany or Austria! At his own regimental duties he is apparently good, though he has no keenness. And he recognizes that even the Blues in future must not expect to go in for shock tactics. He is very different from certain original officers of the Blues, who carried about in their pockets that they were 'to love their neighbours; but hate them that are the Lord's enemies.'

On the Monday we passed Socotra, mountainous, half-explored island, once with an independent Sultan; now possibly with a Sultan, but certainly with English civil servants to tell him what to do.

Tuesday Dec. 6–Saturday Dec. 10

In the Red Sea. We did not touch at Aden. Most of the time we have not been able to see land. What is to be seen is only

227

bare, unimpressive hills, behind which you know Mecca to be lying. The sun once lit the mosques and minarets of one of the towns where the pilgrims land. Otherwise it was German and cricket till we got alongside the Sinai Peninsular. I was up in time to see the morning sun gild the tops of the Sinai range, as it no doubt did when the hoary old law-giver was walking up and down on the top with bent brows working out the inspired common sense of his great code.

We passed the place where some say the waters were piled up for the hosts of Israel to pass over. It is more authentic that a greater general than Pharoah tried to pass with his staff somewhere about 1798 but found the tide just too high, and so had to go round like a common man by the ordinary highway the servants riding behind him and blessing the Gods of Egypt for their escape from drowning.

We got to Suez at night, a poky place on flat sand plains, and started up the canal, which was made by the nation that ought to have had Egypt but have not. They still work the canal, almost all the officials being French, and when a French boat comes along they take great pleasure in giving it precedence. Unfortunately out of some thirty ships we saw passing or in port at either end, about twenty-nine were flying the Union Jack at the stern. Ships pay an enormous price for going through, we on this one voyage paying about £1,500. The Spanish fleet that put to sea and came home again, paid £33,000 for the amusement of its trip to Suez. But as some ¼ of the interest of the whole concern, thanks to Dizzy, goes into the pockets of the British tax-payer, why grumble? It is only one way of taxing the Orient line shareholders, and first-class passengers to India and Australia.

Sunday Dec. 11

The canal is very dull. Huge flocks of pelicans and flamingoes sit in the shallow lakes in large squadrons of pink and white, beginning a mile off to the furthest horizon. Capt. Mann Thompson of the Blues found his mouth watering to have some gun practice on them. You pass a few bright coloured natives. Otherwise it is sand, water, buoys, neat station-houses for the watchers and dredgers. You pass the great highway between Asia and Africa at Kantara. But now the road is untrodden and only a few ruins marks where it used to go, carrying the trade of two continents.

Port Said is a dull town and a villainous. A governor and many thousand Arabs and Egyptians think they rule it. 1,700 Frenchmen think they ought to rule it. 300 English people do rule it. There are crowds of Italians, Maltese, Germans, Portuguese, etc., and innumerable half-castes. It is aid to be vilely corrupt. There are roulette tables, the book-shops are French of the worst sort, and small boys sell indecent literature under the noses of the native policemen. Fortunately we had not long to stay. The ship took four hours coaling, a wonderful sight. Hundreds of natives walk and run up and down narrow planks from the lighters to the ship singing and shouting with baskets of coal on their shoulders till the coal-bunkers are full again. It is said to be the quickest coaling station in the world. I spent the time in visiting the American consul, an Englishman, who was very proud of having stopped Camara coaling at the port. Lord Cromer forbade it at his request and the fleet of two warships, two torpedo-boats and 8 transports had to put out three miles to sea, and there ignominiously to transfer in a rolling sea sufficient coal from the transports to keep the warships going. The English smiled. The French said 'quel dommage'. Then they sailed through to Suez, then back again to the tune of £33,000. The French shrugged their shoulders, and the English smiled again.

Mrs. Bear Crawford, my German teacher, got off to join Mrs. Amos and Maurice at Cairo.

Monday Dec. 12–Wednesday Dec. 14

One day unpleasant and rough off the coast of Crete, just where Paul's ship 'laboured woundily'. The Cretan mountains, now free, were just hazily visible. This afternoon we have passed between Scylla and Charybdis. The whirlpool hardly whirled at all, and it must have been a bad sailor indeed to run on the rock. But it was very attractive, the Calabrian coast being very beautiful and the sea like a lake, dotted with endless sailing craft, coasting no doubt between Syracuse, Messina and Brindisi. The hills, the villas, the cottages, the vines, the large dry water-courses with walled edges were all clearly visible.

The sun set just behind Etna, showing the smoking peak of it, over a big ridge, which had hitherto been hid in cloud. Tomorrow morning we reach Naples, where I hope to see Rolfe and spend a few good hours under his guidance.

Goodbye, then, for another five days my family – I number them now like a returning schoolboy.

Yours aff.

Charles Trevelyan

INDEX

INDEX

233

Scott, 210
Scott, Sir Walter, 17
Seddon, 141, 150, 151, 152,
   154, 160, 166, 169, 179, 219
Sellars, Miss, 179, 180
Senate, 11, 14–17, 19, 25
Severance, 68, 69, 72
Shambow, 96
Shaw, Albert, 12, 18, 19
Shaw, Bernard, 3, 118
Sherwood, 97
Shiloh, 20
Simpson, Congressman, 23
Skerrett, 167, 168
Smith, Dr., 68, 72
Smith, Mr. Barr, 223
Smith, I. L., 18
South Australia, 218, 219, 222
Speaker, The, 21, 22
Springfield, 47, 50, 51
Stead, 48
Stephen, Judge, 224
Stevenson, Robert Louis, 135,
   136
Stickney, 69
Stout, Sir Robert, 154, 155, 167
Strong, Mr., 107, 109
Strong, Rev. Josiah, 10
Suez, 228
Sydney, 167–169, 172, 174, 175,
   189, 190, 194, 204, 208, 218
Sydney University, 176, 189,
   192, 201
Sykes, Richard, 5
Syme, 203, 209
Syromiatnikoff-Signia, Mr.
   J. N., 118

Tacoma, 106
Tammany, 9, 10, 14, 20, 131
Taupo, Lake, 147
Taylor, 185, 186, 187
Taylor, Prof. Graham, 47

Taylor, Tommy, 152, 154, 156
Terry, 173
Thompson, Scotch, 90, 91
Thornton, Mr., 87
Tooley, Judge, 48
Tregear, 153
Trenwith, 201
Trevelyan, R. C. ('Bob'), 3,
   132, 212
Tuckerman, 20, 21
Tuckerman (of St. Louis), 52
Turner, Sir G., 202

Utah, 91, 92, 130

Vaile, 84, 85, 87
Vallenge, Capt., 172
Veale, Capt., 224
Victoria, 202, 209, 210, 217

Wadsworth, Fort, 6
Waiakua, 130
Waikiki, 218
Waite, Governor, 88
Walker, 75, 76
Wall Street, 7, 10, 12
Wallas, Graham, 3
Wallington, Capt., 218, 219,
   223
Wangauri College, 162, 163,
   166
Want, Attorney-General, 169,
   173
Ward, 156
Ward, Capt., 157
Waring, Col., 13
Washington, 13, 14, 24, 25,
   68
Washington, George, 24, 26
Washington Monument, 21
Wason, 160
Waugh, Mrs., 180, 182
Way, Chief Justice, 219

237